A House of Gathering

Tennessee Studies in Literature Volume 34

A House of Gathering
Poets on May Sarton's Poetry

EDITED AND WITH AN INTRODUCTION

BY MARILYN KALLET

The University of Tennessee Press ❦ Knoxville

1605314

"Tennessee Studies in Literature," a distinguished series sponsored by the Department of English at The University of Tennessee, Knoxville, began publication in 1956. Beginning in 1984, with Volume 27, TSL evolved from a series of annual volumes of miscellaneous essays to a series of occasional volumes, each one dealing with a specific theme, period, or genre, for which the editor of that volume has invited contributions from leading scholars in the field.

Inquiries concerning this series should be addressed to the Editorial Board, Tennessee Studies in Literature, Department of English, The University of Tennessee, Knoxville, Tennessee 37996-0430. Those desiring to purchase additional copies of this issue or copies of back issues should address The University of Tennessee Press, 293 Communications Building, Knoxville, Tennessee 37996-0325.

Copyright © 1993 by The University of Tennessee Press / Knoxville. All Rights Reserved. Manufactured in the United States of America. First Edition.

Frontispiece. May Sarton at home, York, Maine, 1991. Provided by May Sarton. Photograph by Bruce Conklin. Used with permission.

"Prayer Before Work," from *Collected Poems* (1930–73), by May Sarton, is reprinted by permission of the author and W. W. Norton & Company, Inc. Copyright © 1974 by May Sarton. "The House of Gathering" and "Old Lovers at the Ballet," from *The Silence Now: New and Collected Earlier Poems,* by May Sarton, are reprinted by permission of the author and W. W. Norton & Company, Inc. Copyright © 1988 by May Sarton. "Friendship & Illness," from *Coming Into Eighty,* is reprinted by permission of the author and William B. Ewert, Publisher, Concord, N.H. Reprinted by permission of W. W. Norton & Company, Inc. from *Endgame, A Journal of the Seventy-ninth Year,* by May Sarton. Copyright © 1992 by May Sarton. Quotations from *H.D. Collected Poems 1912–1944,* copyright © 1982 the Estate of Hilda Doolittle, are reprinted by permission of New Directions Publishing Corp. Excerpt from Hilda Doolittle Aldington's letter of 7 January 1946 to May Sarton is reprinted with permission of the Henry W. and Albert A. Berg Collection, the New York Public Library, Astor, Lenox and Tilden Foundations. With the permission of Perdita Schaffner. Selected quotations from the H.D. Papers appear with permission of the Yale Collection of American Literature, Beinecke Rare Book and Manuscript Library. With the permission of Perdita Schaffner. Excerpts from selected poems published in *The Lion and the Rose* reprinted by permission of Russell & Volkening as agents for the author. Copyright © 1948 by May Sarton, © copyright renewed 1976 by May Sarton.

The paper in this book meets the minimum requirements of the American National Standard for Permanence of Paper for Printed Library Materials. ∞ The binding materials have been chosen for strength and durability.

Library of Congress Cataloging in Publication Data

A house of gathering : poets on May Sarton's poetry / edited and with an introduction by Marilyn Kallet.—1st ed.
     p.   cm. — (Tennessee studies in literature; v. 34)
   Essays written in honor of Sarton's eightieth birthday. Includes bibliographical references and index.
   ISBN 0-87049-785-5 (cloth: alk. paper)
   1. Sarton, May, 1912 –   —Criticism and interpretation.
   I. Sarton, May, 1912 –   . II. Kallet, Marilyn, 1946 –   . III. Series.
PS3537.A832Z7 1993   92-36430
811'.52—dc20   CIP

To Lou and Heather

and

to Bradford Dudley Daziel,
great scholar, great spirit

The House of Gathering

If old age is a house of gathering,
Then the hands are full.
There are old trees to prune
And young plants to plant,
There are seeds to be sown.
Not less of anything
But more of everything
To care for,
To maintain,
To keep sorted out,
A profusion of people
To answer, to respond to.

But we have been ripening
To a greater ease,
Learning to accept
That all hungers cannot be fed,
That saving the world
May be a matter
Of sowing a seed
Not overturning a tyrant,
That we do what we can.

The moment of vision,
The seizure still makes
Its relentless demands:

Work, love, be silent.
Speak.

May Sarton
The Silence Now, 1988

Contents

Illustrations

Acknowledgments

I will always be grateful to Julia Demmin for having suggested this project to me. It would be hard to imagine doing this book without Catherine Emanuel, my research assistant, who provided invaluable editorial and research services as well as moral support. Several other friends and colleagues assisted in the editorial process: Deborah Harper, Keith Norris, and Greg Burkman put in long hours and offered numerous suggestions that helped to shape the book. Thanks to Joyce Carol Thomas for introducing me to the *Before Columbus Review*. J. J. Phillips at the *Before Columbus Review* published my first essay on May Sarton's poetry in 1990, which expanded into this larger work. Carol Orr, formerly Director of the University of Tennessee Press, encouraged me at the outset to do this book. Miller Williams, Director of the University of Arkansas Press, and John Poindexter, Director of Vanderbilt University Press, gave encouragement and practical suggestions. I am grateful to Bradford Dudley Daziel of Westport College, not only for his scholarship on Sarton, but also for his thoughtful advice on editing this manuscript, and for his encouragement. To poet and scholar Constance Hunting, at the University of Maine in Orono, I owe a similar debt of gratitude.

The English Department at the University of Tennessee provided support for this volume of *Tennessee Studies in Literature* in numerous ways. Professor Norman Sanders, Director of the Board for the series, facilitated all aspects of the review process. Professor Allen Carroll, Head of the Department of English and a member of the Board of Directors for *Tennessee Studies in Literature*, offered painstaking editorial comments. I am grateful to the board for the financial support for this volume. In addition, the John C. Hodges Better English Fund provided a summer research grant for my work. Graduate Studies in English awarded me a research assistant for this project, for which I am thankful. Beth Walker came through with final, necessary editorial services. Clarke Russell helped significantly by researching the Chronology. Norma Meredith, secretary to *Tennessee Studies in Literature*, provided invaluable assistance.

I wish to thank Mary Ryan, Permissions Editor at W. W. Norton, for facilitating this volume. William B. Ewert of Concord, New Hampshire, was generous to let us copy "Friendship & Illness" with its original artwork by Mary Azarian. He first published the poem in 1990 in a special edition, and again in 1992 as part of *Coming into Eighty*. Jennifer Siler, Acting Director at UT Press, and Meredith Morgan, Acquisitions Editor, as well as their entire staff at the press, are as congenial and helpful a group as one could hope to work with. All of the fine poets who contributed to this volume worked as a community, in a professional, timely manner—and they rarely complained!

Despite the fact that she is quite ill, May Sarton has been generous about granting me an interview, providing unpublished documents, photographs, granting permissions, and answering endless questions. Deepest gratitude to May for her poetry, and for helping this volume at every turn. And special thanks to Lou and Heather—my family—for putting up with my absenteeism during months of work on this book.

Abbreviations

The following abbreviations of titles of works by May Sarton are used throughout this volume.

AG   *A Grain of Mustard Seed*. New York: Norton, 1971, 1984.

AD   *As Does New Hampshire*. Dublin, N.H: William L. Bauhan, 1967.

AS   *At Seventy: A Journal*. New York: Norton, 1984.

ASP   *A Self-Portrait*. New York: Norton, 1982.

AW   *A World of Light*. New York: Norton, 1976.

EA   *Encounter in April*. Boston: Houghton Mifflin Co., 1937.

HS   *Halfway to Silence*. New York: Norton, 1980.

TH   *The House by the Sea*. New York: Norton, 1977.

IL   *Inner Landscape*. London: The Crescent Press, 1939.

JS   *Journal of a Solitude*. New York: Norton, 1973.

LM   *Letters from Maine*. New York: Norton, 1984.

LR   *The Lion and the Rose*. New York: Rinehart & Co., 1948.

CP   *Collected Poems*. New York: Norton, 1974.

MS   *Mrs. Stevens Hears the Mermaids Singing*. New York: Norton, 1965.

PD   *Plant Dreaming Deep*. New York: Norton, 1968, 1984.

P&D   *The Poet and the Donkey*. New York: Norton, 1969, 1984.

RE   *Recovering*. New York: Norton, 1980.

SP   *Selected Poems of May Sarton*. Hilsinger and Brynes, eds. New York: Norton, 1978.

SSE   *Sarton Selected: An Anthology of the Journals, Novels, and Poems of May Sarton*. Bradford Dudley Daziel, ed. New York: Norton, 1991.

SN   *The Silence Now: New and Uncollected Earlier Poems*. New York: Norton, 1988.

TS   Typescript drafts of "Old Lovers at the Ballet." Provided by May Sarton.

WW   *Writings on Writing*. Orono, Maine: Puckerbrush Press, 1980.

YCAL   Yale Collection of American Literature, Beinecke Rare Book and Manuscript Library, Yale University, New Haven, Connecticut.

Introduction

MARILYN KALLET

I first met May Sarton on a sweltering Sunday afternoon in late July 1980, when I drove from Geneva, New York, to her poetry reading at the Rochester Museum of Art. Several years earlier, my sister had given me *Journal of a Solitude,* and the spiritual struggle in that work had made a strong impression. Like the author, I had chosen to live alone, a woman writer wrestling with the creative angels of solitude. I knew little about Sarton's poetry, and yet I felt condescension toward it—her verses rhymed, didn't they? Having recently completed a dissertation on William Carlos Williams, and having immersed myself in his work, I had learned well his ideas on diction and rhythm—that rhythm is revolutionary ground in contemporary poetry; that the American poet's responsibility is to work in the "American idiom," to translate into our lines the language we hear about us every day. Until hearing May Sarton read, I hadn't realized that traditional verse could accommodate pliable rhythms, could sound idiomatic, or that the quiet music of certain rhymed verses might charm away all thoughts of dogma.

I was unprepared for the emotional experience ahead of me. Despite the heat, the auditorium was packed. The audience was more diverse than I had seen in years of organizing poetry readings. Young people crowded in—presumably many were students at the University of Rochester—but there were also hundreds of middle-aged and elderly people, men and women. Luckily, I found a seat in the front row. Sarton prefaced her reading with remarks about the poet's life, how remaining vulnerable is at the heart of creating poetry. Like Adrienne Rich at her readings, Sarton seemed to be at one with her words; in her expressive voice, she embodied what she was saying about staying "open" to emotional life. Having trained in the theater with Eva Le Gallienne in the early 1930s, and having started a theater of her own in 1932, Sarton brought to her poetry a disciplined, resonant voice. Her rhymes were unobtrusive, subtly underscoring emotion.

After the reading, Sarton signed books in the lobby, and I waited with a crowd of others to have my book—*Journal of a Solitude*—inscribed. The line extended across the lobby and around the corner; I was the last person in line. By the time I reached the poet, I was so nervous I was shaking. I said, "That was the best reading I have ever heard!" Sarton joked with a friend of hers, "This poor woman hasn't heard very many poetry readings, has she! She's been deprived!" We laughed, but I told her that, on the contrary, I had probably heard too many readings. "Are you a poet?" she asked. "Send me some of your work."

I sent her my translations of Paul Eluard's love poetry, as well as a poem about solitude. Two weeks later Sarton responded that she had read my work while waiting for radiation treatments at the hospital; her comments were generous. Thus began an exchange of hundreds of letters over the last twelve years. May Sarton's responsiveness to my work is typical of her generosity toward younger writers; whatever critical neglect her own poetry has endured, Sarton has transmuted her feelings about it into a sensitivity toward the work of others. The vulnerability she spoke of at her reading translates into an openness in her relationships, into the ability to listen, into a capacity for intimacy that is at the heart of effective lyric poetry: the poet speaks to the reader personally, evoking for her in musical language the intimate union of word and mind.

Throughout Sarton's body of work, which spans over sixty years of writing and publishing poetry, the theme of "openness" toward feelings recurs as central to the poet's life and art. In "Letters to Myself," Sarton suggests that our culture regards the capacity to live with strong feeling as pathological: "The terrible fear, the fear of feeling, / Must I hear it defended on every side? / Live like a madman echoing his cell?" (*LM* 55). On the contrary, Sarton asserts, "The fact is I am whole and very well, / Joyful, centered, not to be turned aside, / Full of healing and of self-healing." Sarton refuses to be mythologized as the Romantic, "cursed," poet. She does not cherish suffering, but rather what she has learned from it. As Adrienne Rich states in *The Dream of a Common Language*, "deliberate suicide wasn't my métier" (29). Not merely a survivor, but one who savors life, Sarton assures us that she is "Marvelously open, transparent, and unafraid" (*LM* 24). At times the theme of openness occurs in the context of Sarton's imagery for nature; the poet responds in a graceful measure to the world around her, she breathes with the lines, and her verse becomes playful:

> My breath warms like the sun,
> Melts ice, bursts into song.
> So when that inner one
> Gives life back the power
> To rise up and push through,
> There's nothing to it.
> We simply have to do it,
> As snowdrops know
> When snowdrops flower. (*LM* 40)

Here openness is a kind of transparency, what Keats termed "Negative Capability": the ability to exist "in uncertainties, Mysteries, doubts, without any irritable reaching after fact & reason." In her lyric "April in Maine," Sarton conveys this inspired state:

> But as the dark flows in
> The tree frogs begin
> Their shrill sweet singing,
> And we lie on our beds
> Through the ecstatic night,
> Wide awake, cracked open.

> There will be no going back. (*LM* 44)

In exploring the "hidden tumult" of her feelings, the poet takes enormous risks. When love is as integral as breathing, each breath can cut: "But for today it's true / That I can hardly draw / A solitary breath / That does not hurt me like a little death" ("Mal du Départ," *HS* 28).

The image of the phoenix, recurring throughout Sarton's opus, "has to do with surviving and coming back after one death (metaphorically speaking) after another" (Sarton to Kallet, 7 April 1992). Defying death, the phoenix is emblematic of Sarton's willingness to stay open to feeling and to probe its limits, to be "consumed" by strong emotion. Through its music, its skillful, formal expression, the poem becomes the phoenix, the passionate image that remains. In her essays as well as in her poetry, Sarton reminds us that the poet's vulnerability can be hazardous: "Poetry is a dangerous profession because it demands a very delicate and exhausting balance between conflict and resolution, between feeling and thought . . . and these balances are shifting all the time. We move softly because we tread on swords. . . ." The poet does not allow herself to give in to the instinct for self-protection, since remaining "totally open" to experience offers an opportunity for growth (*WW* 69). In "The Phoenix," Sarton questions whether it is the image, the myth that transforms itself in the poem's dynamic, or whether it is the poet herself who must be painfully transformed: " . . . what if it were not he at all, not he / Who must consume himself to be reborn, / But we ourselves, who drove an angel from us / Because our hearts were torn?" (*SSE* 155)

The poet becomes one with her images—she is the last wolf, with its "touch of wildness," and the "aging unicorn," the mature woman purified by experience, the phoenix who "consumes her own soul" in poetry's fierce probing. She *earns* the poem by being honest and open:

> If we earn metaphor by being extremely open to experience of all kinds, and able to examine it with a cold clear eye, and if we earn form only as we are able to experience at a high level of intensity, then might one not say that the revising of a poem is a constant revising, disciplining and refining of the poet himself? Each true poem has been an act of *growth*. . . . Let me suggest . . . that the art of poetry as a lifetime adventure will demand the capacity to break down over and over

again what has already been created. . . . Creation is revision within the whole person. . . . (*WW* 66)

This willingness to remain open resonates as an ethic and an aesthetic in Sarton's poetry. The last poem in *Halfway to Silence,* "Of the Muse," expresses this in free verse: "There is no poetry in lies, / But in crude honesty / There is hope for poetry" (61). The poem becomes a meditation on immediacy and on preparedness for giving oneself to experience:

> Today, I have learned
> That to become
> A great, cracked,
> Wide-open door
> Into nowhere
> Is wisdom. (*HS* 61)

At Sarton's home in York, Maine, the house overlooks tall grasses that stretch toward the expanse of the sea. There's a path through the field where May Sarton used to walk Tamas, her sheltie, to the edge of the cliffs. The spirits of Tamas and Bramble, Sarton's cat, still inhabit the house, the field, and the garden. The garden offers up a planned profusion of colors throughout the spring and summer. And in the front of the garden, visible from the third-floor writing room where Sarton begins work each morning at eight, is a stone sculpture of the phoenix rising. Without the discipline and hard work that created the garden, the phoenix would be lost in wildness. Even in her most impassioned statements on writing and the writer's life, Sarton returns to the theme of discipline:

> I trust that I have not failed to communicate my faith that poetry is a
> way of life as well as a complex and fascinating intellectual game, that
> poets must serve it as a good servant . . . must revere and woo it as the

mystic reveres and woos God through self-discipline toward joy. And I hope that you may feel under all these words the inexhaustible enthusiasm that drives us on, that willingness to break down in order to refashion closer to the heart's desire that makes the creative process among the most fruitful and awe-inspiring disciplines of the mind. (*WW* 57)

It seems likely that May Sarton's father, George Sarton, distinguished intellectual historian, founder of the history of science, transmitted to his daughter a love of intellectual rigor and discipline. And that her mother, Mabel, who was a gardener, painter, photographer, textile and furniture designer, conveyed to May a profound love for the arts. But family histories are never so cut and dried. Early in his writing career, in his twenties, George Sarton wrote poetry under the pen name of Dominique de Bray. And May Sarton tells us that, like her, he answered every letter—"that was his way of being human" (*AW* 21). Mabel Sarton's letters to her daughter convey a love for writing itself, a love of the smallest aesthetic details as a way of composing a life and creating relationships. The frontispiece of *Letters to May* contains a letter dated "March 19–" in bold, expressive handwriting from Mabel Sarton to her daughter; in the center of the letter she writes, "There are little *groups* of orange-gold crocuses out and one violet one just showing from between its green sheath. . . . I got yours this morning with 'The Window' and am elated. . . . I just love you *more* each time you make some thing so beautiful to hold a pure emotion & thought." Here, flowers, letters, and May Sarton's new poem seem almost equivalents in this world of women nurturing each other. Sarton's poem "The Window," from *The Lion and the Rose* (1938–48), evokes the "mathematical window"—the austere world of careful observation and spare, structured stanzas. But this "abstract window" is invaded by deeper feelings, less contained: ". . . suddenly alive / The rivers of the air / Invade the static square; / As the stars only move/ Obedient to Love, / Heart opens into time" (*CP* 56).

May Sarton says of her mother that she was "*aware* in the deepest sense of what every living thing . . . needed at that moment." (E. M. Sarton ix). In her letters, Mabel Sarton's alertness to detail seems at times to be clairvoyance, as when she expresses sorrow over a friend's

growing blind: "I look at the poppies. I saw one drop its petals yes-
terday, so gently, with the tiniest whispering sound . . . 'these are the
things she will miss, *how will she bear it?*'" (63). It seems likely that
May Sarton inherited from her mother not only a keen aesthetic sense,
a sensitivity to beauty and to art, but also unusual compassion, a kind
of heroism of everyday life. In many of her letters, Mabel Sarton refers to being ill, to her "misères"; yet even when not well, Mabel
Sarton wrote energetic, detailed letters to her daughter, and to others. This self-discipline shows itself in May Sarton's life as well—at
eighty years old, suffering from degenerative heart disease, and other
ailments that cause her unremitting pain, she still writes letters, has
dictated her most recent journal, has started another novel on her new
word processor, and, miraculously, she is writing poetry again:

> After long silence
> An old poet
> Singing again,
> I am a mage myself
> Joy leaps in my throat.
> Glory be to God! ("Renascence," Christmas 1991)

Born in Belgium, May Sarton escaped the war by fleeing with her parents to America in 1916. May was four when her family immigrated,
moving first to Washington, D.C., and then to Cambridge, Massachusetts, where her father began his opus at the Widener Library, and
where May grew up, in a three-room apartment at 5 Avon Street. At
seventeen, Sarton turned down a chance to attend Vassar College in
order to study in New York with Eva Le Gallienne. Sarton became an
actress and later founded her own theater. In 1958, she moved to
Nelson, New Hampshire, where she bought an old farmhouse set in
thirty-six acres. Anyone familiar with Sarton's autobiographical writings, including *Plant Dreaming Deep,* and *Journal of a Solitude,* knows
how important the theme of the "house" is to Sarton. As a woman

writer living alone, claiming her solitude and her art as worthy subject matter for her writings, Sarton has done for women's literature what Rousseau accomplished for the individual sensibility in modern literature—she has validated for us the importance of a woman's life as she experiences and writes it.

In 1973, Sarton moved to York, Maine, where she still lives. For a transplanted person, one who has made such a significant move at an early age, writing itself becomes a kind of home. It is the place of self-creation and self-discovery, where the poet opens her door to others through her language. Sarton has stated that she thinks of poetry as both a journey and an "arrival" (Sarton Interview 96). In "The Work of Happiness" she evokes the way poetry is like weaving, a daily process of inner construction:

> I thought of happiness, how it is woven
> Out of the silence in the empty house each day
> And how it is not sudden and is not given
> But is creation itself like the growth of a tree.
> No one has seen it happen, but inside the bark
> Another circle is growing in the expanding ring.
> No one has heard the root go deeper in the dark,
> But the tree is lifted by this inward work
> And its plumes shine, and its leaves are glittering.
>
> So happiness is woven out of the peace of hours
> And strikes its roots deep in the house alone. . . . (*SSE* 106)

This poem give us images for the intangible, for the inner lining of the "house," the soul woven from the poet's imaginings, from the daily work at her desk. The silent, "inward work" also reminds us of the structure of the poem itself, its variations on iambic pentameter, its alliteration creating sounds that are fluid, mysterious, and resonant. Above all, the rhymes and near-rhymes are subtle, almost invisible like silence, singing to the subconscious, yet solid like the structure of a house: "No one has heard thought or listened to a mind, / But where people have lived in inwardness / The air is charged with blessing and does bless; / Windows look out on mountains and the walls are kind" (*SSE* 106).

The quality of attention Sarton gives to each day, each moment, unites her journals and her poetry. William Stafford's poem "Keeping a Journal" sheds light on this habit of working:

> More important than what was recorded, these evenings
> deepened my life: they framed every event
> or thought and placed it with care by the others.
> As time went on, that scribbled wall—even if
> it stayed blank—became where everything
> recognized itself and passed into meaning. (Stafford 13)

The "house of gathering" suggests not only the rich garnering of old age, but also writing itself—the place of integrating all aspects of a writer's life, as well as the activity of staying conscious.

Elsewhere I have written about the landscape of silence and solitude Sarton has created in her three most recent books, *Halfway to Silence* (1980), *Letters from Maine* (1984), and *The Silence Now* (1988) (Kallet, 1990, 18–21). Native American writer Scott Momaday has helped me to reflect on Sarton's topography; at the end of *The Way to Rainy Mountain* he advises: "Once in his life a man ought . . . to give himself up to a particular landscape . . . to look at it from as many angles as he can, to wonder about it, to dwell upon it. He ought to imagine that he touches it with his hands at every season and listens to the sounds that are made upon it." Like Momaday, Sarton has chosen to focus her attention on a particular landscape—the "once in her life" is not one time, but the whole span of her long writing life. For more than sixty years she has given her attention to the natural world through her poetry. Having lived in New England for almost thirty-five years, she has observed and imagined the creatures of earth, air, and water, tracking the storms from "dead-center," creating her mythology of phoenix-fire.

Sarton's landscape is inner as well, a landscape of strong feeling seeking its perfect form; her songs are set against an immense ocean of silence and solitude no less exacting than the vast plains of Momaday's vision quest. The blank space of the page surrounding her spare verse recalls the wintry silences of Maine. The rigor Sarton imposes on her lyrics shows a profound respect for silence. The "woman made of words" deals with the world on equal terms through her language (Kallet 18). Sarton comments on the scope and vigor of her creation: "So what one hopes, or what I hope, is that the whole work will represent the landscape of a nature which is not primarily intellectual but rather a sensibility quite rich and diverse and large in its capacities to understand and communicate" (Sarton Interview 86).

As of 1992, May Sarton has published forty-seven books, seventeen of which are collections of poetry. The inner place that Sarton has created in this body of work can be compared to a cosmos, like the Navajo "house made of dawn," rather than to an ordinary house. When asked how it felt to be seventy, Sarton acknowledged that "for the first time in my life I have a sense of achievement. I've written all these books and they're there! Nobody can take that from me" (Sarton Interview 102). And though Sarton continues—heroically—to be prolific, her poems from the 1980s and '90s are ruthlessly edited, pared down. She never forgets the law of creation; as Momaday states it, "A word has power in and of itself. It comes from nothing into sound and meaning; it gives origin to all things" (Momaday 33).

For Sarton, as for poets from the oral tradition, silence is an integral part of the creative matrix that permits poetry to be born. It is an awareness in the poet's consciousness, a respect for the silence that predates us and that will follow us. As Keith Norris indicates in his essay "Desiring Silence," silence is a transitional metaphor for Sarton, one that accrues meanings throughout her work, becoming especially eloquent in the poetry of the last ten years. Implicitly we receive the image of silence as we turn the pages of Sarton's poetry, and take in the picture of short-lined poems set in their wide, blank frames. The short lines suggest inwardness, rather than the concern with power that has historically charged the longer, prophetic, Whitmanesque line in its competition with silence. Far from being a small, contained image, "silence" for Sarton holds a positive depth-charge: going deep enough, silence is the meeting-place with the Goddess: "Old Woman I meet you deep inside myself. / There in the rootbed of fertility, / World without end, as the legend tells it. / Under the words you are my silence" (*LM* 23). Sarton's short lines can also be prophetic: in its most terrifying aspect, silence imagined by Sarton contains what Jane Miller calls "the post-apocalyptic moment," a vision of the world's end.

May Sarton has chosen to work with the silences in her life, both the metaphorical and the literal ones. As a child, May was required to remain silent while her father worked on his research: "When I was small I learned to be very silent, for he worked at home and the slightest noise interrupted his concentration" (*AW* 17–18). As the writer, May Sarton takes charge of her silences, choosing a house in a quiet place by the sea, ordering her life around the activity of writing.

Silence in a woman's life is charged, both with what society expects of her, and with what she will create for herself, turning silence around so that it reflects what she chooses—a place of "rich silence," where the Goddess reveals the "voice itself and not the language spoken" (HS 24, 21).

Sarton's "New Year Resolve," the opening poem of *The Silence Now,* begins with the poet's assertion of her need to restore order and to be spare: "The time has come / To stop allowing the clutter / To clutter my mind. . . ." The poet resolves to "find / Clear time. . ." (15). Four words per line is typical of Sarton's spareness in recent poems, with two primary stresses per line, one on each side of the caesura. Sarton works with and against a steady iambic, as in the first two lines of this poem concerning time and state of mind. Her phrasing in recent years has become more and more idiomatic, closer to the spoken American language, thus appealing to those of us for whom William Carlos Williams's work has had such impact. When Sarton varies her line, giving us fewer than four words, we pay careful attention, as in the beginning of stanza three: "Let silence in." Here the poet leaves only three stresses, "Let," "si," and "in." "In" gets equal time and attention with "Let silence," if we read this the way Williams might have, counting one beat per line, measuring the time elapsed for each phrase in the line. The rhythmical emphasis on "in" reminds us that the poem consists of inner work, of "soul-making."

Sarton's short lines reveal the strictness of her editing. In her writings on writing, she has emphasized the process of editing: "The advantage of form, far from being 'formal' and sort of off-putting and intellectual, is that through form you reach the subliminal level. I love form. It makes you cut down." Free verse requires even more paring: "The greatest peril in free verse seems to be that of over-charging, or of rambling along, so that cutting to the bone becomes mandatory. It must feel shaped, though in a far less obvious way than in a sonnet, for instance" (*WW* 71; rpt *SSE* 81–82).

Readers who have not made the effort to acquaint themselves with the body of Sarton's work tend to pigeonhole her as a poet writing only in traditional forms. Yet in her essay "On Growth and Change," Sarton eloquently describes the creative process involved in composing free verse (*WW* 67–72; rpt *SSE* 78–82). Speaking of her work on the poems in *A Private Mythology* (1961–66), she explains how she felt about the transition from traditional forms:

> . . . I took a deep breath and plunged into a new element . . . ; it was all risk and tremor at first. I had to break down a grooved response to meter; iambic pentameter had become my natural way to write poems. This fluid element of free verse was frightening. I found that its value for the reader of apparent spontaneity, casualness, was just as hard to come by as the sustained dancing quality of formal structure. . . . These poems felt not like rocks in my hand, but like water flowing over it (*WW* 70–71; rpt. *SSE* 81).

She experienced a sense of release while working with free verse: "little by little I learned to breathe with the line; I enjoyed the sensation of being floated on an image. . . ." Sarton shows remarkable agility

and sure-handedness in her work, varying her repertoire over the years
in poems that sing, whether shaped into strict verse or into free verse,
where spare lines are all the more resonant.

Paring down is everywhere apparent in Sarton's poetry. One reference to this discipline embedded in her texts is Sarton's repetition of
the word *bone* in her last three books. "Bone" is to Sarton's work
what "esprit" or "souvenirs" is to Baudelaire's, a touchstone, a refrain, a way of evoking the poet's central concerns. The image of
"bone" suggests that the poet wants to probe her thoughts and feelings to the quick, to take them to the depths of her understanding.
And as the poet ages, the recurring references to the skeletal structure
cannot be coincidental. Sarton's poetry is informed by her body; and
the aging body, though engaged in "soul-making" song, still insists
on its ties to earth. "Bone" reminds us of Sarton's work on form, her
concern with structure; the image suggests both moral and aesthetic
qualities of "spine" or character. The "bone" is the structure of feeling and thought integrated in the poem, an experience of form that is
hard-won. It appears when Sarton feels the thrill of mortality: "I
caught my breath, alone, / Abandoned like a lover / With winter at
the bone / To see the geese go over" (HS 48). But the image also
comes back when Sarton uses poetry like prayer, to lean into the unknown and timeless; the last poem in *The Silence Now* sings the poem's
refusal to be trapped in time: "It struggles now alone / Against death
and self-doubt, / But underneath the bone/ The wings are pushing
out" (76).

Sarton's first poems, the opening five sonnets from *Encounter in
April*, were published in *Poetry* magazine, when she was seventeen.
Sarton's poetry volume *In Time Like Air* was nominated for a National Book Award in 1958, along with *Faithful Are the Hounds*, one
of her novels. For the first time an author had been nominated in the
same year for two different genres. Poetry reviews up until 1958 contain numerous positive notices. Martha Bacon's review of *The Lion*

and the Rose, in *The Saturday Review of Literature,* would seem to herald May Sarton's career as a major postwar poet:

> May Sarton is an artist of remarkable powers. She is one of those rare poets who, in making use of simple combinations of words—and of the words of our common speech at that—has achieved a vocabulary and style as distinctly her own as any poet now writing. . . . She has drawn upon the whole stream of English literature to develop her subtle cadences and delicate, all-but-inaudible rhymes. . . . One wonders at the extreme simplicity of her statement (for such simplicity needs courage), and the more one wonders the more one is aware of the great gifts set forth. . . ." (50)

This review suggests that Sarton's poetry is complex, bringing to bear both the directness of idiomatic American speech, and the richness of the English literary tradition.

Yet a review of Sarton's *The Lion and the Rose* in the *Kirkus Reviews* sounds a more biased note: "Like so many women poets, her poems are not held together by any ordered continuity of thought. . . ." (44). Along with such scornful remarks about women writers, this review mixes in high praise for Sarton: "May Sarton takes her place among a remarkably gifted group of modern American poets—Elizabeth Bishop, Edith Hinrichs, Marguerite Young to mention a few" (44). After 1958, even the "good" reviews of Sarton's poetry often reveal this kind of confusion; traditional critics seem to struggle against the impulse to praise Sarton's work. James Dickey's review of *In Time Like Air* expresses a mixed mind about Sarton's success. Ostensibly positive, Dickey begins by dismissing, stereotyping, and turning Sarton into a "token" of female acceptability: "May Sarton is not a profoundly original writer, but she is a beautiful one, with the casual balance, the womanly assurance and judiciousness that we look for in vain in many of our other women poets." Next Dickey dismisses Muriel Rukeyser and Edith Sitwell along with other women writers whose names "come flocking." He begins a sentence with strong praise of Sarton: "In almost every poem she attains a delicate simplicity as quickenly direct as it is deeply-given," but ends with qualifiers, comparing the poet to "the queen of a small well-ordered country" (Dickey 306).

Despite the vast body of poetry created by Sarton and the remarkable variety of forms she has achieved, her work has received scant critical attention in the last forty years. Her poetry has been all but ignored by the academy. Constance Hunting's collection of essays, *May Sarton: Woman and Poet,* published in 1982 by the National Poetry Foundation at the University of Maine, was the first and—until 1993—the only collection of criticism on Sarton's work. Hunting's volume includes five essays on Sarton's poetry, all favorable, most of them appreciative and formalist in method. Though they focus on other genres, two feminist essays in this volume, "May Sarton's Memoirs" by Carolyn Heilbrun (43–53) and "A French View of May Sarton" by Mary Lydon (61–79), help the reader of Sarton's poetry to appreciate Sarton's risk-taking in all aspects of her work. *Sarton Selected,* edited by Bradford Dudley Daziel in 1991, contains three of Sarton's essays on her poetics. Here, as often happens when a poet falls outside the canon, the poet is her own best critic. In 1993, the University of Michigan Press plans to issue a volume of critical essays on Sarton, *That Great Sanity,* edited by Susan Schwartzlander and Marilyn R. Mumford. Hopefully 1993 will bring in a new tide of criticism on Sarton's work.

That relentless negative criticism or critical indifference can blight an artist's career, we know from Tillie Olsen's *Silences* and from Joanna Russ's *How to Suppress Women's Writing.* William Carlos Williams spoke of the negative impact on a poet's imagination of critical neglect, of how his work had been "buried" by the critics (Williams, *Interviews* 30–31; *Selected Letters* 257). Despite his feelings of "resentment against them all," Williams's response to the critics was stubborn and creative: "Poetry, an art, is what answer I have. . . . all I can do (growing old) is to compose. It is the only recourse, the only intellectual recourse for an artist, to make, to make, to make, and to go on making—*never* to reply *in kind* to their strictures" (*Selected Letters* 238–239). Like Williams, Sarton has answered the critics by persisting in her art. While Sarton's readership, especially of her prose, has grown enormously over the last fifteen years, critical ignorance of her poetry remains pretty much the rule. Some well-known critics have been frankly abusive toward her poetry. Despite the thousands of favorable letters Sarton has received over the years from what Daziel aptly calls "the common reader" (*SSE* 22), rough treatment by the critics can deeply wound.

John Ciardi's review of Sarton's *The Land of Silence* in *The Nation* (1954), becomes agitated, almost frenzied, as he blasts Sarton's work for being "high-pitched," "an aesthetic position," Ciardi continues, "to which I must register myself as absolutely, fiercely, implacably, violently opposed." Why "violently"? His rhetoric—a model of what he says he abhors—seems more intended to intimidate the poet than to enlighten the reader. When I asked Richard Wilbur to contribute to this Sarton volume, he wrote a gracious response, creating a miniature portrait of their writing group; Wilbur's response illuminates us as to Ciardi's position:

> Yes, back in the late 40's and early 50's there was a Cambridge group (John Holmes, May Sarton, John Ciardi, Richard Eberhart and I) which met once a month at one house or another; we talked about poetry, read our new poems aloud, suffered criticism, and drank a bit of whiskey. Robert Frost once asked me about these meetings: "Do you come together to fix up each other's poems," he asked, "or are you just hoping to be praised?" I said that we were mostly looking for praise, and he said, "Well, that's all right, then." Certainly the men in our group did not do a great deal of fixing up in the light of objections. Dick Eberhart was by his nature incapable of revision, and John Holmes was so prolific that he could cheerfully discard anything which failed to please. May, perhaps because she was then more accomplished as a fiction writer, and wished to improve her secondary talent as a poet, played fairer than the rest of us; she took criticism seriously, and often appeared at our meetings with poems which had been reworked and bettered. Our comments on each other's work were often quite harsh: I recall Eberhart's listening with smiling obduracy while we all insisted that he could *not* commit such a mad inversion as "Everyone a mother and a father has." The main flaw in John Ciardi's warm and good character was that, out of some fear that poetry was a sissy profession, he was always rather hard on woman poets, May included.

Wilbur wraps up this last startling comment by adding: "She was, however, a good sport about his criticisms, and those of the rest of us, and she was at all times a charming and valuable presence" (Wilbur to Kallet, 20 August 1991).

That there are some poems less successful than others in Sarton's vast body of work seems undeniable. This would be true for the works of any poet with considerable output. Wordsworth has the most entries in *The Stuffed Owl,* an anthology of bad verse; the title comes from one of his poems. Yeats's early work can seem misty compared to the polished gleam of the later poems. But readers would not refuse to read any of Wordsworth or Yeats because of certain less successful poems. Why then, the overreaction of distaste concerning Sarton's work?

The bias I brought to that reading in Rochester had to do with free verse as opposed to traditional forms; William Carlos Williams's fanaticism served as a survival technique for him—he was blazing a path—but such fervor no longer seems to be a necessity for contemporary poets. Even if one writes nontraditional verse, one can still read other kinds of forms without being "contaminated." Dacey and Jauss's anthology *Strong Measures,* which presents traditional forms by contemporary poets, has done much to prepare a new generation of readers for May Sarton's poetry. By including poems from a wide range of poets, among them Cid Corman, Robert Creeley, Louise Glück, Etheridge Knight, and Allen Ginsberg, *Strong Measures* makes a strong case for admiring variety in contemporary poetry.

Had Sarton been born a few years earlier, of the generation of Wylie and Millay, her use of traditional forms might have seemed less of an anachronism. Since her work spans the decades from the thirties into the nineties, her poetry has at times seemed unfashionable. Sarton's *In Time Like Air* appeared two years after Ginsberg's *Howl,* one of the major poetic documents of the fifties and sixties, a poem that blasted away most remnants of traditional forms. Yet there are also contemporary aspects to Sarton's poetry, to her grappling with "silence" and solitude, as Keith Norris points out in his essay on postmodernism, and as Jane Miller indicates in her essay "The Simple Day." Sarton brings her own version of Romanticism into modern and contemporary poetry, a Romanticism more oriented toward the present than the past. Sarton's European background gives some of her work a traditional flavor, and makes her a spiritual and aesthetic companion to Valéry and Yeats, rather than to Sharon Olds or Galway Kinnell. And yet, Sarton sings of the Goddess, a theme that we will not find in Valéry; the intimate tone of her poetry creates warmth even in the midst of the formal distillations of her lyrics. Intimacy is a hallmark of Sarton's poetry, and in this respect her verse takes its place in contemporary poetry alongside the poems of Olds and Kinnell.

Stronger biases against Sarton than those having to do with difficulties in historical placement, reveal themselves in overreactions like Ciardi's, or in Karl Shapiro's abrupt dismissal: "Her poetry is ladypoetry at its worst—this at a time when poetry is very much the art of women" (5). "The woman thing," Sarton calls this tendency of some critics to "bash" women's writings. As Richard Chess points out in his essay "The Straight Gaze," Adrienne Rich's work has helped us to understand the cultural bias against homosexuality and the very real dangers lesbian women face. Though Sarton's lyric poetry is not explicitly about sexual preference, her "coming out" in *Mrs. Stevens* has made her vulnerable to homophobia as well as to sexism. Mrs. Stevens and Harriet Hatfield wear "masks"—thinly disguised ones, perhaps, to express the author's feelings; and these writings have a bearing on Sarton's lyric poems. The poet knows well that privacy in the lyric is an illusion, one that she requires to write poetry at all. The poet is "out," but the poems do not belabor her being an "outsider"—they go on singing the subtleties of feelings engaged by many subjects—love, nature, spirituality, grief, illness, aging, and release. Being "out" is another facet of the openness that Sarton has always embraced.

Among the poets who wrote essays for this volume, William Stafford is closest in age. There's a quiet, meditative spirit to his poetry that seems a good companion to Sarton's, though their forms are far apart. Most of the authors whose essays appear in this collection are "younger" poets who show appreciation for Sarton's work, though they themselves do not work primarily in strict forms. As poets, they express admiration for the music in her language, for her discipline and meticulous craft, for her sense of humanity. They are intrigued by the open-ended theme of "silence" in Sarton's work, particularly as silence becomes more eloquent in the last three books. They speak out of respect for Sarton's courage in being "out" there, alone, writing faithfully each day over the last sixty years. As poet Robert Hass inscribed aptly in May Sarton's copy of *Human Wishes:* "For May, Who teaches us all by *writing.*"

In America, we tend to give our poets—especially our women poets—serious consideration only after they are dead. While this collection of essays does not contain praise only, it does bring to bear careful, respectful consideration of Sarton's verse. Our close attention to Sarton's recent work serves to illuminate the finely wrought forms of her "upward years." As the aging poet Williams reflected: "I like to think of the Japanese print maker Hokusai who said that (he lived to be ninety-nine) when he arrived at age a hundred, every dot on his paper would be significant. . . . I think the older you get, provided you don't abuse your faculties, the better you're likely to be as an artist" (Williams, *Interviews* 62). At eighty, after a lifetime of work at writing, May Sarton has achieved the artistry Hokusai looked toward. The poets gathered here—and numerous others we could not include—wish her abundant poems and light-filled hours in the years ahead.

Knoxville, March 1992

Works Cited

Bacon, Martha. "Marvels of Interwoven Syllables." Rev. of *The Lion and the Rose,* by May Sarton. *Saturday Review* (Apr. 1948): 50.

Ciardi, John. "Recent Verse." Rev. of *The Land of Silence,* by May Sarton. *Nation* 178 (1954): 183–84.

Dacey, Philip, and David Jauss, eds. *Strong Measures: An Anthology of American Poetry in Traditional Forms.* New York: Harper and Row, 1986.

Daziel, Bradford Dudley. "May Sarton and the Common Reader." *Sarton Selected: An Anthology of the Journals, Novels, and Poems of May Sarton.* Ed. Daziel. New York: Norton, 1991. 19–61.

Dickey, James. "In the Presence of Anthologies." *Sewanee Review* 66 (1958): 306.

Heilbrun, Carolyn. "May Sarton's Memoirs." *May Sarton: Woman and Poet.* Ed. Hunting. 43–52.

Hunting, Constance, ed. *May Sarton: Woman and Poet.* Orono, Maine: National Poetry Foundation, University of Maine at Orono, 1982.

Kallet, Marilyn. *Honest Simplicity in William Carlos Williams' "Asphodel, That Greeny Flower."* Baton Rouge: Louisiana State UP, 1985.

———. "The Silence Then and Now: May Sarton's Poetry." *Before Columbus Review* 1.3–4 (1990): 18–21.

Momaday, Scott. *The Way to Rainy Mountain.* Albuquerque: U of New Mexico P, 1969.

Olsen, Tillie. *Silences.* New York: Delacorte Press/Seymour Lawrence, 1978.

Rev. of *The Lion and the Rose,* by May Sarton. *Kirkus Reviews* 16 (1948): 44.

Rich, Adrienne. *The Dream of a Common Language: Poems 1974–1977.* New York: Norton, 1978.

Russ, Joanna. *How to Suppress Women's Writing.* Austin: U of Texas P, 1983.

Sarton, Eleanor Mabel. *Letters to May.* Orono: Puckerbrush P, 1986.

Sarton, May. *Collected Poems (1930–1973).* New York: Norton, 1974.

———. *Halfway to Silence.* New York: Norton, 1980.

———. Interview. "The Art of Poetry XXXII: May Sarton." With Karen Saum. *Paris Review* 89 (1983): 80–110.

———. *Journal of a Solitude.* New York: Norton, 1973.

———. *Letters from Maine.* New York: Norton, 1984.

———. Letter to the author. 7 Apr. 1992.

———. *Sarton Selected: An Anthology of the Journals, Novels, and Poems of May Sarton.* Ed. Bradford Dudley Daziel. New York: Norton, 1991.

———. *The Silence Now: New and Uncollected Earlier Poems.* New York: Norton, 1988.

———. *A World of Light.* New York: Norton, 1976.

———. *Writings on Writing.* Orono: Puckerbrush Press, 1980.

Schwartzlander, Susan, and Marilyn R. Mumford, eds. *That Great Sanity: Critical Essays on May Sarton.* Ann Arbor: UP of Michigan, 1993.

Shapiro, Karl. "Voices That Speak to the Critic in Very Different Rhythms." Rev. of *Cloud, Stone, Sun, Vine,* by May Sarton. *New York Times Book Review* 24 Dec. 1961, Sun. ed.: 4–5.

Stafford, William. *An Oregon Message.* New York: Harper and Row, 1989.

Williams, William Carlos. *Interviews with William Carlos Williams: "Speaking Straight Ahead."* Ed. Linda Wagner. New York: New Directions, 1976.

———. *The Selected Letters of William Carlos Williams.* Ed. John C. Thirwall. New York: McDowell, Obolensky, 1957.

FRIENDSHIP & ILLNESS

Christmas, 1990

Through the silences,
The long empty days
You have sat beside me
Watching the finches feed,
The tremor in the leaves.
You have not left my mind.

Friendship supplied the root–
It was planted years ago–
To bring me flowers and seed
Through the long drought.

Far-flung as you are
You have seemed to sit beside me.
You have not left my mind.

Will you come in the new year?
To share the wind in the leaves
And the finches lacing the air
To savor the silence with me?
It's been a long time.

— *May Sarton*

Fig. 1. *"Friendship & Illness," 1990. Christmas poem by May Sarton, reprinted from a special edition by William B. Ewert, Publisher, Concord, N.H. Design by Mary Azarian. Used with permission.*

An Interview with May Sarton

MARILYN KALLET

The following interview took place on Sunday, 21 July 1991, at May Sarton's home in York, Maine. As Sarton had been feeling very ill, I promised to make this a brief interview. She began by telling me that she had written only one poem since the summer of 1990, "Friendship & Illness," which she sent out to her friends as her customary "Christmas poem." Happily, since our conversation, May Sarton has been writing poetry again. Several of her new poems from 1990–92, including "Friendship & Illness," appear in a special edition entitled *Coming Into Eighty,* published in 1992 for May Sarton's eightieth birthday by William B. Ewert, Publisher, Concord, New Hampshire.

Kallet: You wrote a beautiful poem called "Friendship & Illness" in 1990. Was that your last poem?

Sarton: Yes, last year. I wrote it in August.

Kallet: Have there been others since then?

Sarton: No. The one great advantage of having to write a Christmas poem is that I do it. And if I didn't have that compulsion and feel I must get it done, I probably wouldn't have written some of my best poems. "The Nativity," the one about the painter Piero della Francesca, who affected me so deeply, that was a Christmas poem [*SSE* 157].

Kallet: "Christmas Light," with its quiet lines, ". . . pure light/ Stayed on, stayed on"—that's another [*SN* 27]. So sometimes in order to get to your inspiration, you have to get kick-started. How long have you been doing the Christmas poems?

Sarton: Thirty years or so. But I stopped for a long time, when the list got to be a thousand. I felt: I'm not a factory. Just writing the addresses was exhausting. I had no secretary. And so I gave it up for twenty years. Only quite recently a fan, William Ewert, who loves to do special editions, said, "Wouldn't you write a poem, and we'd do it for you?" He does it for nothing, and then he sells them. It's wonderful. He gets wonderful people to illustrate. It's just great!

Kallet: "Friendship & Illness" is very spare, resonant, and moving. It seemed to be an invitation to your friends to come and see you. Literally, that we should take you up on it.

Sarton: Yes, I think it really was. . . . I was afraid of sending it. It seemed too personal, not enough about Christmas. But people have loved it. Many people tell me that they've framed it. Amazing!

Kallet: Let's talk about "the muse," a subject that has been crucial to your work. . . . Has the muse always been a passionate, feminine source for you?

Sarton: Yes, the muse has always been a woman. I have had more than one male lover, but never a male muse. And the muses, the women, were, by no means, all lovers. The muse is someone who captures the imagination. . . .

Kallet: Yet, in your writings the donkey has been a muse. Bramble [Sarton's cat] was a muse.

Sarton: Animals more than people.

Kallet: And trees.

Sarton: Trees. Yes, that's true. It's very puzzling. I just don't know. I really don't. The muse is possession by the imagination. It was very often someone older than I, though not always someone obvious like Eva Le Gallienne, whom I adored, and who was very glamorous. But I think I wrote only one poem for her. One of the great muses in my life was Katharine Taylor, the head of Shady Hill School when I was ten or eleven. I wrote many poems for her. . . . I started to say that it was not until I was over forty that I could begin to think of myself as a woman and not a young man. So, in all the early poems, the romantic poems, I am "he."

Kallet: I went through that also. I didn't realize I was a "she" in my work until 1968, as ridiculous as that sounds.

Sarton: There you are! I'm so glad to hear that. . . . We didn't believe in ourselves as women.

Kallet: It's not necessarily that. At the time, it just wasn't part of the common currency of speech to differentiate our pronouns; we didn't think about the implications of using "he" as a generic pronoun. We naïvely thought "he" was everybody.

Sarton: Yes, exactly. . . . Finally, someone said to me about the last, fairly recent "Phoenix" poem—which ended with something about "sing his thrilling song"—she said: "Why don't you say *'her'?"* ["The Phoenix Again," *SN* 76]. And I said to myself, "Why not?" [laughter].

Kallet: I think we've all come through that. Even Adrienne Rich's poems are traditional in the beginning; her models are traditional male poets. She moved on.

Sarton: Yes. I knew her then. She was the same kind of poet as I was— like Millay and Elinor Wylie. Rich has certainly grown!

Kallet: Before I move on to ask about the historical placement of your work, I want to ask you if the muse is still here for you.

Sarton: No.

Kallet: Yet, on some level it must be, because you wrote that poem, "Friendship & Illness."

Sarton: But then *I* was the muse. Someone said to me, "You must become your own muse." I think in a way that's true. That's what happens.

Kallet: I love that idea! We embrace ourselves.

Sarton: Yes, in a way. There is a poem about the last muse being the sea. The poem begins, "Never has the sea been maternal to me or kind" [*SN* 73]. But, in a way, perhaps the last muse has been this house, this environment where I've written a great deal. . . . Juliette Huxley has been a muse, but you see I haven't written poems for her for thirty years. She was one of the great muses. I wrote the sonnet sequences for her in Paris. "Those images remain"—that sequence, those were to her. There were many poems to her [*CP* 144–47].

Kallet: Is she still living?

Sarton: Yes, she's over ninety. There's a whole book of my letters to her that Norton will publish when she dies. She gave permission to me, but I'm sure she doesn't realize what's there. They're really lovely letters, not sexual. But I think if she saw the book, she might say, "I never said that!" It's too ticklish.

Kallet: We had talked before about the difficulty of placing your work in a historical context, since your writing spans sixty years. In fact, you saw this difficulty as one reason why there has been some neglect of the poetry, more so than of the other genres you have worked in. Having begun to write poetry in the 1930s, you might be dismissed by contemporary critics as being old-fashioned—without their taking a more serious look.

Sarton: I think that's so. Helen Vendler, poetry critic for the *New Yorker,* said of my work in a review: "derivative and not interesting" [556]. I think that was the general attitude. It looked as though I were like everyone else, but I really wasn't. I was doing things like "A Divorce of Lovers" [*CP* 201–8], saying things that hadn't been said before. And that *they* didn't get.

Kallet: Then Vendler did not read your work closely?

Sarton: That's right.

Kallet: Your work shows the pervasive influence of the modern poets Yeats and Valéry.

Sarton: Yes, Yeats and Valéry were the two major influences, absolutely. Yeats, partly because he grew so much and changed his style.

Kallet: And he was lyrical.

Sarton: Lyrical too. He was everything. His last poems are like rocks.

Kallet: The language has been "worked." Your poems are polished, too.

Sarton: That's what I feel. That's what I want.

Kallet: Was Valéry more of an influence than Mallarmé?

Sarton: Mallarmé was not an influence. No, Valéry. Louise Bogan and I translated a lot of Valéry together. . . . *Metamorphosis* was one literary magazine that printed quite a few [seven]. I did all the work. This tickled Louise. She would go over the poems and make a few suggestions. I would have worked ten hours on a poem. She couldn't put them into form; I could. She was a good critic in some ways. She was helpful. But she got the credit for a lot she didn't do. . . . I didn't mind; I enjoyed it. . . . We both enjoyed this working relationship.

Kallet: Did the poetry cross-pollinate?

Sarton: She was a muse, certainly. She wasn't writing then. She was at a very bad time in her life when we met. This was in the 1950s and '60s. Her poetry was out of print. You know how terrible that feels.

Kallet: I know how it feels. It doesn't seem right. I mean, here you are still alive and yet the book is dead!

Sarton: Yes, yes. Then they did a selected poems, thank God, and she got back. . . . And she got very good reviews, deserved, well deserved.

Kallet: Did you influence one another in your work?

Sarton: She influenced me by her poetry enormously, She was extremely—I think now I can say it—jealous of me. So, she never gave me a good review. And this was at a time when she could have made all the difference. She chose not to. It was very painful.

Kallet: You mentioned in one interview that you were influenced by Walt Whitman.

Sarton: He was one of the poets I knew best and loved most when I was fourteen. One of my first great influences. . . . And then I went to other poets to study form. . . . I read Donne and Marvell. I got very excited about all that.

Kallet: Are there any contemporary poets you feel strongly about?

Sarton: There aren't many . . . Constance Hunting, who has just had a book of poetry brought out. I think she's an absolutely remarkable poet. She edits Puckerbrush Press, and she has many books. . . . William Heyen, I also admire him tremendously. He's a German who's been able to write about the Holocaust. That's so rare.

Kallet: William Stafford was kind enough to copy over a note that you had written to him, where you say that regularly you receive a letter from some reader who is just discovering your poetry. I was happy to hear that.

Sarton: I think I said I get such a letter at least once a week. Yes. Once a week is a lot!

Kallet: Does that make you feel better about this whole enterprise?

Sarton: Yes, it does. It does!

Kallet: It seems like you've always been a poet foremost—heart, soul and mind, a poet.

Sarton: That's right. That's why you must read the first novel. . . .

Kallet: Recently, I had a talk with Joy Harjo, who is Native American, and some of her poems are influenced by prayers, specifically by the form of a Navajo prayer. I asked her whether she saw a connection between poetry and prayer, and she said, "Yes, of course," as though this were perfectly obvious. I would like to ask you the same question.

Sarton: I feel that too. I feel it very much. Yes, I've gone so far as to say my poems are between me and God; my novels are communication with other people. I would write poems even if I were in solitary confinement, but I would not write novels, and I don't think I would write a journal.

Kallet: At some points of your life, you must have felt like you were in solitary confinement.

Sarton: Yes, I have. I went to Nelson because I felt that I had to withdraw, that the literary world would eventually come to me. At that moment I was in the wilderness, and I thought I'd better go to the real wilderness and be there. And it has worked out. But I've just been reading my letters to Bogan to help Susan Sherman make some choices for the book of letters she is editing. There were some very painful letters after the Shapiro review of the selected poems came out at Christmas. The collection was *Cloud, Stone, Sun, Vine,* six volumes of my poems selected. The review appeared in the *New York Times*: "May Sarton is a bad poet" . . . That was it. And he ended the review, "I'm sorry to have had to do this" [5].

Kallet: At least he realized he had something to apologize for.

Sarton: Yes. I was terribly ill, I became violently sick. I almost died of it; I really did.

Kallet: The review attacked you at the core—how could you not be affected?

Sarton: Yes, that's right. In front of 5 million people, I was called "a bad poet." He blamed me for doing sonnets, and he did a whole book of sonnets ten years later. Oh, what a rat! Well, this is the anti-woman thing.

Kallet: You think that's it?

Sarton: Oh, I'm sure it was. When you think of Ciardi. . . . We were all in a group together—Wilbur, Eberhart, Ciardi, and John Holmes. We met five times a year to criticize each other's poems. . . . It was very interesting. . . . Well, Ciardi wrote a book about writing poetry and in the introduction he told all about that group and never mentioned that I was in it! . . . I didn't exist, period.

Kallet: For those of us for whom poetry is such a meaningful activity, and for whom this recession amounts to a repression of the arts, it's heartening to have a model of someone who's been kicked down so many times and for such a long time and whose poetry has thrived.

Sarton: I kept going—well, I had to. I think it's because I finally decided to give up all ideas of ever being successful or read or criticized. That was when I went to Nelson. I sort of closed the door on ambition, I think that's what I'm saying. And so finally, recognition came. But it might not have. And that's the hell!

Kallet: Whether it comes or doesn't—whatever "it" is—at least having taken control of your life you can be more at peace with yourself.

Sarton: Yes, that's right.

Works Cited

Heyen, William. *Erika: Poems of the Holocaust.* St. Louis: Time Being Books, 1990.

Hunting, Constance. *Between The Worlds: Poems, 1983–1988.* Orono: Puckerbrush Press, 1990.

Sarton, May. *Collected Poems (1930–1973).* New York: Norton, 1974.

———. *May Sarton: Among the Usual Days: Illustrated Portrait of the Poet in Unpublished Letters, Journals, and Poems.* Ed. Susan Sherman. New York: Norton, 1993.

———. *Sarton Selected: An Anthology of the Journals, Novels, and Poems of May Sarton.* Ed. Bradford Dudley Daziel. New York: Norton, 1991.

———. *The Silence Now.* New York: Norton, 1988.

———, trans. "Palm." By Paul Valéry. *Metamorphosis* 4 (1964): 7.

Shapiro, Karl. "Voices That Speak to the Critic in Very Different Rhythms." Rev. of *Cloud, Stone, Sun, Vine: Poems, Selected and New,* by May Sarton. *New York Times Book Review* 24 Dec. 1961, Sun. ed.: 4–5.

Vendler, Helen. "Recent American Poetry." *Massachusetts Review* 8 (1967): 541–60.

Palme

A Jeannie

De sa grâce redoutable
Voilant à peine l'éclat,
Un ange met sur ma table
Le pain tendre, le lait plat;
Il me fait de la paupière
Le signe d'une prière
Qui parle à ma vision:
—Calme, calme, reste calme!
Connais le poids d'une palme
Portant sa profusion!

Pour autant qu'elle se plie
A l'abondance des biens,
Sa figure est accomplie,
Ses fruits lourds sont ses liens.
Admire comme elle vibre,
Et comme une lente fibre
Qui divise le moment,
Départage sans mystère
L'attirance de la terre
Et le poids du firmament!

Ce bel arbitre mobile
Entre l'ombre et le soleil,
Simule d'une sibylle
La sagesse et le sommeil.
Autour d'une même place
L'ample palme ne se lasse
Des appels ni des adieux . . .
Qu'elle est noble, qu'elle est tendre!
Qu'elle est digne de s'attendre
A la seule main des dieux!

L'or léger qu'elle murmure
Sonne au simple doigt de l'air,
Et d'une soyeuse armure
Charge l'âme du désert.
Une voix impérissable
Qu'elle rend au vent de sable
Qui l'arrose des ses grains,
A soi-même sert d'oracle,
Et se flatte du miracle
Que se chantent les chagrins.

Cependant qu'elle s'ignore
Entre le sable et le ciel,
Chaque jour qui luit encore
Lui compose un peu de miel.
Sa douceur est mesurée
Par la divine durée
Qui ne compte pas les jours,
Mais bien qui les dissimule
Dans un suc où s'accumule
Toute l'arôme des amours.

Parfois si l'on désespère,
Si l'adorable rigueur
Malgré tes larmes n'opère
Que sous ombre de langueur,
N'accuse pas d'être avare
Une Sage qui prépare
Tant d'or et d'autorité:
Par la sève solennelle
Une espérance éternelle
Monte à la maturité!

Ces jours qui te semblent vides
Et perdus pour l'univers
Ont des racines avides
Qui travaillent les déserts.
La substance chevelue
Par les ténèbres élue
Ne peut s'arrêter jamais,
Jusqu'aux entrailles du monde,
De poursuivre l'eau profonde
Que demandent les sommets.

Patience, patience,
Patience dans l'azur!
Chaque atome de silence
Est la chance d'un fruit mûr!
Viendra l'heureuse surprise:
Une colombe, la brise,
L'ébranlement le plus doux,
Une femme qui s'appuie,
Feront tomber cette pluie
Où l'on se jette à genoux!

Qu'un peuple à présent s'écroule,
Palme! . . . irrésistiblement!
Dans la poudre qui'il se roule
Sur les fruits du firmament!
Tu n'as pas perdu ces heures
Si légère tu demeures
Après ces beaux abandons;
Pareille à celui qui pense
Et dont l'âme se dépense
A s'accroître de se dons!

Paul Valéry, Charmes, 1922

Palm

To Jeannie

Veiling only a little
The bright awe of his gift,
An angel to the table
Brings fresh bread and smooth milk.
But the grave eyelids there
Gently summon to prayer,
The vision's inwardness:
—Calm, calm, be calm!
Learn the weight of the palm
Supporting its largesse.

Just as the tree is bent
Under its heavy fruit,
Just so is all assent,
Leaning on its own weight;
Lovely the slight vibration,
The threading in slow motion
As it divides the moment
And learns to arbitrate
Between earth's pulling weight
And the vast firmament.

Between the sun and shade,
Wise as a sybil's sleep,
This judgement lightly made
Still rests upon the deep.
Patient, it never tires
Of farewells or desires,
But, centered, the palm stands.
Oh, tender noble one
Worthy to wait alone
For the gods' fertile hands.

The light gold is a murmur
Fingered by simple air
To weave a silken armor
For desert soul to wear,
Gives to the brittle wind
Shot through with shifting sand
A voice that's never done,
Is its own oracle,
A self-made miracle
When grief sings on alone.

And still itself unknowing
Between sand and the sky
While each day shines, is growing
And makes a little honey.
This sweetness of sensation
Is timeless in duration
Through days that hardly move,
Uncounted hours of presence
Secrete the living essence
And the full weight of love.

Sometimes severe endeavor
Yields only that despair
Of shadow and of languor
In spite of many a tear.
Yet do not then accuse
The tree of avarice,
Oh Gold, Authority!
Gravely the rising sap
And the eternal hope
Grow to maturity.

These seeming-empty hours
When the whole world is gone
Send avid roots and powers
Down through the desert, down
Like myriad fine hairs
The fruitful darkness bears;
Working their way through sand
To the entrails of earth
Where sources come to birth
That the high peaks demand.

Patience, and patience,
Patience across the blue.
Each atom of your silence
Ripens the fruit in you.
The grave mercy is near,
A dove, a breath of air,
The gentlest feeling,
There where a woman leans
The light rain begins
And you are kneeling.

If now a people fall
Palm—irresistibly!
Powdered like dust to roll
With the stars in the sky!
You have not lost those hours
So lightly bear your powers
After the great outgoing;
As does the thinking one
Who spends his spirit on
The gifts of his own growing.

Translation of Valéry's "Palme" by May Sarton, 1954

I

The Gift of Discipline

The Gift of Discipline:
Miss Sarton in 1950

LINDA PASTAN

May Sarton gave me the first B I had ever received in an English class, and for a long time I didn't forgive her for it. I had come to Radcliffe from a small progressive high school in New York City where much had been made of my "individuality," my so-called talent, and I thought that every word I wrote, every poem, was so nearly perfect that it shouldn't under any circumstances be tampered with. I had even read somewhere that the words that spring naturally to a real poet's mind are sacrosanct, that changing them would be an act of dishonesty and could only do some kind of moral damage. A poem of mine had been printed on the back of our high school graduation program, so wasn't I already a real poet?

"The day was like a newly washed bedspread, hanging out to dry," I wrote in the first piece I handed in for her section of the obligatory freshman course, English A, and I have to confess that I still have a certain affection for that line, but May Sarton was having none of it.

"I know it sounds good," she told me, "but it is just too imprecise."

"There is sorrow and lonely and dark and still lonely. . . ." I can still hear the wonderful bark of her laugh when I tried that one on her.

I remember the first day of class. All my other classes were large lectures, taught in darkened auditoriums by imposing Harvard professors, all male, and with sheaves of well-worn notes in their hands. Miss Sarton, as we called her, was small, even slight, with a boyish air, a strong, engaging laugh, and a kind of assertive shyness. Could this be a "real" class? I worried. Would we learn anything worthwhile?

Was one supposed to take notes on the kind of informal talking it was clear was going to go on here? And was anything going to be worth taking notes on?

I think May Sarton wore trousers on that day as well as on subsequent days. We were not allowed to wear anything but skirts outside the dormitory, and I like to think she was immune to, or else ignored, such strictures, but I don't really remember much more than the tailored cut of her clothes, gray or tan usually, relieved by a colored scarf at the neck, or a bright handkerchief. It was a small class, all women, or girls as we were called then. "We are going to do a semester on witches," Miss Sarton told us, all intensity and wearing a sly, bewitching kind of smile herself as she spread out on her desk an assortment of books and manuscripts dealing with the Salem witch trials: facsimiles of original notebooks, diaries, documents of that time. There was also a glass of water with a bunch of vivid fall flowers in it on the corner of that desk, or am I simply inventing those flowers because I cannot think of May Sarton without at least a few flowers somewhere nearby?

Why did I go into such a panic about studying and writing about witchcraft trials? I knew nothing of Arthur Miller's *The Crucible*. I hadn't even read Hawthorne yet, and in this, my first composition class in college, I wanted to write about what I wanted to write about, that is, my own feelings; my fledgling love affairs; my cloudy thoughts about life; myself. May Sarton, perhaps unwisely, let me have my way, after a bit of negotiation. I would attend class and all of the discussions about Salem and the witch trials, but instead of using that material for my compositions, I would write whatever I wanted to write for my weekly assignments.

Thus began a kind of tutorial for me with an accomplished and meticulous poet, whose own work, I'm ashamed to say, I didn't read or even know about until years after that class was over, for May Sarton did not talk about her own poetry. I would hand in something, a poem or a story or a short essay, and she would write comments on it, gentle, tactful criticism at first that became firmer as the weeks went by, and I was still showing little inclination for taking advice. "I don't believe in these emotions," she would say finally, in exasperation, "give me some details," "let me see what you're describing," "this isn't a poem yet," "show me!"

"How can a tree have 'antlered branches' on one line and 'summer-scented fingers' on the next?" I remember her writing in her tiny precise script on the bottom of one of my poems. And "that's a lot of blather," I think she was even driven to once.

Miss Sarton was almost always right. Still, I argued and resisted, and defended my every comma. Days and weeks went by. In the documents we talked about in class, children accused old women of being witches, women were actually put to death, and I was in love for the second or third time and writing long, emotion-clogged poems about it.

Somewhere around Thanksgiving, I think it was, when the astringent New England winter was starting to wake me up, it must finally have gotten through to me that perhaps I could actually change what I had first put down on paper; that Waterman ink washed off a little more easily than blood, though it felt like blood that I was writing in. And as the leaves fell away, as the first snow followed, what was slowly and painfully and wondrously born in me was my enduring love for, my enduring love affair with, revision. I don't remember the precise day I first decided that I could make my work better by thinking of it as work, by sitting down and working on it. But one teacher's patient, intelligent persistence finally got through to me. Poetry was a matter of inspiration, but it was also a matter of craft. Years later, when I came upon May Sarton's own work almost by accident, I saw that this idea of craft was more than an abstraction for her, for I saw the meticulous care that certainly went into the shaping of her own crystalline lyrics.

The gift, then, of discipline and craftsmanship was hers to me. And somehow along the way a kind of fascination with the subject of witches was subliminally transmitted too, so that lately real witches have been insinuating themselves, spells, brooms, and all, into some of my own poems.

II

Chaos Unbewildered:
Sarton and Her Craft

To See the Chaos Unbewildered:
May Sarton's Earliest Collections

CHARLOTTE MANDEL

A painter's hand may actuate characteristic spirals, angles, or brush strokes to create a form of writing as singular as her legal signature. For a poet, associations of image with sound, syllabic rhythms, and syntactical oddities may design unique patterns of artistic verbalization. Working poets begin to recognize and accept the intrusion of certain similes and metaphors into first drafts and learn to draw upon these familiar (often "family") sources as welcome clues toward creative discovery. Out of the never-resolved argument between values previously absorbed and perceptions of the moment, the poet plays her keyboard of inner history with language in virtuoso control of feeling and thought. May Sarton's achievements demonstrate such evolution.

A close reading of Sarton's three earliest published collections offers insight into the dynamics of her identifiable poetic signature. Essential to the integrity of her poetic process is choice of form, mostly traditional, yet with notable approaches to free verse. Themes that will occupy Sarton's poetry throughout her long career are evident from the beginning: love, sensitivity to landscape, social concerns, poetry as a sacred art, emergence of the self as woman.

Since 1937, May Sarton has published seventeen books of poetry, including volumes of selected and collected poems. Poetry is, to Sarton, her most significant work, and her first published book was a poetry collection, *Encounter in April; Inner Landscape* was published two years later in 1939; and *The Lion and the Rose* in 1948. An examination of the three books in chronological order reveals the poet already in the process of creating signature work. The first collection shows style and subject matter derived from poets read, admired, and memorized since childhood—interspersed, nevertheless, with strong flashes of her individual powers. Evolutionary changes are visible in her second collection, and, as might be expected, a leap in development marks the difference between the second and third volumes, written nine years apart.

Of the fifty-five poems published in her first book, *Encounter in April,* thirty-two are conventional sonnets. Other poems establish a form by consistencies of line length and use of end rhyme, sometimes as whole word repetition. Unevenly handled free verse appears as a series of haiku-like observations, a longer meditation on a Japanese print, tributes to Georgia O'Keeffe and Eleonora Duse, the heartfelt paean "For Keats and Mozart," and Sarton's famous "She Shall Be Called Woman." The last-named is a ten-part lyrical narrative that explores the consciousness of Eve newly created, and holds to its weave without rhymed or metered patterns. The poem celebrates Woman's discovery of her sexual energies, "the wound of desire" and the cyclical "surging miracle / of blood" in tune with rhythms of earth's turnings. Clearly, no inherited forms could suffice for this powerful new feminist statement.

Instances of creative growth can never be located as statistical points on a graph, yet there is a direction to Sarton's journey: the forms she chooses often reflect degrees of shyness or confidence in her self emergence. In the interview, "I live alone in a very beautiful place," she says, "Far from being conscious and willed, form is what is given me when I'm inspired" (Kaplan and Neiderbach 249–60).

Her earliest love poems, however, rely on forms and references inspired by the politeness of inherited givens. *Encounter in April* opens with a sonnet sequence of five love poems and closes with a longer sonnet sequence of fifteen love poems. The lovers of the first sequence, who "came together softly," are not identified as to gender; in the second sequence, one poem speaks of the lovers as "man and woman." When Sarton was in her twenties, and for close to a quarter of a century after, the poet's bisexuality was not publicly acknowledged. In her early love poetry, the influence of socially approved convention is allowed to color, and therefore weaken, the content of her poetic statement. Whether writing poetry or prose, Sarton has never approved the inclusion of frank sexual material into her work, but the strength of her later love poems has not depended on such detail. "A Divorce of Lovers," for instance, a sequence of twenty sonnets published in 1958, declares the poet's direct emotional experience through images that are actual and incontrovertibly real—"long bands of light . . . across the floor," the weekend that was "circled on the calendars," the act of touching "mosses under balsam" as she walks the woods (*CP* 201–9).

In contrast, the love sonnet sequences published in 1937 do not, in the main, speak with the poet's identifiable voice. Although a sudden typically sensuous-specific Sarton image such as "The puckermouth crab-apple" punctuates a line with pleasure for the reader, points of reference, lacking autobiographical framework, remain vague. The lovers are distanced from individuality by metaphor. Similes chosen to represent love or the lover sound a catalog of animal, plant, mineral, or weather comparisons. The lovers are "two deer"; "two Dresden figurines"; a fox about to leap that loses "feet of an antelope"; they are seen "as fauns"; "as early wheat"; "one leaf on another leaf"; one's "vermilion heart [is] crystal . . . to be filled by a bee's golden milk"; the lover's hand in hers feels "like a smooth stone on the smooth sand"; the lover is abstracted as "my tropic and my south." Such gestures as (in the voice of the porcelain figurine) "I curtsied, darling, and you kissed my hand" distance the reader from the personal reality of this relationship. The forms, all Shakespearian sonnets but for one, and half of another, in Petrarchan rhyme scheme, have a dutiful ring to them.

In maturity, Sarton recognized that these early sonnets were overly imitative and, for that reason, excluded them all from *Collected Poems (1930–1973)* published in 1974 (Kaplan and Neiderbach 254). Only three poems from *Encounter in April* may be seen in *Collected Poems,* most prominently, "She Shall Be Called Woman." Yet nine of the early love sonnets were still important enough to Sarton at the time she published her second volume for her to feature them again, in the British edition, as a section with nine other poems from the first book. *Encounter in April* had come out only in the American edition published by Houghton Mifflin, and the same publisher's edition of *Inner Landscape* does not, therefore, reprint any of the poems from the first book. Because the earlier volume had not yet appeared in England, Sarton wished to present a fuller view of her work (for the British publisher, Cresset Press) by selecting a group of poems from her first collection. "She Shall Be Called Woman" is included under the title "Conception."

The texts of reprinted poems remain unchanged, a practice followed by Sarton in later years, consistent with her poetic aims.[1] The poem is an act of control—the control of passion by form. Sarton does not release a poem for publication until the work feels, to her, alive in its final arrangement. In childhood, she absorbed poetic forms as rhythms organic to the processes of daily living from a father who spent his lifetime assembling words on paper and from a mother who sang and who could weave embroideries of color into unique designs flowing into apparent effortlessness only by means of painstaking hours of stitching. Her mother also had a talent for coaxing glowing blooms of color out of moist, fertile earth, dark roots and stems. Each parent worked from rich materials given, and the work they did was sacred in dedication: Art requires discipline. Words are inseparable from knowledge and beauty, and a poem requires pattern and design. A kind of synesthesia comes into play, where stimulations of color and touch may be heard by the inner ear. May Sarton's inner ear vibrated in that environment to melodies of poems read aloud to her and that she herself recited and memorized. As for many poets, an unconscious sense of hearing shapes the final directions of a poem.

Beginning with intense but amorphous emotional need, Sarton has used traditional forms as creative starting points—the sonnet, for instance, as a tool to extract syllables of sound and idea while weaving patterns of permanent order. A child of the twentieth century, she seems, at first glance, oddly untouched by modernism's precepts, which rejected metronomic iambics or the wrenching of syntax into obligatory rhyme. Influenced by avid, omnivorous reading of such varied poets as George Herbert, Blake, Dickinson, Yeats, Hopkins, Keats, H.D., and Walt Whitman, her method sought integrative reworking of forms and rhythms rather than denial of the past. At twenty-

nine, Sarton vociferously defended her attraction to traditional forms
in a letter to the novelist and editor Bryher (Winifred Ellerman), close
friend of the poet H.D. (Hilda Doolittle): "A great deal has to do
with what the state of poetry is or was at the time of one's emergence
into it—you, and . . . Hilda [H.D.] emerged earlier than I, at a time
when poetry was form-ridden and inwardly faded. I am already the
reactionary against your reaction." In the same paragraph, she defines
the principle that will continue to energize her lifelong poetic mis-
sion: "I believe . . . that one of the things art does is to translate the
chaos for a moment into a form so one can see it, un-bewildered"
(YCAL, 13 Feb. 1942).

The language of Sarton's first collection enacts the unevenness of
her struggle toward transcendence into form. "For Keats and Mozart,"
while contemplating the immortal music and poetry of geniuses who
died young, speaks to a generic "you" who might be the reader, who
might be herself. The first half of the poem, written in expositional
free verse, consists of eleven nonrhyming lines with from eight to thirteen irregularly stressed syllables. Midway, however, the poem seems
to find itself in an ardent litany of twelve shorter lines beating a delicate percussion of end rhymes to meaningful conclusion. Here, Sarton's
brush strokes may be traced—turns of stress and sound that evidence
her orchestration of language:

> Lift up your hearts to the young dead.
> They will give you knowledge of
> something like love
> (O to be comforted!)
> They will be hosts to your pain,
> the wine and the bread,
> a pillow under your head:
> Give praise to those who are dead,
> who have created
> with human breath
> something outside of life, outside of death—
> the heart translated. (*EA* 64)

The pattern may best be seen by isolating and lining up the final word of each line, as follows:

dead	a
of	b
love	b
comforted	a2
pain	x
bread	a
head	a
dead	a
created	a2
breath	d
death	d
translated	a2

The rhymes follow no pattern of quatrain or couplet that may be anticipated, yet, slowly, we become conscious of a weave. By intoning the final words, one after the other, the essence of the poem's meaning is spoken. The dead are of love, comforted, and by their created breath is death translated. The technique—which I have named "rhyming of idea," may not be conscious design on the poet's part, yet such poetic reinforcement subtly strengthens her lifetime work.

It is also characteristic of Sarton to vary stress on end rhymes. "For Keats and Mozart" ends most of the lines quoted above on a stressed rhyming word of one syllable, such as "dead" or "bread," but for three end words of three syllables each—"comforted," "created," "translated"—all of which fall to unstressed softening with the chiming syllable "ted." "Breath" and "death" sound a further variation—a consonantal alteration of rhyme from hard to soft dentals. The progression of stresses and sounds repeated with slight, but significant, variation plays an elegiac drum; slow beats interspersed with gentle brush/roll to the poem's final consolation. Yet, sharp and atonal, the word "pain" disrupts the rhyming pattern on the fifth line like a sudden cry; then, three lines later, "pain" chimes aurally and visually with the word "praise." This internal rhyme shift emphasizes meaning—pain has been eased by transcendence into praise.

In an essay written thirty years later, Sarton speaks of the "risk and tremor" of writing free verse, that for her to tap energy in a poem, "tension presupposed formal structuring" (*WW* 69–70). She expresses this belief after having published six collections of poetry. Yet in her fifties she began to break free, seeking to hear the "silences within" made audible by working in free verse. Since 1966, with an increasing sense of daring, Sarton has expanded more often into free verse to capture the direct interplay of feeling with thought, letting her language rewrite maps of her personal geography. Free verse may be an expression of the greater permission she has given herself to seek, as she puts it, "horizon" rather than "boundary" (*WW* 71). Horizon opens and retreats through the years. When, as a young writer in her twenties, Sarton created "She Shall Be Called Woman," she had let that particular feeling/thought interplay achieve perfect harmony with her female self, unnamed, unencumbered by traditional exhortations toward forms—in free verse, therefore, unbewildered.

If "For Keats and Mozart" reflects an intermediate stage of Sarton's personal genesis, there are no halfway positions in her evocation of the first woman's emergence. In sequence one, idea is inseparable from rhythm as each of the five opening stanzas leads off with the capitalized female referent "She." This unmistakably feminine pronoun is the key that unlocks this poem—the title, quoting the biblical injunction, emphasizes that her name is "Woman":

> She did not cry out
> nor move.
> She lay quite still
> and leaned
> against the great curve
> of the earth,
> and her breast
> was like a fruit
> bursten of its own sweetness. (*EA* 13)

Here, too, "rhyming of idea" sings along the vertical play of end words, a confirmation of image with meaning: "still leaned curve earth breast fruit sweetness."

The second stanza opens with another distinguishing mark of Sarton's poetry—repetition of a line or phrase with slight shifts in word order. The repetition will step time backward, yet with variation that carries the narrative forward: "She did not move / nor cry out—." As the "delicate savage" lays hand to her breast, she is coping with discovery of her body and its "first ache of fullness."

The fifth and final stanza of this sequence repeats its opening phrase:

> She did not move
> nor cry out.
> She lay beneath the hand
> conceiving of a flower,
> a little white flower,
> the flower of love—
> she bore it like a child. (*EA* 14)

"She" who has been somehow conceived is capable of conception. The above stanza shows another characteristic swirl of Sarton's poetic handwriting: words are urged into contextual positions that may stretch their capabilities of meaning. "She bore it like a child" may signify to have endured (the touch of the other) or to have given birth. Later, in the poem's third sequence, "She bore the wound of desire" continues the word's double meaning, as Woman conceives of her own capacity for sexual desire, a painful but ultimately wonderful honoring of her own body. She studies her hand, literally seeing it for the first time:

> the mesh
> with its multitude of lines,
> the exquisite small hairs,
> the veins
> finding their way
> down to the nails,
> the nails themselves
> set in so firmly
> with half-moons
> at their base, (*EA* 19)

and she uses those hands to "clothe herself" in knowledge by touch of her own bodily form.

The poem's final sequence extols the female cyclical reality—of "seeds / that burst at intervals"—menstruation as "a surging miracle / of blood," a time to:

> re-identify herself,
> each time more closely
> with the heart of life
> . . . .
> And she would lean
> again as once
> on the great curve of the earth,
> part of its turning. . . . (*EA* 22)

Enacting the female cycle, words have circled back to the poem's— and to Woman's—beginning. "She Shall Be Called Woman" is pioneer and presage to the growing canon of forthright feminist poetry where the poem becomes an act of giving birth to the woman writing. The central truth of this meaning for Sarton was ratified by her own renaming of the poem, reprinted in her second book under the title "Conception."

Of the fifty-four new poems (1936–38) published in *Inner Landscape,* only three are written in free verse. Of fifty-nine published in *The Lion and the Rose* (1948), only one, "Celebrations," depends on conversational pace without fitting words into meter and rhyme.[2] Sarton's poetic fiber now sought the loom of visible form—the working frame that would govern her poetry almost entirely for many years.

"Prayer Before Work," the poem that opens her second book, plays as a motif the goal that energizes her poetic process. This short poem has received superb metrical explication by Constance Hunting (*Woman and Poet* 201–9; rpt. *SSE*). Yet the poem rewards even further study by revealing instances of the signature techniques that have been discussed above—rhyming of idea, repetition with slight shifts in word order, doubled weight given to a word by placement. Here is the entire "Prayer Before Work":

Great one, austere,
By whose intent the distant star
Holds its course clear,
Now make this spirit soar—
Give it that ease.

Out of the absolute,
Abstracted grief, comfortless, mute,
Sound the clear note,
Pure, piercing as the flute:
Give it precision.

Austere, great one,
By whose grace the inalterable song
May still be wrested from
The corrupt lung:
Give it strict form. (*IL* 3)

Reading the last syllable of each line downwards, we see and hear the poem's meaning reinforced, most declarative in the final stanza which asks for "one song from lung: form." Exhortation to the "great one" is repeated with variation: "Give it that ease. . . . Give it precision. . . . Give it strict form." Hunting rightly points to the exquisite transposition of "from" to "form" (203). A doubled meaning surely also may be contained in the last stanza's third line where "May," a simple verb, by the convention of its capitalization as the first word of the line, transforms verb into the poet's name, and therefore asks that the poet herself may be "song—May—wrested from the corrupt lung."

The contents of *Inner Landscape,* as the book's title implies, cohere more decisively than Sarton's earlier poems to an individual voice the poet has been shaping for herself. Images touch the reader with inviting physicality: "Remembrance . . . like light upon the eyelids of the blind," (*IL* 50). The poems vary from emulative love sonnets to more personal specifics of feeling expressed in the diction of quotidian life. Number 11 of a group called "Canticles" opens conversationally—someone is telling a story—this is how it was: [3]

We sat smoking at a table by the river
And then suddenly in the silence someone said,
"Look at the sunlight on the apple tree there shiver:
I shall remember that long after I am dead." (*IL* 48)

The poem goes on to relate an image of the sparkling light and concomitant glow of the lovers' faces, each reflecting the other's love. The lines move in easy pentameter as the unstressed syllables, varying in number and order, precede or follow the consistent beat of five stresses to a line. Sarton's multilingual sources govern her habits of stressed syllables—native Flemish and Belgian French, her mother's native Welsh and English. The strongest diction of all to be "wrested" into poetic control was the language of the United States of America. Although absorbed since her early childhood, American speech was, nonetheless, an adopted language. These contradictory linguistic variants entered the struggle to which every poet must consent—forcing silence to speak.

Sarton's third book, *The Lion and the Rose* (1948), embraces the paradox—it is by having toured the width of the American landscape that she begins to feel rooted in the silence of her own inner landscape. Reading her poems and working with students across the country has helped Sarton to reconcile self-divisions and calm her sense of exile. Because her poetry cannot be willed but must be received as given, landscape has been a profound source of spiritual energy. A section of the volume is even subtitled "American Landscapes," with reflections on Jefferson's Monticello; an abandoned plantation in South Carolina; a former mansion in Natchez, Mississippi; Boulder Dam; Texas; New Mexico.

Gazing at the beautiful changings of light upon the mountain landscapes of New Mexico, Sarton feels uplifted. The book opens with "Meditation in Sunlight," simply worded in seven short trimeter quatrains. The meter is basically iambic, yet stress patterns subtly punctuate patterns of her thought. Apart from stanza separations and conventionally capitalized first words, the stresses are, in fact, the only punctuation. No periods or commas are given to the eye; the punctuation of this poem must be heard.

> In space in time I sit
> Thousands of feet above
> The sea and meditate
> On solitude on love (*LR* 3)

The second line stresses the first syllable, lengthening and emphasizing the awe of "thousands" after the opening line's regular iambic
beat. The poem concludes:

> And I happy alone
> The place the time together
> The sun upon the stone. (*LR* 4)

The stressed syllables place "I" and "happy" together in "the place
the time" of the poem, and the closing line rests in rhythmical agreement with the opening line's quiet iambic statement.[4]

Sarton completely alters the pace in the poem "In Texas" to evoke
the region's landscape and culture in long rangy seamless lines. Without stanza breaks, the poem flows in rhyming enjambments, apparently at ease as an expert cowboy on a good-natured palomino, yet in
absolute control of its destination. Too long to quote in full, "In
Texas" marks a turn in Sarton's development—perception, thought,
feeling, and diction freed of linguistic disjunctions and unified into
one original voice:

> In Texas there's so much space words have a way
> Of getting lost in the silence before they're spoken
> So people hang on a long time to what they have to say;
> And when they say it the silence is not broken,
> But it absorbs the words and slowly gives them
> Over to miles of white-gold plains and gray-green hills,
> And they are part of the silence that outlives them.
> . . . .
> . . . But the earth slowly swings
> In time like a great swelling never-ending ocean,
> And the houses that ride the tawny waves get smaller . . .
> . . . .

In Texas you look at America with a patient eye.
. . . .
. . . You wonder why
People must talk and strain so much about a nation
That lives in spaces vaster than a man's dream and can go
Five hundred miles through wilderness, meeting only the hawk
And the dead rabbit in the road. What happens must be slow,
Must go deeper even than hand's work or tongue's talk,
Must rise out of the flesh like sweat after a hard day,
Must come slowly, in its own time, in its own way.
(*LR* 20-21)

At the conclusion of this poem, Sarton seems to be learning to be patient with herself as well, giving respect to her future poetry that will "rise out of the flesh" and "come slowly, in its own time, in its own way."

In this volume, Sarton shows a conscious ability to select and vary those traditional forms that will best enable her poems to "breathe within their strict design," an image she uses in "The Window" (*LR* 7). An epigraph by Petrarch keys the three-part elegy for her friend Edith Forbes Kennedy, "In Memoriam." This structure recalls W. H. Auden's "In Memory of W. B. Yeats," but Sarton's poetic handwriting is clearly identifiable. The first part of the poem hinges on progressive repetitions:

Think, weep, love, O watch
This casket that no keys unlatch
And may your eyes once locked in her
Gently release their prisoner.

Watch, love, weep, O think
Till it is thought not tears you drink
And thought can keep all pain apart
From her dissolved and open heart.

> Love, watch, think, O weep
> For her no love nor watch could keep
> And may your tears be the release
> Of what kept you not her from peace.

> Weep, think, watch, O love
> Her who lies here and cannot move
> And may your love rest lightly on
> Her quiet consummation. (*LR* 51)

The shifts in word order as each new stanza opens elicit the echo-chiming pleasure of a sestina, where words return in different order, but compel attention by the quiet imperative of one-syllable verbs, each a funereal drumbeat, breath caught between third and fourth beat by the grieving cry of pure vowel "O" and then resumed. The end word of the first line twice begins another stanza, interconnecting thought with sound. As "love" begins the third stanza, it moves "weep" to the forefront at the start of the final stanza. Rhyming subtly rings within the body of the poem. Each verb has a turn at setting the end rhyme for its stanza, yet like notes held by a piano pedal, continues to resonate, rhyming internally with those that precede or follow. The poem opens wider and deeper and higher as it progresses through the next sequences, reaching triumph in the third, evoking the traditional address of pastoral elegies to whatever may be powerful and holy in the elements. The conclusion of "In Memoriam" rises in a crescendo:

> Leap from the green gloom of the summer trees,
> Leap from the grasses and glittering seas,
> O terrible, life-giving marvelous shock,
> The source that jets up from the rigid rock,
> You, Praise, break from our hearts and change all grief
> Into the living rivers of belief! (*LR* 53)

In "For Keats and Mozart" published a decade earlier, a poem in tribute to "the young dead" of previous centuries, "pain" was transcended through a delicate consonantal shift into "praise." In the face of actual grief for her friend, Sarton calls upon that ideal, deepened by experience.

The Lion and the Rose features two well-known Sarton poems that exemplify, in very different styles, Sarton's personalization of society's injustices. "Who Wakes" reacts to racial violence in Detroit, June 1943, with self-examination. The poem's voice asks: "Who wakes now who lay blind with sleep?" and answers:

> I do. I, the plain citizen. . . .
> . . . .
>
> This is the harvest. The seeds sown long ago—
> The careless word, sly thought, excusing glance. . . .
> . . . .
>
> I, the plain citizen, have grown disorder
> In my own world. It is not what I meant.
> But dreams and images are potent and can murder.
> I stand accused of them. I am not innocent. (*LR* 92)

This poem of five quatrains faces up to the serious reality of thought, "the dream's responsibility," the power of mind. Human events—the actions of people—are also part of her American landscape. Here, the word "disorder" rhymes with "murder." Sarton's poetic process incorporates off-rhymes that bind together as signifiers.

"My Sisters, O My Sisters" expands the process of woman's self-creation Sarton had first discovered in "She Shall Be Called Woman" to dramatic fulfillment in a world of Sisters (*LR* 56–62). Appropriately, the poem opens with a sequence of rhyming couplets—the poet is not alone, the word "I" does not appear, the first-person pronoun is the plural "we."[5] Sarton lists Dorothy Wordsworth, Dickinson, Rossetti, Sappho, George Sand, and others as "women who have wanted to break out / Of the prison of consciousness to sing or shout." This perceptive poem sounds a clarion call of hope for "we who are writing women and strange monsters":

> To be through what we make more simply human,
> To come to the deep place where poet becomes woman. . . .
> (*LR* 57)

Off-rhyme binds "woman" with "human."

Sequence Two changes pace. An address of praise in shorter lines of two or three stresses, its end rhymes fall in variable order, dependent on cadence rather than fixed pattern. "Let us rejoice," the poem says, "And trust what we know":

> First the green hand
> That can open flowers
> In the deathly bone,
> And the magic breast
> That can feed the child. . . . (*LR* 59)

Sequence Three returns to couplets:

> Eve and Mary the mother are our stem;
> All our centuries go back to them. (*LR* 59)

But this sequence moves comfortably into free verse in sections where direct statement fits the path of thought/feeling:

> For it is surely a lifetime work,
> This learning to be a woman.
> Until at the end what is clear
> Is the marvelous skill to make
> Life grow in all its forms. (*LR* 60)

Sequence Four returns, with variations, to iambic pentameter, stating at the last:

> And we shall never find ourselves again
> Until we ask men's greatness back from men,
> Until we make the fertile god our own,
> And giving up our lives, receive his own. (*LR* 62)

The woman poet has appropriated the vocal instrument of traditional meter and rhyme. Organic to the poet's meaning, language necessary for "the masculine and violent joy of pure creation" has become feminine, recreated by Sarton on her own terms. Nevertheless, Sarton may have felt the message was too subtle. Contrary to her usual practice of keeping poems in their original form, she revised "My Sisters, O My Sisters" for her *Collected Poems*. Sarton states that she "changed the last two lines to be more feminist" (letter to Mandel, 2 Oct. 1991). The poem now uses repetition with significant shifts of wording to conclude:

> For we shall never find ourselves again
> Until we ask men's greatness back from men,
> And we shall never find ourselves again
> Until we match men's greatness with our own.
> (*CP* 77; rpt. *SS* 112)

In this revision, iambic pentameter weaves with off-rhyme to publish unequivocal, assertive meaning.

Forty-three years of productive work have elapsed since the publication of *The Lion and The Rose,* and May Sarton's poetry has continued to evolve, particularly toward greater use of free-verse form. Nevertheless, rhyme, meter, and other measured patterns of repetition have stayed at her service no less than cadence and subtleties of sound patterns. Writing these poems, she came to know how the incessant contradictions of silence and speech may be wrestled into poems of constantly changing form. The dynamics of Sarton's poetic forms enact the evolving directions of her struggle to draw unafraid upon self-knowledge, conscious of gifts of heritage no less than unique powers of body and mind. Inner self and outer world interplay as one instrument. The musical bonding of thought with feeling woven into the best of her early poems does not unravel.

Notes

Correspondence from May Sarton to Bryher is quoted with permission of May Sarton, and the Beinecke Rare Book and Manuscript Library, Yale University. Many thanks to May Sarton for graciously providing permissions, information, and corrections of detail. Thanks are given to Patricia Willis and Vincent Giroud, Curators, Beinecke Library. The assistance of Millicent Abell, University Librarian at Yale, and Carol Mandel, Director of Technical Services, Columbia University Libraries, is also appreciated.

1. There are two exceptions: for her *Collected Poems,* Sarton revised the endings of "My Sisters, O My Sisters" and "Meditation in Sunlight," discussed later in this essay.
2. "Celebrations" uses long lines and cadenced repetitions reminiscent of Muriel Rukeyser, such as "For all creators everywhere in this time," repeated in five of the stanzas.
3. Of thirteen poems in the sequence, this is the only one Sarton included in *Collected Poems,* under the title "Canticle"; also in *Sarton Selected.*
4. These two lines do not appear in *Collected Poems;* Sarton cut the poem's last two lines to remove what then seemed to her to give a "didactic" sense of closure (letter to Mandel, 7 Aug. 1992). The stanzas are restored in *Sarton Selected.*
5. For a perceptive analysis of the ways contemporary women poets conceive of the self as plural, see Ostriker, *Stealing the Language* (234–38).

Works Cited

Hunting, Constance. "'The Risk Is Very Great': The Poetry of May Sarton," *May Sarton: Woman and Poet.* Ed. Constance Hunting. Orono, Maine: National Poetry Foundation, University of Maine at Orono, 1982. 201–9. Rpt. in *Sarton Selected,* listed below.

Ostriker, Alicia Suskin. *Stealing the Language: The Emergence of Women's Poetry in America.* Boston: Beacon Press, 1986.

Sarton, May. *Collected Poems (1930–1973).* New York: Norton, 1974.

———. *Encounter in April.* Boston: Houghton Mifflin Co., 1937.

———. "'I Live Alone in a Very Beautiful Place': Interview with May Sarton." With Robin Kaplan and Shelley Neiderbach. *Motheroot Journal: A Women's Review of Small Presses* 1.4 (1979): 1, 10–11. Rpt. in *May Sarton: Woman and Poet.* Ed. Hunting, listed above.

———. *Inner Landscape.* London: Cresset Press, 1939; American edition, Boston: Houghton Mifflin Co., 1939.

———. Letter to Bryher. 13 Feb. 1942. Beinecke Rare Book and Manuscript Library, Yale University, New Haven, Conn.

———. Letter to Charlotte Mandel. 2 Oct. 1991.

———. *The Lion and the Rose.* New York: Rinehart & Co., 1948.

———. "On Growth and Change." *Writings on Writing.* Orono, Maine: Puckerbrush Press, 1980. 67–72.

———. *Sarton Selected: An Anthology of the Journals, Novels, and Poems of May Sarton.* Ed. Bradford Dudley Daziel. New York: Norton, 1991.

The Straight Gaze:
On the Poems of May Sarton

RICHARD CHESS

"The writing of poetry," according to May Sarton, "is first of all a way of life and only secondarily a means of expression" (*SSE* 52). As a way of life, the discipline of poetry aids Sarton in clarifying and deepening her experiences. Drawing on the totality of her life—intellectual, emotional, physical—her poems explore the process of life, the journey, rather than serving as a platform from which she merely expresses feelings. Though they explore processes, the poems represent distillations of experience, forms from which raw facts have been cleared away, leaving essential images and rhythms. The crafted poems may seem impersonal but, paradoxically, remain deeply personal. They dramatize and clarify various moments of an individual's life without imposing the author's experiences on the reader. The effect achieved invites the reader to accept the essence of his or her own experience rather than to measure that experience against the author's. Sarton's passionate, intellectually and aesthetically disciplined poems leave room for the reader to breathe deeply, to feel the weight of his or her own solitary existence.

Sarton characterizes the process by which one arrives at essential experience in the poem "In Time Like Air," the title poem from her 1958 volume of poetry:

> Consider the mysterious salt:
> In water it must disappear.
> It has no self. It knows no fault.
> Not even sight may apprehend it. . . .
> It is dissolved and everywhere.

But, out of water into air,
It must resolve into a presence . . .
It crystallizes in our sight
And has defined itself to essence. (*SP* 63)

"Salt" serves as a metaphor for "soul" as the poem continues. "What element dissolves the soul / So it may be both found and lost, / In what suspended as a whole?"—love, the poem replies, itself subject to transformations over time. "In its early transformation" the self, like salt in water, "dissolves" in love. The self is without "a future or a past, / And a whole life [is] suspended in it." The "faultless crystal of detachment / Comes after," though it "cannot be created / Without the first intense attachment." Finally, the poem contrasts saints to less holy humans, "us," for whom essence is stated in time, similar to the way the essence of salt "is stated" in air.

Natural, organic, and inevitable as the process may seem, Sarton presents it in a meticulously crafted form—rhymed sestets of iambic tetrameter. This artfulness adds to the credibility of the vision, for the poem's form, crystallized like salt in air, together with its impersonal voice, suggests that the poet has achieved detachment similar to that of which she writes. Indeed, artistic creation, in Sarton's view, occurs at the second stage of experience, after the necessary "first intense attachment." Rather than an immediate, unprocessed response, Sarton's poems reflect a distillation of experience. Sarton describes this method in *Journal of a Solitude:* "My own belief is that one regards oneself, if one is a serious writer, as an instrument for experiencing. Life—all of it—flows through this instrument and is distilled through it into works of art" (*JS* 77).

But for a poem to move the reader, it must engage her or him on both an intellectual *and* emotional level. And Sarton understands that form may be the most effective way to reach the reader's emotions.

Form is not fashionable these days. What's being thrown out, of course, is music, which reaches the reader through his senses. In meter, the whole force is on the beat and reaches the reader, or the listener, below the rational level. If you don't use meter, you are throwing away one of the biggest weapons to get at the reader's subconscious and move him. The advantage of form, far from being "formal" and sort of off-putting and intellectual, is that through form you reach the reader on this subliminal level. (Sarton Interview 97)

This poem's form does convey on an experiential as well as conceptual level the process whereby one moves from intense attachment to detachment. Consider the *a-b-a-c-c-b* rhyme scheme. Following the first three lines, readers may suspect the return of the *b* rhyme to fulfill an *a-b-a-b* pattern. That pattern, however, is "suspended" in the second half of the sestet, causing the reader to wait for the return of the *b* rhyme. Thus, we note the coincidence of rhyme pattern to theme. The "first intense attachment" of love is suggested by the *a-b-a* half of the sestet, while the latter "crystal of detachment" is suggested by the distance between the two *b* rhymes.

The rhyme scheme subtly draws our attention to the poem's progress through time, the very context within which we experience essence, soul, and timelessness. "In time like air is essence stated." Of course, human life outside time does not exist. In love's early transformation we may feel "dissolved," "without a future or past." But this feeling is illusory. Only during the second, time-bound stage will love's essence clarify and present itself. Thus, Sarton embraces time rather than timelessness as that dimension in which truly human essences may be stated.

Sarton explores similar experiences in "Evening Music," a love poem in which she proposes that the ideal state of being is like an "interval where all seems possible," a moment of "order within time when action is suspended / And we are pure in heart, perfect in will" (*SP* 49). The lovely metaphor here refers literally to a quartet in which carefully timed silences, "interval[s] where all seems possible," please a listener. A pause, a silence—an ideal moment of pure potential. As in other poems, in "Evening Music" Sarton proposes art as the model from which we must learn to live and love: "love must learn . . . to move like formal music through the heart, / To be achieved like some high difficult art." Thus love must learn when to be silent, when to suspend action.

Indeed, the poem centers on limitations and imperfections (of action, speech, and music), contrasted to imagined and longed-for perfections and purity (of stillness, "when action is suspended"; and silence, "a special gift," "a detached joy that flowers" and blooms). This dialectic—speech/silence, active/inactive—suggests another, namely content/form. The successful composition of a work of art (music or poem) requires an attentiveness to formal aesthetic necessities even while the subject makes its own claims on the creator. The successful composition of love requires a similar attentiveness to restraint and free expression of one's feelings, to distance and intimacy, or ironically the intimacy of distance ("intense detachment").

> We enter the evening whole and well-defended
> But at the quick of self, intense detachment
> That is a point of burning far from passion—
> And this, we know, is what we always meant
> And even love must learn it in some fashion. . . . (*SP* 49)

Again, Sarton seeks intense experience. But unlike in "In Time Like Air," here the speaker seems unable to give in and lose herself in the Other—music or companion—as a necessary step toward becoming more fully herself. She longs for the ideal—"to move like formal music through the heart"—though she fails to surrender to the process that would enable her to approach that ideal. She remains "well-defended," "detached" but not yet realized. Consequently, at the conclusion of the poem the poet tells us she remains dependent on the other for her satisfaction: "There would be no music if you left."

Artists—visual, musical, literary—have often striven to produce "high difficult art" that would appeal to universal human emotions, though paradoxically through cool, impersonal voices. In "Nativity," based on the painting by Piero della Francesca, Sarton recognizes that aesthetic that represents common human emotions such as "comfort and joy" not in the usual ways, "personal and expected," but "utterly distilled and spare / Like a cool breath upon the air. / Emotion, it would seem, has been rejected / For a clear geometric praise" (*SP* 17).

Later in the same poem Sarton observes that "the strange impersonal does not relent." But must one reject emotion in order to achieve pure geometry? And is the impersonal voice the desired goal of high art, or an indication that the pursuit of high art can lead to self-estrangement? Her commitment to classical forms has not led Sarton away from an equally deep commitment to explore the organic process of art and life, a process at once familiar and strange, personal and impersonal.

"Because What I Want Most Is Permanence" expresses a classic theme in poetry—the desire for immortality. But in characterizing it as a "long unwinding and continuous flow / Of subterranean rivers out of sense" (*SP* 82), Sarton proposes an unconventional concept of permanence: not monumental but fluid, organic. The concept extends through the second image of permanence the poem offers: "Poetry, prayer, or call it what you choose / That frees the complicated act of will / And makes the whole world both intense and still." Sarton does not simply praise the poem as object—she does not idolize the poem; rather she praises the process, the liberating act of composing the poem/prayer.

The equation of poem to prayer seems appropriate. Both poems and prayers, as Sarton views them, bring one to a state of attentiveness through which one can contact the deepest sense of self. Also, through the very act of prayer or composing or even reading a poem, the individual may arrive at an experience of the transcendent. Of course, Sarton understands that the notion of poem as prayer is unfashionable in the current climate. Thus she permits her readers to call "it" what they choose. But to what grammatically does this "it" refer? "It" could refer to "prayer," or "poetry," or even "permanence." But the ambiguity does not suggest carelessness. Rather, it de-objectifies the "it," which in context cannot be reduced to a single *object*. The experiencing self—whether as writer, worshipper, or reader—interests Sarton here. Through prayer or poetry one can free oneself of the "complicated act of will" and experience a world that is "whole," "intense," and "still"—the transcendent experience.

The transcendent or essential experience Sarton seeks must be found within the flux of time: "Because what I want most is permanence . . . I set my mind to artful work and craft." Through work, she experiences permanence. And she continues, "I set my heart on friendship, hard and fast / Against the wild inflaming wink of chance / And all sensations opened in a glance." Here as in other poems Sarton emphasizes the importance of devoting oneself only to that which endures, art and friendship. Friendship, not romantic love. Even in an individual volume of poetry devoted almost entirely to tracking the course of love (*Halfway to Silence*), it is in fact the *course* of love, love's transformations Sarton highlights, rather than the peculiar comings and goings of any individual beloved.

In "Because What I Want Most Is Permanence," she contrasts her course with that of sailors on the "blue Atlantis" who "dream their girls under the waves and in the foam." "I move another course," Sarton states, "I'll not look down." She rejects the illusions of male mythology, then proposes an alternate method to achieve permanence:

> Because what I most want is permanence,
> What I do best is bury fire now,
> To bank the blaze within, and out of sense,
> Where hidden fires and rivers burn and flow,
> Create a world that is still and intense.
> I come to you with only the straight gaze.
> These are not hours of fire but years of praise,
> The glass full to the brim, completely full,
> But held in balance so no drop can spill. (*SP* 22)

She buries fire within her to ensure its endurance, for the permanence that matters does not come with eternity but must be experienced on mortal terms, that is, within time: in "time like air is essence stated." But the passion—fire and river—is not merely banked within, it is hidden. Why withhold the passion? Does Sarton believe that as in art, in life, too, passion is intensified when restrained, or that passion too openly expressed will be diffused? Is she protecting herself from harm, as if the explicit expression of her passion—its particular causes and possible manifestations—would endanger her?

"I come to you with only the straight gaze," she states. Read within the context of lesbianism in a homophobic society, we could appreciate the necessity of approaching the reader with "only the straight gaze." The poem was originally published early in the 1950s, before Allen Ginsberg's "Howl," a celebrated, influential poem in which homosexuality is treated explicitly, and before other American women poets such as Adrienne Rich begin writing frankly about lesbianism. Sarton herself took great risks in publishing *Mrs. Stevens Hears the Mermaids Singing,* her 1965 novel whose heroine is a "woman homosexual." "The fear of homosexuality is so great," Sarton reflects, "that it took great courage to write *Mrs. Stevens. . . .* I am well aware that I probably could not have 'leveled' as I did in that book had I had any family (my parents were dead when I wrote it), and perhaps not if I had had a regular job" (*JS* 91-92). Indeed, to this day the dangers of writing openly about homosexuality remain great. In a recent review of an award-winning book of poetry by a lesbian poet, Adrienne Rich commented: "It should go without saying, but probably doesn't, . . . that no lesbian or gay bedroom—in whatever gentrified neighborhood or tent pitched off the Appalachian trail—is a safe harbor from bigotry (and for some, not only bigotry but lethal violence)." If even in 1992 a lesbian writer must fear for her life, how much greater the real dangers must have seemed to Sarton writing "Permanence" in the early 1950s.

Nevertheless, the implications of the "straight gaze" are wider than this and include a consistent aesthetic stance found throughout Sarton's poetry. Immediately after feelings of romantic love and sexual desire erupt through the poem's surface ("the sailors dream / Their girls under the waves"), an interruption occurs, a stanza break, a gap, a pause, a silence. Rather than censorship, this brief silence can be felt as the moment the poet takes to reflect on her own desires. Through that gap, we imagine, the personal life teems with passion. But the details of that passionate life remain buried, withheld. The poet pauses to reflect before, composed, she resumes composing her artful poem.

We could argue that Sarton's reluctance to write more explicitly and literally of her life in her lyrical poetry limits its impact. But the reverse is true. The poems gain power precisely because they do not impose the life of one person on another. Rather, they position themselves in a space, as it were, between writer and reader. In this impersonal space between, the intimate reveals itself. In this space the "I" of the writer meets with a straight gaze the "Thou" of the reader. The writer engages the other (reader, beloved) with a direct, frank gaze. To meet openly the outer world, she draws strength from her fortified inner life. The poem concludes:

> These are not hours of fire but years of praise,
> The glass full to the brim, completely full,
> But held in balance so no drop can spill. (*SP* 82)

As the journals have amply demonstrated, Sarton "balances" the needs of her inner life against the demands of the world, and in this poem celebrates a moment of fulfillment.

"The impersonal wing," Sarton writes in "Christmas Letter to a Psychiatrist," "provides a place, a climate, / Where the soul can meet itself at last" (*SP* 71). Here she characterizes a therapist under whose "impersonal wing" Sarton takes shelter. We can apply the metaphor to Sarton's poetry itself, which serves as a kind of "impersonal wing" providing a place where the reader's "soul can meet itself." The impersonal does not imply an absence of feeling, rather the impersonal invites passion. To the psychiatrist, the patient brings wounds and complaints, "shy wild animals" with "sharp infant teeth," and "sharp old antlers" (70-71). The doctor herself, who heals the "animal pain / So the soul may live," works impassioned.

> This angel must be anarchic,
> Fierce, full of laughter,
> Will neither punish
> Nor give absolution,
> Is always acute, sometimes harsh. (*SP* 71)

Sarton uses both archetypal images and imagery from nature to characterize the therapeutic experience. In the final section of the poem, for instance, she recalls having watched a "jay flopping, help-less" outside a window (72). So she brought the jay in, and "man-aged to pull out the quill / Shot through just under the eye. . . . / Then it was Easter and I saw the jay / Fly off whole into the resurrected air." She sees in this anecdote a metaphor for the analyst's methods: "I know what it is to have to be brutal / Toward the badly crippled / In order to set them free." In this poem, the speaker experiences herself as "a complex whole," finding natural connections between her inner and outer life, balancing archetypal imagery and imagery from nature. Many of Sarton's poems explore grief, suffering, frustration, and de-spair. Even at that, her work is finally "The Work of Happiness," the growth of which she describes in an early poem with that title, from *The Lion and the Rose.*

> No one has seen it happen, but inside the bark
> Another circle is growing in the expanding ring.
> No one has heard the root go deeper in the dark,
> But the tree is lifted by this inward work
> And its plumes shine, and its leaves are glittering. (*SP* 189)

Happiness comes of solitude, the best condition for "inward work." And happiness, which *can* be experienced in a domestic environment, brings one "the timeless sense of time when furniture / Has stood a life's span in a single place." She quietly praises "the dear familiar gods of home," where the "work of faith can best be done":

> . . . where people have lived in inwardness
> The air is charged with blessing and does bless;
> Windows look out on mountains and the walls are kind.
> (*SP* 189)

Sarton's poems seem at once windows and walls. Although she states in this very poem that "no one has heard thought or listened to a mind," her poems are in actuality lyrical notations of the music of her mind. But the poems also are constructs, walls, containments of strong feeling rather than mere "blurting" out. These walls kindly protect the one who dwells inside, Sarton herself, and they are equally kind to those of us on the outside: we respect the privacy of what goes on behind the poems, and we are inspired by them to listen to the music of our own souls.

Works Cited

Rich, Adrienne. "Sliding Stone from the Cave's Mouth," a review-essay. *The American Poetry Review* 19.5 (1990): 11–17.

Sarton, May. *Journal of a Solitude.* New York: Norton, 1977.

———. *Selected Poems of May Sarton.* Ed. Serena Sue Hilsinger and Lois Brynes. New York: Norton, 1978.

———. *Sarton Selected: An Anthology of the Journals, Novels, and Poems of May Sarton.* Ed. Bradford Dudley Daziel. New York: Norton, 1991.

———. Interview. "The Art of Poetry XXXII: May Sarton." With Karen Saum. *Paris Review* 89 (1983): 80–110.

Available to the World

WILLIAM STAFFORD

Some writers come out of their books and speak for their time, some as public leaders, or as champions of strenuously new attitudes, or as consciously instructive guides. May Sarton has provided leadership of a special sort. She relates to our need to have a champion of private life, an intellectual life with wholehearted human involvement but without the trappings of office or acclaim. In her books a person who appears to be just one of us encounters what distinguishes life in our time—war, social turmoil, changes in attitudes toward success, race, sex, politics.

In May Sarton the private citizen has a champion, one who takes the missiles that the years fling at us all: she parries them, survives, and lives as a model, not of the unusual but of the usual, the person beleaguered but staunch. The big abstractions—war, pain, age, disappointment—find a lodging in one life and are there considered and confronted in an exemplary way.

And this intense involvement as our kind of human being comes delivered to us readers in its best, most succinct way in the big, rich package of her *Collected Poems (1930–1973),* a winnowing of eleven books made into one hefty volume over four hundred pages long.

Until letting this book have its way with me, I held off giving full allegiance to the Sarton my friends kept telling me about. The glanced-at pieces of hers, both poetry and prose, that came my way over the years slipped past without fully impacting. It seemed to me that in these pieces people liked each other too much, like in-groups elated at a party; they celebrated being human in a standard, almost postcardlike way. I had often been chilled by reading poised authors who characteristically said, "Look at me; I'm a writer, but I have the same characteristics and problems as you ordinary people."

The Sarton I assumed I knew was intelligent, industrious, some-how "right," but a juggler of literary forms, too relentlessly busy turn-ing over human feelings, and passing experience along in a mothery-smothery way.

Then by good luck I spent sustained reading time on her collected poems, and became a disciple. Especially convincing, *A Private My-thology* (poems 1961-1966) struck me as crucial. These poems come in the middle of May Sarton's writing life, around her fiftieth year, and they mark a breakthrough. These poems reveal a new depth and resonance.

It was her eighth collection. She had begun in the 1930s, with books that displayed her control of forms and her facility with "po-etic" subjects:

> There have been two strangers
> Who met within a wood
> And looked once at each other
> Where they stood. ("Strangers," *CP* 27)

Many of those poems turned inward and depended on the author's appeal to others of like mind. A large element in the poems was an appeal to abstractions like life, hope, loyalty—or so it seemed to me.

But in *A Private Mythology* a mature writer turned outward. On an extended visit abroad, May Sarton's sensibility encounters the bracing cultures of Japan, Greece, and other exotic, alert-making places. In an early poem in this book, "A Child's Japan," the speaker tells of her childhood home and its influences that readied her for a rich encoun-ter with Japan. She says:

> When I flew out into the huge night,
> Bearing with me a freight of memory,
> My parents were dead.
>
> I was going toward
> All they had left behind
> In the houses where we had lived,

In the artful measure
And sweet austerity
Of their lives—
That extravagance of work
And flowers,
Of work and music,
Of work and faith. (*CP* 225)

Japan tumbles May Sarton into a marvelous series of illuminations. It almost seems as if she is guided toward just what she needs as an artist at this stage of her development. In one poem she tells of observing foreign ways distantly and then actually falling, bruising herself, being picked up and helped by the people she had been apart from. They brush her off; they smile; they come close and thus come to life:

I had been the woman
With the camera eye
Who notices everything
And is always watched,
The stranger on whom
No one smiled.
Then I slipped,
Fell headlong
In the red dust,
And at once the rickshaw boy
Is there at my side.
Thin expert hands
Feel hard for a break,
Then wipe the blood off
With a filthy cloth.
Worth a scraped knee
To land on this earth at last,
To be helped alive,
To be, in fact,
Touched! (*CP* 246)

In India she encounters "The Sleeping God" and is transformed. Her life changes through the influence of a civilization that releases her:

> And I, the Western One, was lost in thought,
> Felt the lock spring, demons fly out,
> And, all cracked open as the image caught,
>
> Knew I was dreamed back to some ancient school
> Where we are held within a single rule:
> True power is given to the vulnerable. (*CP* 250)

This poem, "The Sleeping God," displays in one brief passage the many convergent talents that May Sarton has brought to her poetry. She is working with form, with flexible rhyme; she has found an overarching image in the sleeping god (an apt connection with this whole set of poems about an awakening); and she is using her daring, principled commitment to direct, clear statement (power is given to the vulnerable).

From the collected observer, this traveler changes into one caught up in new, intense realizations. The sequence in this book takes her onward to Greece, where another part of the past, a brilliant, rational part, confronts her:

> Too sudden, too brilliant,
> Who can bear this shining?
> The pitiless clarity?
> Each bone felt the shock.
> I was broken in two
> by sheer definition. . . . (*CP* 251–252)

She perceives dangers in this new culture, so sunlit and removed from the spirituality she felt in the Orient:

> When measure is conscious,
> Who is to protect us from arrogance? (*CP* 253)

The clarity of Greece has to be balanced by something else; and though "It was the right year / To confront / The smile beyond suffering," she has to hark back to the shadow and movement of life in India:

> I am suddenly homesick for
> The Indian night
> And my dark cell
> In Orissa
> Where I was visited
> By a white lizard
> With emerald eyes,
> By an articulate frog,
> And sometimes, very late,
> By a wandering shrew.
> The lizard chittered
> And danced;
> The shrew ran compulsively
> Along the wall;
> The frog,
> When I lifted him up,
> Gave a single heart-rending cry
> In my unmysterious
> White room,
> I miss the chittering,
> The cry of despair,
> The silent, lunatic trot—
> It is too sane here for words. (CP 254)

In this wonderful sequence of poems May Sarton explores her life outward; she escapes from the carefully introspective poems of her earlier collections. She yokes geography and its discoveries to the expanding of consciousness—on successive islands, for instance, she encounters the past, John on Patmos, the magic of Delphi ("Everyone stands here alone. / I tell you the gods are still alive / And they are not consoling") (CP 259).

The collection ends with poems that take this enlightened traveler on into Europe and then—changed and more available to that outside world—back home.

To my mind this book in the middle of May Sarton's writing life is a breakthrough. The steady intelligence, the sympathy, the humaneness that characterize all her writing become richer and more effective. How could this expansiveness come about? What can we as writers, readers, human companions, discover inside this document of awareness?

I propose great comfort from the book itself and from what it displays about steadiness and honesty and development. We often tell ourselves that the daily practice of art-full living, the application of our own feelings to the experiences that come along, the forthright communicating of unfaked and generous impulses—all of these activities and qualities that May Sarton has lived by—will result in lasting gifts from the muse. An author's rectitude will be repaid by a convergence between life and the art. May Sarton practiced that life of art, and in the fullness of time she was welcomed into a kind of holy community of authors, those whose natural impulses turn into magic.

How else to account for such gifts as emerge in these poems?

As if guided by a familiar spirit the author embarks on a journey, offering her images that come to hand readily while also proving to be apt for the journey of her life. She ascribes that balance of past and present to her parents, but it also fits her own life and practice ("I was going toward / All they had left behind. . . / In the artful measure / And sweet austerity / Of their lives—" *(CP* 225). In just such a life journey May Sarton has achieved a state of resonance; past, present, and future converge in an "extravagance of work / And flowers, / Of work and music, / Of work and faith."

A well-made and seasoned violin will forward and enhance the musicianship of its user, just as the trust of an artist, the faith of an artist, portends a like state for those who serve the muse well.

It seems as if May Sarton's travels guided her, as if the world provided just what she needed for this stage in her writing, but we know that a shaping intelligence is here, that years of generous commitment have gone into such a partnership with the world.

A Private Mythology confirms and strengthens the body of writing that puts this author in place as one of the builders of culture, a friend to her readers, an explorer of what it means to live in our time.

Paradox and Plenitude:
A Grain of Mustard Seed

MARJORIE STELMACH

In book after book of striking observations and quiet affirmations of my own thinking, May Sarton's voice has become an important presence in my life, a presence that began with *A Grain of Mustard Seed*. Although this volume of poems was published in 1971, it wasn't until 1972 that it first appeared in my favorite bookstore—the year that Marianne Moore, Ezra Pound, and *Life* magazine died, the year that ended with Watergate and a landslide victory for Richard Nixon, and yet marked the end of the draft and the last full year of America's official presence in Vietnam. It was the first year in which my "loud-mouthed protester-friends" and I felt justified in claiming victory in the moral wars. For me, personally, it meant the end of campus life, with its stimulating mix of political unrest and personal leisure, and the beginning of both marriage and a full-time teaching position. That year marked the beginning of my journey.

At the start, we travel a solitary road—and solitude is something for which many in my generation were ill prepared. Identified and amassed to be named as *Time*'s Man of the Year in 1967, we clustered easily in dorms and communes, sit-ins and marches; we learned that as a group we had considerable power. But alone? May Sarton, knowing firsthand of the power contained in our groups, knew more; she knew a great deal about solitude.

And I knew that day in my bookstore, paging through Part 1 of *A Grain of Mustard Seed,* that this woman whose name had never appeared on the syllabus of any of my college English courses, knew a great deal about my local terrain. I bought ($1.95) and read the book. To my pleasure, the poems in Part 1 agreed with me in all my vast political and spiritual wisdom, and they did so elegantly, offering examples of the use of rhyme in an age when such lessons from living women poets were not readily available. I did not study the book— perhaps I had had enough of studying for a time, or perhaps I did not think this woman whose merits had been overlooked by my professors was a poet to *study*. I did, however, read it well. Then, I shelved it.

Like all the real voices of my life, however, May Sarton's voice did not fade. People fall in love for both deep and trivial reasons. Some of our early enthusiasms wear thin, and real reasons, more worthy and lasting, surface, if we're lucky, to cover the bald spots. Over the next two decades I found myself returning to this "dated" book, usually after the purchase of a "new" Sarton, and gradually I found that the traits I had admired at twenty-two were small things; that there were larger things to admire. I discovered the intelligence of the voice— speculative, always learning something herself in the course of the poem; I began to admire the unfailing felicity of language; I found poems that displayed a fine precision of imagery (and perhaps more important, I found alternatives to the image as the organizing principle of a poem); and with each new reading, a new poem became my "favorite." This time, I find myself in awe of the book's structure, and appropriately, my attention is drawn to "Dutch Interior," a poem that I learn (counting the poems in the Table of Contents for the first time), is the book's centerpiece, the nineteenth poem in a volume of thirty-seven. It should have been obvious; *A Grain of Mustard Seed* is more than a collection of individual poems, it is a *work*. This late discovery allows me now to view each element of the volume with fresh appreciation.

First, the title is perfect. I know that now, though a biblical allusion was enough to put me off that first day in the bookstore. Faith was not high on my list of admirable personal qualities; in fact, it might have made my private list of seven deadly sins. I recognized the title, though. A product of two decades of church and Sunday-school attendance, I knew the whole story. According to Matthew, Jesus' disciples had been trying their hand at healing, specifically, attempting to cast out a stubborn devil. I always envisioned this occurring in somewhat the same spirit as my own early eagerness to mow our steep back lawn; it looks like a lark until you try it. Freud claimed three impossible tasks: to rule, to heal, to teach. Healing is hard work; the disciples failed. "What did we do wrong? Why didn't it work?" they want to know. In the Revised Standard Version of the Bible, Jesus' answer sounds peeved (teaching, too, is impossible): He said to them, "Because of your little faith. For truly I say to you, if you have faith as a grain of mustard seed, you will say to this mountain, 'Move hence to yonder place,' and it will move; and nothing will be impossible to you" (Matt. 17.20–22).

A gospel filled with impossible rules and impossible promises, Matthew is far from child's play, though the fact somehow escaped the notice of my Sunday-school teachers. Paradox and plenitude. To overcome the paradox and access the plenitude, to make the impossible possible, requires only one thing: a bit of faith. But *that* seems the most impossible thing of all, just as it must have seemed to the disciples. Sarton, like Matthew, concerns herself throughout this book with paradox and plenitude. By confronting and ultimately embracing the paradoxes, she claims in our name (her habitual use of the first person plural includes us in her victory) an inheritance, a burgeoning wealth of loaves and fishes, a miraculous plenitude. Moreover, she makes it look easy. In the Gnostic Gospel According to Saint Thomas, Jesus is a bit more direct, though no less paradoxical, when he claims that the kingdom "is spread out on earth, but people do not see it" (Saying 112). Or, to stay with Matthew: "Seek and you will find" (Matt. 7.7). When the eye is opened, everything enters. "The eye is the lamp of the body. So, if your eye is sound, your whole body will be full of light" (Matt. 6.22).

Like any obedient Sunday-school student, I knew all that, but at twenty-two, I didn't see the world through faith-filled eyes. What I saw was nothing so large and challenging as paradox. What I saw was hypocrisy, and I saw it most clearly in society because it's easier to point blame's finger *out* than *in*. Soon, though, it's necessary to see that we too are flawed, wanting equality for all citizens *and* superior conditions for ourselves and those we love. How can we reconcile these opposite desires? We can't; it's impossible. We become to ourselves, a paradox. It is in this recognition that the solitary portion of the journey begins.

So: a guidebook that confirms the hypocrisy in the local terrain and provides instruction on how to "get out," how to escape a confining vision and advance to a wider view that embraces opposites, allowing us, thereby, to heal the split in ourselves.

A Grain of Mustard Seed meets both needs. The first of its four parts is overtly political, including poems on the Kent State shootings, on the forced integration of Boston's schools, on Martin Luther King's death—poems written in the latter half of the sixties and concerned with the fire of the times. As the opening lines of the opening poem, "Ballad of the Sixties," remind us, little has changed from biblical times; like it or not, we are still "In the West . . . / Hoping for some good news" (*AG* 11). But good news is not forthcoming. The world still fails to meet our expectations for sanity and order: the "sad truth plain," is that "only the ill are well, / And only the mad are sane" (11). Repeatedly, throughout Part 1 we are reminded that this is a "terrible place" (20), a place in which, emphatically *not* the state, but instead, "Our love has withered away" (12).

In Part 1, Sarton fixes a steady gaze on this impossible place, a steadiness that accounts for the civility of tone so at odds with the disturbing content. Poems about racial prejudice and the self-loathing instilled in black children may run the risk of sounding glib when pressed into ballad stanzas, but in the context of this book, that opening gamble is justified. Though Part 1 offers a deceptively simple starting point, Sarton refuses to provide easy answers; there is too much heart in these poems, and too much intelligence, for glib accusations or easy solutions. Other poems in Part 1 add a touch of humor that saves; in "The Ballad of Johnny," Sarton tells the tale of a child's loss of identity, a deep and powerful terror that occurs when his name tag is eaten by a goat—a creature renowned for its ability to stomach anything, even the unpalatable identities we have pinned to our jackets.

The range of these poems is great—from Christ to Kali, from Martin Luther King to the Nazi death camps. There is much here, too, about poetry itself. In "The Invocation to Kali," Sarton employs a birth metaphor, one among many, to observe that

> Every creation is born out of the dark.
> Every birth is bloody. Something gets torn.
> Kali is there to do her sovereign work
> Or else the living child will be still-born. (*AG* 20)

If nothing appears less bloody than her measured lines in these poems, it may be that she is showing us in this way that appearances may
be disguises. These decorous lines seem themselves to have been born,
as the best poems are, out of the darkness of the poet's disturbing
vision. This poem is the first to ask the book's question: "How live
with the terrible god?" (*AG* 19) and to answer it: the god cannot be
destroyed, must be faced: "We must stay, open-eyed, in the terrible
place" (*AG* 20). The god of poetry, too, can be terrible, and yet the
poet has no choice but to keep her eyes open, to accept the bloody
birth, in order that the creation may be a vital one.

No longer among my favorites in the volume, these poems still
resonate for me with the outrage my friends and I felt in 1972 toward
the world we had entered and now found so difficult to live in without making a scene; subtlety was never the strong suit of the sixties.
Sarton, with decorum and control, documented our outrage: Yes, this
is "the terrible place" (*AG* 20); and yet in the final poem of this section, her persona in "Night Watch" speaks of learning to "Take the
sick world in" (*AG* 30). By the end of Part 1 Sarton speaks with the
voice the decade itself managed to find at the end:

> Wide awake in the hospital
> In the morning light,
> I weighed one thing against the other.
> I took a deep breath. (30)

In a world that seems at times riddled with illness, we must learn
somehow to stay "wide awake" to reality and, having faced our personal and societal truths, to take "a deep breath" and go on.

In Part 2 the paradoxes continue, but human events replace current events, and images of water and sky ("The Great Transparen-
cies") and earth (both landscape and geography) replace the images
of fire. Sarton also considers less-localized issues: art ("Proteus" and

"Girl with 'Cello") and human relationships, both personal ("For Rosalind" and "Friendship: The Storms") and mythic ("An Intruder" and "The Muse as Medusa"). We are, in short, ushered out of the claustrophobic hospital room of Part 1 and into the spaces of history, geography, the arts. We can breathe. The final three poems in Part 2 deal most directly with the paradoxes and promises of this widened vision. In all three, the controlling image is strongly feminine and strongly located. In "Evening Walk in France" the measured couplets lead us through a heavy gate into vineyards where we wander among "late bees and late people" (42) until all the landmarks—the distant cypresses and finally even the farm itself, "dissolv[e] into dusk" (42). All this, in one sentence. Then, under a single lamp, a woman appears who will gather the last light into one clear image: she stands "at rest, / Cutting a loaf of bread across her breast" (42). The two figures in the poem cross *her* light, *her* breast is crossed by the knife, and yet, she is "at rest." We are left, as we are in many of Sarton's finest poems, with just the smallest trace of uneasiness. The image of a blade drawn across the breast is unsettling, and yet inhabits a landscape of calm. The gesture is simple and natural, removed from the realm of immediate dangers by its very smallness, its domesticity. In this fading exterior light, the two walkers glimpse objects—bread and the knife—belonging to an interior, that, though absent, haunts the scene.

In the last of the three poems, Sarton paints "A Vision of Holland," a Dutch landscape of her own, entirely in the open and breathtaking in both senses. The persona experiences this landscape as a "horizontal infinite" and a "rush of height" (44). Storm and illumination sweep the persona away (along with the reader, brought into the scene by a sudden use of the first-person-plural pronoun):

> . . . "Oh sky, sky,
> Earth, earth, and nothing else," we cry,
> Knowing once more how absolutes exalt. (44)

But no one in this poem walks up into the sky, no one breaks into blossom. We do the decorous thing. Or rather, the *eye* does the decorous thing, for the final stanzas of the poem use no defining pronouns at all. Both the persona and we ourselves are "the eye [that] comes back again to rest," mooring "The visionary moment" (42) in "a house, canal, cows in a field"—appropriate symbols of the domestic realm. But this return, even in its impersonality, contains a blessing:

> Come back from that cracked-open psychic place,
> [The eye] is alive to wonders freshly seen:
> After the earthquake, gentle pastures green,
> And that great miracle, a human face. (42)

"A human face" ends Part 2. Together, these three poems have made a single statement about the light we see by and the light we are sometimes permitted to see. Visions notwithstanding, we are human and must return to an interior, which, as we will be shown in Part 4, is the home of the great solitude, that dark waiting room we inhabit between moments of exultation. Our task will be to find blessing in that return.

In Part 2, "Dutch Interior," the central poem of this triptych, marks the structural center of the book. Sarton selected it as the final poem in the 1982 volume, *May Sarton: A Self-Portrait*. In this small book commemorating her seventieth birthday, she speaks of "Dutch Interior": "I have a great feeling, of course, about the Dutch painters because of my having been born in Belgium; it's in my blood. The apparent calm of these paintings holds in it so much feeling" (78).

"Dutch Interior" is not only a fully achieved work of grace and strength, of philosophy and vision, but it serves well as a lens through which to view the thematic content of the entire book. It is a poem about the tiny grain of faith that allows, even insists upon, the possibility of the impossible.

Written in tercets, the poem moves in leisurely sentences through a description of Pieter de Hooch's framed painting of a "Dutch Interior." It is a familiar genre to the persona, who opens with the statement:

I recognize the quiet and the charm,
This safe enclosed room where a woman sews
And life is tempered, orderly, and calm. (*AG* 43)

As details accumulate in the first four stanzas, the reader, too, recognizes the tradition: the sun-washed room where a woman sews, the dreaming dog, the enclosed bed, the glowing copper, the deep sense of peace. The couple we imagine to occupy this home will be "safe from harm" (43) even in their cupboarded bed, where the privacy of their lovemaking and the peacefulness of their dreams are guaranteed. The scene is wholesome, touched like the copper with "the warm flush of roses" (43). The adjectives employed in the first four stanzas include: "safe," "cozy," "sheltered," "domestic," "enclosed," "tempered," "orderly," "calm" (43)—all ingredients of a recognizable tradition. Perhaps most familiar of all is the light, for the Dutch tradition speaks most eloquently about light.

However, Sarton is about to speak of the darkness discovered inside the enclosed cupboard of the woman's heart, for this is not a natural calm. Instead, it is "Chaos subdued by the sheer power of need" (43). Necessity is the architect of such sanctuaries; outside them, chaos reigns. At this point in the poem, the artistic tradition is abandoned for a tradition that belongs to the real world and to womankind. "This is a room where I have lived as woman," the persona claims, and here the missing article tells all. This is Sarton speaking not as *a* woman, but as *woman*. When, after the stanza break, she goes on: "Lived too what the Dutch painter does not tell—" (43), the poem has taken a vital turn. As woman, the persona claims knowledge of the force that remains outside the picture and yet is the force that necessitated the creation of the framed world we are shown.

Here the poem changes, picking up speed, stacking up participles ("dissolving [the calm]" "breaking [the light]"), raising the voice in exclamation ("What bitter tumult, treacherous and cold . . . !"), repeating the question ("How many . . . ? . . . How many . . . ? . . . How many . . . ?"), and generally creating a sense of gathering storm. But this storm is no passing phenomenon; for this painting to exist, storm and calm must always be equally present—and most powerfully present in woman herself, who has "won and maintained" her own peace "Against . . . terrible antagonists" (43).

And at what cost? "How many from this quiet room have drowned?" the persona asks. Because Sarton presents us with a domestic scene from which the man (like the storm) is missing, our thoughts turn first to the grief inherent in a world where men go out "drunk on the wind, / And take their ships into heartbreaking seas" despite attempts by these strong, sheltering women to "bind" them. But there are other ways to read this question. This "room where I have lived as woman" is an interior that some women—drunk on that intoxicating air so well described in Part 2 and unable to settle for a claustrophobic peace—would not, could not, endure (43). Such women, enclosed in "this quiet room," may have felt themselves, first, "drenched in calm," and ultimately, "drowned" (43).

This woman? She has disciplined her grief, yes, but the final sentence of the poem questions all peace:

> But in her heart this woman is the storm;
> Alive, deep in herself, holds wind and rain,
> Remaking chaos into an intimate order
> Where sometimes light flows through a windowpane. (43)

"In her heart this woman is the storm." It is worth approaching this phrase with both interpretations in mind. Societal roles, not modified significantly since the seventeenth-century Holland of this painting, decree that woman guard the interior, and man risk the broken light of the chaotic world. But such divisions are fictions. Early in the poem we are shown, by way of the Dutch door—half closed upon, half opened to, the elements—that even in building our sanctuaries, we acknowledge the impossibility of such divisions and exclusions. If there is calm in this Dutch interior, in the *interior* of that interior lives a woman who "is the storm." And inside her? As if opening nested boxes, we can continue as long as we like, getting deeper and smaller, but in the end we will arrive at a mystery: a still small voice or a grain of mustard seed or darkness or the Void.

What is deepest inside us remains a mystery. We may not have conventional words or symbols for this alternative knowledge, but we recognize it. And the odd diction, the odd turns of phrase in the final triplet, do not restore the calm of the opening lines, though they may for a moment appear to: "Alive" (43), this woman.

Though drenched, she has not drowned; instead she has dived and "deep in herself, holds" the elements of chaos (43). She, who has tamed the wild black dog, the wild northern world, even the wildness of lovemaking and nightmare, she is the storm—the wild eye of the calm. By the end of the poem, we see that chaos has not been "subdued," but rather "remade" (a creative act, not a repressive one) into an "intimate order" where "sometimes light flows through a windowpane" (43).

The interior of this Dutch woman is not static as in the painted interior. "Sometimes" (43), there is light. On those occasions when the light flows through the half-opened door, the male genre-artist may gather it up to make of it a traditional peaceful Dutch interior, but these are rooms women have lived in, and they know better. They know only "sometimes" light comes to the intimate order of the home, or the interior order of the heart—and comes through a windowpane, a glass that, unlike a Dutch door, cannot be closed and may represent the clearer, more total, vision of the female artist. Perhaps, allowing the pun, even the *pain*ful vision.

The importance of this single poem resides in its insistence that the twin truths of chaos and calm be acknowledged; insistence that there resides a violence in the eye of the storm—in the eye of the woman. Violence may *be* the eye that permits vision. None of this is clear, though the last line is crystalline, the sentence transparent. There is more truth here than the syntax can hold; a paradox that brings me back to this poem again and again. Convention has been broken open to admit the light and the storm together.

Reminded in the final line of Part 2 that the "great miracle" is "a human face," we enter Part 3, where we are brought face to face with a few of our close relatives, expected, perhaps, to keep an eye out for the family features (44). The poems in this section are playful: we are introduced to a bear, "childhood's rug come true" (47), a nearly unbelievable "Rousseau" (49) parrot, photographic frogs, musical snails, all trotted out for our amusement—and for Sarton's, who clearly enjoys the escapades of her creatures as they evade our arts, showing a bemused tolerance of human foolishness. The section does not exclude vegetable life, either; the final poems focus on one daring fig and one dancing Hawaiian palm. By drawing our attention to less-impassioned, less-intentioned creatures than ourselves, these poems allow us the breath we need before Part 4.

Part 4 begins with a look at the largest "impossible" we know: Death. Our own is, of course, inconceivable, but even those we try hardest to fathom—our parents' perhaps—escape us. In "A Hard Death," Sarton examines the pain of accepting the fact that our human love cannot be equal to the tasks we have given it. In Matthew, we are promised that "faith, as a grain of mustard seed," will allow us to do the impossible, but we do not have that faith.

In lines reminiscent of Matthew Arnold as he accepts the huge compromise forced upon an exiled mankind, Sarton ends this poem with the words:

> Let us be gentle to each other this brief time
> For we shall die in exile far from home,
> Where even the flowers can no longer save.
> Only the living can be healed by love. (58)

This important poem, written for the death of her mother, has moments of luminosity:

> God's Grace, given freely, we do not deserve,
> But we can choose at least to see its ghost
> On every face. . . . (57)

In the phrase "God's Grace, given freely," Sarton introduces the important idea of plenitude. Having accepted the abundance of God's grace as a "given," she concludes that it matters greatly the manner in which we see and the words we say about death: ". . . when the petals fall / Say it is beautiful and good, say it is well." The care with which she chooses and orders her own words testifies to the importance she attaches to the act of breaking the world's silence.

In the fine second poem of the section, Sarton examines the character of "The Silence." "At first the silence is a silence only" (59), but by the poem's final lines, "huge lack bears huge something through the dark" (60). Between complete silence and the "huge something," the persona discovers what is required of her:

> . . . Somehow I must get through
> Into the universe where stars still flock,
> To the rich world not empty but wide open,
> Where soul quietly breathes and is at home. (59)

A birth, then, is required of us—a rebirth into the universe full of everything we will ever need.

Everywhere in this fourth section we are reminded that to claim the plenitude, we must only see that it exists, without our efforts. The third poem, "Annunciation," with something of the flavor of Rilke, reminds us again of the "nothing" that we can do: Mary, in this poem, can do

> Nothing at all but to believe and bear,
> Nothing but to foresee that in the ending
> Would lie the true beginning and the birth. . . ." (61)

Mary must understand, like Kali in the earlier poem, that "every birth is bloody" (20). She must affirm the identity of vast destruction and endless creation, or, in more Western terms, must allow "the human heart's descent to Hell" (61).

In the first of the two Chartres poems, again, there is nothing "we" can do: ". . . we cannot move, / Nor be consoled or saved. But only see" (62). The persona in "Once More at Chartres" pushes, not through the silence into the stars, but through the gates of Chartres, only to find another shelter (like the Dutch interior) that refuses to be the whole of it. Chartres, having taken in the childlike persona, "still demands [the child's] re-birth" (63).

But Chartres is more than a mother figure; it is "reason beyond any faith," and "The prayer we make who never learned to pray" (63). These are the paradoxes of faith: the prayer precedes us, spoken already in stone; the child who passes through those gates, though "suffering" and "desperate" (63), must become the mother. Until the persona can embrace these incomprehensible facts, all action is suspended.

The first seven poems in Part 4 are placed in Judeo-Christian contexts, and all document a point of suspension. Again and again the poem occurs at the doorway that holds all beginnings, all endings. In "Easter Morning," the day itself is a prayer and a warning, for the world is both holy and imperiled. The poems of this book have made both states clear to us, and now the answer comes and is the single word "Wait" (65).

Throughout Part 4, the suspension is extended; "we," the chief protagonist of all these poems, are held between two states. We have something to learn. If humankind cannot be compassionate (and again and again the poems in this volume claim that true compassion is truly an impossibility), at least there is in "Jonah" a "compassionate sky" (64); in "Once More at Chartres," the cathedral is an "enclosure [that] opens and transcends" (63); in "At Chartres," the house itself, is "huge with faith" (62).

The oddity in Part 4 is "The Godhead as Lynx"—a poem that mirrors God and beast in their "absolute attention," that quality that Simone Weil tells us is the same as prayer (66). "The Godhead as Lynx" leaves the biblical context and picks up an earlier theme—the state of being face to face. In it, we watch the pure attention of the beast flow from "Mysterious sad eyes," that are nonetheless mindless (66). There is a longing here:

> To submerge self in that essential fur,
> And sleep close to this ancient world of grace,
> As if there could be healing next to her,
> The mother-lynx in her pre-human place.
> Yet that pure beauty does not know compassion— (66)

According to this poem, it was a pretty good world before we came with our human faces—a world suited to Kali, a cruel god that claims only "I am" (66). But we cannot give up our faces; we can only use them to look hard. "Our own / God" insists of us that we "become" (66). And more, our God gives us the means of becoming. He lives in us, "Imperfect as we are, and never whole,"

> . . . like a fertile seed,
> Always becoming, and asking of the soul
> To stretch beyond sweet nature, answer need. . . . (67)

By the "sheer power of need" (43) humans build Chartres and the Dutch interiors, or write "At Chartres" and "Dutch Interior." And if to do so we must "lay aside the beauty of the lynx," there is beauty, too, in the "laboring self who groans and thinks" (67). Sarton has come to terms with Kali in this poem, facing down directly the "golden gaze," of the "guiltless" (66).

Once again, the final three poems of the section, uniform in theme, provide a lens through which to view the whole. In "The Waves," a reprise of "Dover Beach" brings us the familiar eternal note of sadness, but Sarton offers a solution quite different from Matthew Arnold's:

> Oh love, let us be true then to this will—
> Not to each other, human and defeated,
> But to great power, our Heaven and our Hell,
> That thunders out its triumph unabated,
> And is never still. (68)

As in Arnold's poem, the "great power" here is the ocean, itself (68). Beyond our understanding, it yet allows us to stand and take it in. "At Chartres" advises us to "only see" (62); "Easter Morning" delivers the instruction: "Wait" (65); this poem asks that we "Listen once more!" (68). Simply see, simply listen, attend—these are our duties. We cannot act. We *can* take in the perceptions we are offered in such abundance and affirm them in all their paradoxical fullness.

If in the end we still feel we must ask what we asked in Part 1, "What is to be done?" we are given that answer, too, in "Beyond the Question." In this five-part poem—free verse at last after all that control—we are offered explicit instructions, reminiscent of Eliot's in

"East Coker," to "wait without hope." A phoebe teaches us in section one: first, become small and quietly attentive; "weave a nest for silence" (69) out of listening; learn the simplicity of "warm faithful waiting, / Contained in one's smallness" (69).

When all expectation has been suspended, in the second section the message comes: Silence. For the persona, "each thing is haloed. / I live in a Book of Hours" (70). In section three, the peony, centerpiece of the poem, must die, as the flowers died in "A Hard Death." To this peony's death the answer is yes. Part four tells us the source of the voices—they speak, not from the cloud, but in the blood: "we are inhabited" (71). And in part five the dialogue, hungered for throughout this book, begins. Five simple steps. They are not what we expected. The answer comes from "much deeper down" (71):

> Answer?
> But the answer is happening,
> Flows through every crevice, . . . (71)

through air, water, earth.

In the first three stanzas of the final poem, "Invocation," the poet in-vokes in turn "the dark earth," "the strong wave," and "the pure air" (72). The missing element enters the final stanza, not as it appeared in the Part 1 poems, but transformed, as love. The book ends then, by invoking our human fire: "Love, touch us everywhere / With primeval candor" (72).

A Grain of Mustard Seed is a book of seeking, of examining and casting off the old answers—while always the answer waits in the wings for us to exhaust our questioning. The answer is, as we find in "Beyond the Question," that "the answer is happening" (71). The whole book is a single suspension of disbelief in its most spiritual form—a suspension between death and rebirth, the silence of the confirmation that precedes the celebration of communion.

There are heroes of the human journey—often not the famous names we hear spoken and soon hear ourselves speaking aloud; just as often the heroes are the names we keep silent about, the women and men who have taught us how to live, how to find qualities in ourselves to love, how to stumble and get up gracefully, how to retire from a life's work, how to attend a death, how to guard our integrity and our sense of humor.

These women and men travel ahead of us on the road, mapping our journey. May Sarton has been such a hero for me, helping me to grow up—"By thinking." I suspect she has done the same for many others who carry her books as quietly as they carry their own faith, who quote her words with gratitude, if not always with accuracy. I keep running into her admirers in unlikely places. I suspect they are legion; if so, it bodes well for the world.

Works Cited

The Bible. Revised Standard Version, 1946.

Sarton, May. *A Grain of Mustard Seed: New Poems.* New York: Norton, 1971.

———. *A Self Portrait.* New York: Norton, 1982.

The Secret Teachings of Jesus: Four Gnostic Gospels. Trans. Marvin W. Meyer. New York: Vintage Books, 1984.

Imagining the Unicorn:
Poetic Sequence in May Sarton's
Letters from Maine

BOBBY CAUDLE ROGERS

"Who has spoken of the unicorn in old age?" asks May Sarton in the seventh poem of her sequence "Letters from Maine," an assemblage of ten lyrics comprising the opening section of her 1984 book of the same name (*LM* 24). The question itself is strange, for the unicorn, like the muse—another mythical allusion in this rich poem—is supposedly outside of time, eternal. We do not consider either of these beings in terms of age; we cannot conceive that inspiration or uniqueness may be subject to aging and decline. But Sarton's poem submits that age and its concomitant loss enrich beauty, bring purification. This seventh lyric in the sequence ends by asking, "Who has imagined the unicorn grown old?" In breaking open the unicorn myth, appropriating it for our own world, our own days of seeking, Sarton provides a model of the poet: "She who was hunted for her strangeness, / Androgynous, fleeing her pursuers . . . ," but who has learned "to look for wisdom / And experience rather than innocence . . ." (24). And while the unicorn is most certainly the poet—the poem reads like the notes of an impassioned memoirist—the beast is also all of us. Is it any wonder that the unicorn has not found an innocent in the forest? This is not tragic, however. Another more valid purity exists, one that does not depend on ignorance. It is the earned purity of age, the attainment of a woman who has "suffered / And become like gold, the dross beaten out . . ." (24).

I was first introduced to May Sarton's work in college. I was young and inexperienced, not far removed from adolescence and high school, a young, lost poet and an opportunistic reader seeking guidance and models for my own work. I felt distanced from Sarton's poems, and not only by the immaturity of my initial readings of them. I sensed that I was barred from the experience she was writing of, that I had no business reading these plaintive lyrics sung to the accompaniment of a lifetime's knowledge. I remember thinking I was too young for these poems, and I was right, but only partially and not for the reasons I initially supposed. When I picked them up again not many months later, I realized I had suddenly grown into them. Anyone who has come to understand a loss of any kind and its permanence is qualified to read these poems. The narratives of loss in "Letters from Maine," the images of longing, no longer seemed alien to me. I was still removed in age and gender from the poet, but I felt suddenly admitted into the confidences of Sarton's work. I had learned how to listen to a poem of loss.

We are moved by poems for so many reasons: because of their sheer beauty and their energy, because of their sinew, because of their bitterness and hope, perhaps most of all because of their courage. The poems of May Sarton are courageous. Sarton has accrued a formidable canon throughout a tenacious career, a lifetime of creativity that has been roundly overlooked by the critical community. The ease and brevity with which she is dismissed as sentimental by David Perkins in his *History of Modern Poetry* is an indication of how she has been ignored (367). Her poems, compositions of rigor and inventiveness, demand closer attention, require a more exacting consideration.

But we are moved, finally, because we need to be. May Sarton's poems offer much. Her later poems are especially full of a vigorous appraisal of her present, where one might expect the backward-gazing sentimentality that clouds the twilights of some careers. "Letters from Maine" is an example of her strong later work, a sequence marked by honesty and an intricacy that is a path rather than a puzzle, a sequence that distinguishes itself also through its formal concerns, a sequence built of poems that inscribe themselves in our minds deeply and with purpose.

The poem "A Farewell" forms an effective prologue to "Letters from

Maine." The three-stanza introduction is a formal lament of parting, tightly bound in the strictures of meter and rhyme. Stanza 2:

> After a while we shall be cut in two
> Between real islands where you live
> And a far shore where I'll no longer keep
> The haunting image of your eyes, and you,
> As pupils widen, widen to deep black
> And I am able neither to love or grieve
> Between fulfillment and heartbreak.
> The time will come when I can go to sleep. (*LM* 17)

In a time when neoformalists and practitioners of the free verse line continually feud at professional conferences and in the pages of the *Chronicle of the Associated Writing Programs,* Sarton practices both forms to solid effect. The rhyme scheme (*a-b-c-a-d-b-d-c*) in "A Farewell" is at once staid and unbalanced, as the emotions underlying the events reported in these stanzas must have been. The final line of each stanza must reach back to the third line for its rhyme, its resolution, a separation so distant in the sounding of the poem that the correspondence is almost forgotten. The form is appropriate to initiate the ten free verse poems of buoyant transcendence and plunging confession that will follow.

Within this restrained formality the voice speaks of being "for a while now all alive . . . ," an ironically timed affirmation in the wake of a separation, a loss, a de facto death (17). The sequence is a song in the midst of death, yet it is only partially a dirge. In this prefatory poem, Sarton asserts a determination not to return to the "murderous past" or indulge in the dream of "some safe landing." She is interested in the *now,* in "this moment of communion / Entranced, astonished by pure understanding . . ." (17).

This introductory poem speaks of death with directness. The first and second stanzas end with the two simplest declarative sentences: "It was like seeing and going blind" and "The time will come when I can go to sleep," the second assertion heavy in its Miltonic iambic pentameter and dark overtone. The image of "a far shore," if a bit evangelical in its connotation, presents a compelling horizon behind all the water imagery that will be employed. Sarton's intentions are to "float upon this moment of communion," adrift on a sea of "Passionate love dissolved like summer snow" (17). But this poem is not adrift or aimless; its journey is a skillfully navigated passage.

The details of the relationship lamented here are secondary and so deeply submerged below the poet's struggle against doubt as to be almost irrelevant. The scraps of lovers' conversation and the sketches of action are recorded most graphically in the eighth poem of the sequence, but no effort is made to render them idiosyncratic or specific to this one relationship. The dialogue offered is expected, mundane: "'Perhaps we should never meet again.'" The gestures approach cliché: "when we met and stared into each other's eyes" (25). The relationship's seeming ordinariness pulls it closer to universality, a source of the poem's power. The particulars are sparsely mentioned and unspectacular, interwoven among Sarton's doubts, which seem far more tactile than any remembered gesture or uttered word.

The eighth poem is a chronicle of conquered doubts. "I must try to speak words," Sarton says, "when the reality / Is an immense silence, and nothing can be said" (25). This is the situation of any poet, is it not? This is the daily prayer of a poet sitting down to the work, the grace that must be said. The voice in this poem doubts even the veracity of the indelible past, which is here being so meticulously considered: "Perhaps it is, after all, delusion and madness" (25). But the function of the poem is to conquer doubt, to redeem the past, to make lost history concrete and hold it to us as we move into further uncertainties. The poet wages a battle to recapture the past, the poem her piece of blooded ground. Sarton has chosen to ignore the advice Louise Bogan wrote to her thirty years earlier, that "it is impossible really to argue, in lyric poetry, because too many abstractions tend to creep in" (Bogan 295). The voice in Sarton's poem conjures and does verbal battle with the absent *other,* debating the lost person who abandoned her: "Nothing is possible. Nothing is real, you think." Sarton provides a poet's answer: *Nevertheless* repeated three times like the prayer of a believer. *"Nevertheless* is my answer to your *never"* (*LM* 25). This suggests Marianne Moore's poem, a poem that speaks of life, its secrets, its continuations—the mysterious "fruit / within the fruit" (Moore 125–26). The fruit within the fruit interests both these poets, the force that makes the prickly-pear leaf send a root down to seek the earth. "Victory won't come / to me unless I go / to it," Moore tells us in "Nevertheless" (126). Sarton's approach in "Letters from Maine" is no different. The ineffable "sap" in Moore's poem is rising still in the bereaved speaker in Sarton's sequence.

Is it writing, then, that will save us? Perhaps. In the sixth poem, the speaker is looking for "the saving word from so deep in the past" (*LM* 23). But the word seems elusive. It is a redemptive word that is already buried and must be exhumed from

> . . . as deep as the ancient root of the redwood,
> From as deep as the primal bed of the ocean,
> From as deep as a woman's heart sprung open
> Again through a hard birth or a hard death. (23)

Sarton suggests three possibilities: *strength, laughter, endurance.* These are merely the words she hears, we are told, perhaps words particular to her own experience. But each word corresponds with a source she identifies for us: *strength* with the redwood, *laughter* with the private currents of the ocean, and, most emphatically, *endurance* corresponds with the woman's heart.

The world is upside down for someone who has lived it, drained it. The motions of the world are viewed backwards, viewed from the depths yet seen with clarity. The leaves have fallen. The earth itself holds beauty and wonder, the ground beneath her feet becomes "golden while above / The maples are stripped of all color" (18). What is above signifies death. An inversion. It is the summer that is "sterile" (20). The fall and winter, seasons of death, hold the possibilities. Life may become new at any moment. Age and weariness can slip away, become no more than a message "cast away" into a sea of longing (21). For in this poem, time is a sea and not a river, a pool in which we are immersed and not a continual stream of loss. Our lives are chronicles of becoming lost and then found and lost again.

The fifth poem of the sequence provides a self-portrait of the artist. The ocean described in this poem takes on a personality, possesses traits of the poet:

> From a distance the ocean looks calm,
> Gray and unbroken stretching out to Spain,
> But it is seamed with hidden tumult. (22)

The gray and lined sea is only calm when observed from a distance. The poem draws us in. The description undoubtedly suggests age. The ocean currents build slowly like the most inexorable passions, swept by the convection of "some deep pulse far away" (22). The word "pulse" cannot be separated from the human heart. Our heart-driven passions are terrible, "ominous," the force driving the ocean in this poem to strike against its boundaries.

But to see the poem, and indeed the whole sequence, as specific to the trials of aging is to give it an unjust and poor reading. "Letters from Maine" rewards a broader analysis. This fifth poem is also a rumination on language. The ocean striking rocks sends up "shattered towers of white foam" (22). Immediately, the muse is questioned. The towers may as well be the Tower of Babel; communication is at stake; this is the conflict theory of poetry, catastrophism, a world brought into being through violent upheaval. Poems extend from the earth when the surging emotions of the ocean strike the resistance and form of the rocks, a metaphor played out on Sarton's Maine coast.

Poetry never becomes a safe business, even to someone of Sarton's experience and knowledge. She is awash on this ocean

> . . . like one of the black ducks
> Bobbing out there, must keep my balance,
> Stay clear of the rocks as they do
> Who know how to ride this tumult safely
> And play its perils like a game. (22)

This is no mere game for the poet. She has not learned the compromise of safety. "Letters from Maine" is not an easeful five-finger exercise, at least not in the sense that Tennyson's same-sex lament, *In Memoriam*, served as an anodyne. Tennyson confesses:

> But, for the unquiet heart and brain,
> A use in measured language lies;
> The sad mechanic exercise,
> Like dull narcotics, numbing pain. (5.5-8)

Sarton's poem is no "mechanic exercise." She quickly abandons the meter and rhyme of "A Farewell" for a more open form in the numbered lyrics of "Letters from Maine." The free verse line does not essay to numb the reader. If anything, Sarton employs this form as a strategy to heighten the pain, to preserve it (which was surely Tennyson's purpose as well). Writing of grief in free verse is an act of courage—in some notable cases, masochism—rather than an attempt at anesthesia.

"Letters from Maine" is primarily about grief. In "A Farewell," Sarton speaks of being "able neither to love or grieve," seemingly opposing as antitheses the two infinitives in that statement (*LM* 17). Love and grief are extremes between which the poet oscillates—"between fulfillment and heartbreak" (17). But this opposition is misleading. Love and grief are akin to each other in this poem. They become essentially the same act when the object of love has been removed; fulfillment is not so far from heartbreak. Grief can bring its own fulfillment and must if it is to be successful. Love and grief are the keys to redemption for the speaker in these poems. The sequence is a movement toward these acts.

Tess Gallagher's essay "The Poem as a Reservoir for Grief" contains some helpful insights for reading a poem of this type. Gallagher sees poems as "multi-directional" vehicles. The poem "reaches richly into the past and forms linkages with the present and with other isolated pasts. The poem searches into the future. It reminds us of 'longings'" (107). The poem is a synthesizing device, according to Gallagher, which may bridge our past and our future and connect the fragments of our lives. She remarks how poems use myth, on a deeper level, to connect the conscious and unconscious (107). To return to the past, at least provisionally, is essential, "For only through such returns may one hope for the very real gain of transforming losses of various kinds into meaningful contributions to our own becoming" (103). Gallagher recognizes that we need more than release, more than mere catharsis—we need understanding, comprehension, "the need to feel, as in the word *mourning*" (103).

To write a poem (or to read one) takes us beyond understanding—as does the act of mourning. The effects a poem causes in a reader are sometimes untraceable. We feel we have in part made something from nothing, brought forth a world *ex nihilo*. Sarton tells us in the first lyric of her sequence that she will "Make poems out of nothing, out of loss, / And at times hear your healing laughter" (*LM* 18). The poem may travel into the past, as Gallagher says. Sarton's group of poems is a monument built in a void, a construction created from nothingness to fill an absence.

Mourning is the critical act in "Letters from Maine." Sarton's sequence begins in disorientation, a dislocation caused by an inability to mourn. The speaker has returned home, but to a home that is somehow transformed and threatening. Her "cultivated space" is no longer her own. She feels "at a loss, / Disoriented" (18). This displacement is caused by her inability to grieve, to come to terms with a painful past. She does not know which direction to turn, into the past or future: "Where can I go? / Not toward you . . ." (18). But poems are multidirectional, as Gallagher has said, and may transport us forwards and backwards at once, a capability that must be taken advantage of in order to achieve healing. The past must be explored like a terrain, as Sarton explores her Maine coast and the dark waters pushing against it.

This grief, like her love, must be "torn out" of the poet. The metaphor Sarton employs in the poem is that of an eagle's dive. Surely we are meant to see more than the eagle's predatory dive, "His fierce head flashing among the white gulls"; we are intended to visualize the act to its completion, the seizure of his catch from beneath the surface of the water, an image prevalent throughout the poems of this sequence (19). The poet will have to take hold of her own grief with the same ferocity.

The movement through grief toward understanding is difficult and painful. Sarton achieves it with much hesitancy. It is not until the eighth poem of the sequence that the object of grief becomes embodied fully and actually speaks in direct quotation. Having finally found the courage, a courage seemingly derived from the composition of the poem itself, the poet relives the moment of loss: "I could feel the blood withering in my veins, / A breakdown of cells, death in my body" (24). The poet enters into a dialogue with this lost *other*, with "your voice alive in the room" (25). "Letters from Maine" may be placed in a long tradition of apostrophes. But every poem is in a sense an apostrophe, addressing a world that cannot be beside it on the bleached page and that will more than likely never answer. Sarton's poem becomes both argument and rebuttal. She attacks the reason, the hard logic, that has left her bereft. "Reason is not the master of the moment," she asserts; another logic was at work when they met "Like sleepers woken suddenly out of a dream, / Suffering a blaze of light" (25). It was neither madness nor delusion, she tells us, but rather "a gift from the goddess." "Nothing is possible," the voice counters, "Nothing is real" (25). But the poem has redeemed reality. An artifact, a made object now exists. The poem, the "gift from the goddess" (25), spreads across the page as possible and real as the dark sea washing against Sarton's coast.

By the end of the sequence, the muse has become indistinguishable from the ex-lover, the object of loss. Is it that all poetry must be part elegy? The muse, cold as the dead love affair, has returned "as abruptly as a meteor fallen in an open field," the ashes now to be mulled over, discussed, read like tea leaves or interpreted like bird sign. The present has been invaded by the past with the luminosity of a meteorite burning through the atmosphere, a "falling star" (27). The image is appropriate. The speaker reads the stars, our fates mapped in their distant design. She speaks of looking for something "Under the words" as though the words were stars, light years above the humble actions they are intended to describe, occasionally blazing downward through a dark night to touch this ground (27).

Tess Gallagher theorizes that a poem may function as a "live-in church," a place of worship and meditation, a repository of icons (104). Sarton's sequence is infused with religious language and takes on a certain fervor at some points. The poem sets itself up as a study of a "moment of communion" and one may even detect a thirst for redemption (17). "What is the saving word . . . ?" she asks (23). The last two stanzas of the sequence seem to call for this reading:

> Never curse the curse, or forget the blessing.
> Since all things move together to grave ends
> We need not even ask where we are bound.
>
> Let the muse bury the dead. For that she came.
> Who walks the earth in joy and poverty?
> Who then has risen? The tomb is empty. (27)

We are forced to read the poem on a more spiritual level. "The tomb is empty" is at once a foreboding statement, presaging the poet's and everyone else's mortality, and a suggestion of rebirth. The waters of this poem suddenly become baptismal. The waters on which the speaker floats, waters that at first seem daunting but later bring about a purgation, are the poem itself. "Everything stops except the poem. It rises / In an unbroken wave and topples to silence," as constant as the restless sea (26).

Rather than being a tangential voice, May Sarton is in the mainstream of her century, both formally and in her choice and use of content. "Letters from Maine" helps establish her position. She treats her subject matter, the wound by a personal loss, with frankness and courage, mining an unhappy vein of experience for a lode of pathos and transcendence. But we have come to see this kind of courage as no great feat. And it is so much practiced from the "Confessional" poets onward, that it is now de rigueur in the small magazines and the slim volumes offered from the university presses. We tend to forget the emotional costs and the technical difficulties involved in this kind of poetry. The poem of personal grief is a "solitary and most often lonely act . . . [demanding] huge leaps of faith and audacity as a writer to ask that one be followed, be understood, felt . . . , because each loss is ultimately singular, an 'only'" (Gallagher 116).

This sort of emotional disrobing for the sake of art is rarely questioned as Adrienne Rich questions herself in her sequence "21 Love Poems." She looks at her own exhibitionism with a morbid sense of fascination:

What kind of beast would turn its life into words?
What atonement is this all about?
—and yet, writing words like these, I'm also living.
(Rich 28)

Sarton doubts her own impulses as well, calls into question her motivations for turning her life into words, admitting that maybe she is doing it entirely for poetical reasons, "forcing her muse to pay attention, / Forcing too much out of an hour of bliss" (*LM* 25).

Perhaps more surprising for a poem written so late in a career, "Letters from Maine" is interesting and adventuresome formally. If we are to believe M. L. Rosenthal and Sally M. Gall in their book *The Modern Poetic Sequence: The Genius of Modern Poetry,* the sequence form is endemic to modern poets and the supreme indicator of their achievement. Practically all the great modern poets have written in the form of the poetic sequence, and often as the capping achievement of their careers (vii). Rosenthal and Gall's case is a compelling one. They quote Poe's maxim that all longer poems are merely a succession of short poems sutured together, that intense poetic effects are of necessity brief, eventually making the point that Poe's remarks presaged the modern dissatisfaction with the long poem and suggested a strategy through which the poet may controvert these problems (6).

Rosenthal and Gall point to Whitman's *Song of Myself* and Pound's *Cantos* as examples of the modern sequence. More contemporary works such as Lowell's *Life Studies* and Berryman's *77 Dream Songs* also utilize the form. Sarton's sequence must be considered in the same terms. Rosenthal and Gall loosely define the modern sequence as "a grouping of mainly lyric poems and passages, rarely uniform in pattern, which tend to interact as an organic whole" (9). The structure allows for the synthesis of disparate experience and emotion, what is referred to as "powerfully opposed tonalities and energies," a capacity necessary in a form that hopes to capture modern experience (3). Sarton undoubtedly practices this form in "Letters from Maine." She has endeavored to "reconceive reality in humanly reassuring ways rather than in chillingly impersonal ones" (Rosenthal 11). Sarton's structure is not arbitrary or externally imposed. It is, rather, internal and organic, "based on dynamics: the succession and interaction of units of affect" (Rosenthal 15).

Sarton's sequence resides in the company of those by such prominent poets as Charles Wright, whose twenty-poem sequences "Tattoos" and "Skins" in his 1975 book *Bloodlines* have been described by Helen Vendler as "exquisitely finished sequences aiming for inevitability of effect" (393). These poems are less grand in scale than the works by Whitman and Pound which Rosenthal and Gall cite, but they are more contemporary and personal in their quietly ruminative voices and their quotidian approaches to art. Wright's poems arrest the detritus of life and render it spiritual. "Tattoos" is a veritable dustbin of images (clipped camellias, snake markings, overheard Jewish prayers, memories and dreams, dogwood blossoms, many kinds of trees), each isolated and given power (*Country Music* 56-77).

Sarton's and Wright's sequences parallel in several ways. "Letters from Maine" is as concerned with form as Wright's "Tattoos," which is written in a very precise fifteen-line measure, and his "Skins," composed in an approximation of the sonnet form. Though the two poets approach narrative differently—Wright's sequences are made of narratively disjoint materials, each poem isolate, another bead on the rosary, whereas Sarton's sequence extends its story in a continuous and cumulative telling, each unit building upon the previous one—a parallel of intention may be noted in their sequences. Both poets seek the expressly spiritual. Wright has said in interview that "Oh yes, all my poems are prayers and songs. Hymns" (*Halflife* 130). Both poets also generate their sequences from experience. The footnotes to "Tattoos" are intended to show that each poem is derived from an actual occurrence, each unit of the sequence is, as Wright comments, "a psychic tattoo in my life that would always be with me" (*Halflife* 67). And both poets consider death. "Tattoos" begins with an image of death, the white camellia worn at Easter. It, too, is a poem of parting: "Your sound is the sound of good-bye. / Your poem is a poem of pain" (*Country Music* 70).

Without appealing to an appendix of notes, Sarton's poem is equally grounded. Why her work has been written of so little is hard to understand. Her themes are important and her execution of them is skillful. "Letters from Maine" resounds with the conviction of a witness, a participant in the world. Sarton tells us in the final poem of the sequence that she has "always known, the paths / of grace cannot be forced, yet meteors will fall, / A blaze of light, and always when least looked for" (*LM* 27). Her work deserves a longer-lasting illumination.

Works Cited

Bogan, Louise. *What the Woman Lived: Selected Letters of Louise Bogan, 1920–1970*. Ed. Ruth Limmer. New York: Harcourt Brace Jovanovich, Inc., 1973.

Gallagher, Tess. *A Concert of Tenses: Essays on Poetry*. Ann Arbor: U of Michigan P, 1986.

Moore, Marianne. *The Complete Poems of Marianne Moore*. New York: Macmillan/Viking Press, 1967.

Perkins, David. *A History of Modern Poetry: Modernism and After*. Cambridge, Mass.: Belknap Press, 1987.

Rich, Adrienne. *The Dream of a Common Language*. New York: Norton, 1978.

Rosenthal, M. L., and Sally M. Gall. *The Modern Poetic Sequence: The Genius of Modern Poetry*. New York: Oxford UP, 1983.

Sarton, May. *Letters from Maine*. New York: Norton, 1984.

Tennyson, Alfred, Lord. *In Memoriam*. Ed. Robert H. Ross. New York: Norton, 1973.

Vendler, Helen. *The Music of What Happens: Poems, Poets, Critics*. Cambridge, Mass.: Harvard UP, 1988.

Wright, Charles. *Country Music: Selected Early Poems*. Middletown, Conn.: Wesleyan UP, 1982.

———. *Halflife: Improvisations and Interviews: 1977–87*. Ann Arbor: U of Michigan P, 1988.

III

Other Shores:
Vision and Revision

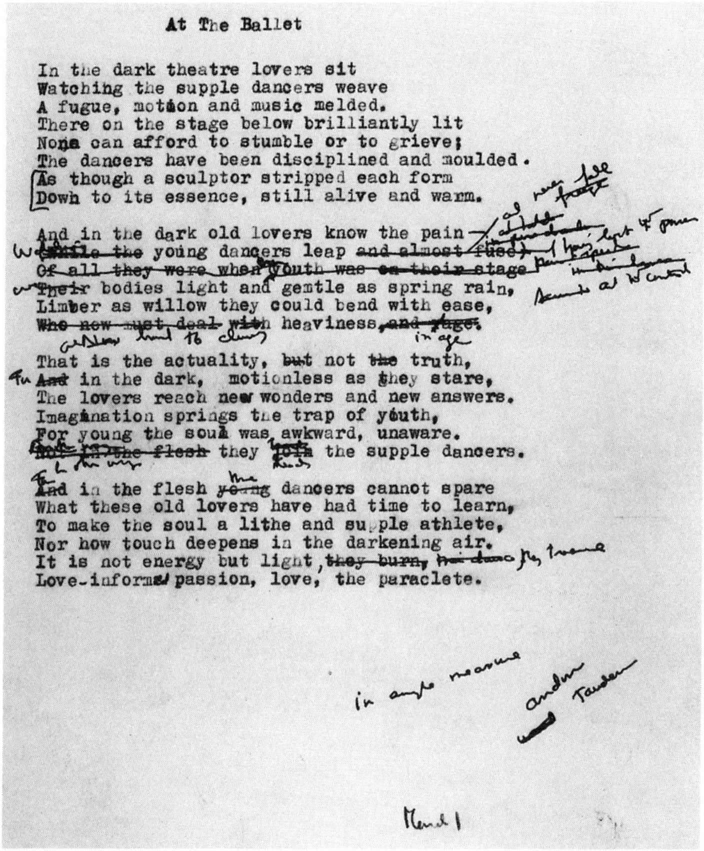

At The Ballet

In the dark theatre lovers sit
Watching the supple dancers weave
A fugue, motion and music melded.
There on the stage below brilliantly lit
None can afford to stumble or to grieve;
The dancers have been disciplined and moulded.
As though a sculptor stripped each form
Down to its essence, still alive and warm.

And in the dark old lovers know the pain
While the young dancers leap and almost fuse
Of all they were when youth was on their stage
Their bodies light and gentle as spring rain,
Limber as willow they could bend with ease,
Who now must deal with heaviness and rage.
That is the actuality, but not the truth,
And in the dark, motionless as they stare,
The lovers reach new wonders and new answers.
Imagination springs the trap of youth,
For young the soul was awkward, unaware.
And in the flesh they join the supple dancers.

And in the flesh young dancers cannot spare
What these old lovers have had time to learn,
To make the soul a lithe and supple athlete,
Nor how touch deepens in the darkening air.
It is not energy but light, they burn, he dance
Love-informed passion, love, the paraclete.

Fig. 2. "At the Ballet," rough draft of "Old Lovers at the Ballet." Draft three of seven. From the files of May Sarton. Used with permission.

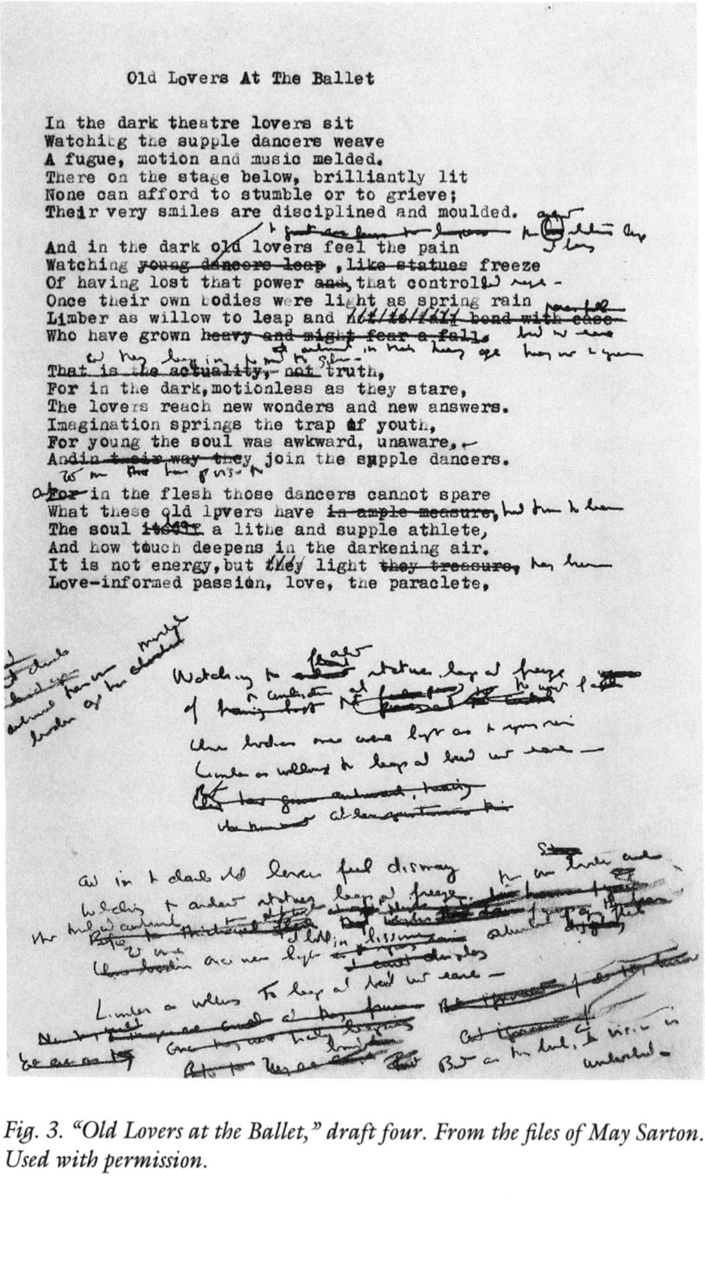

Old Lovers At The Ballet

In the dark theatre lovers sit
Watching the supple dancers weave
A fugue, motion and music melded.
There on the stage below, brilliantly lit
None can afford to stumble or to grieve;
Their very smiles are disciplined and moulded.

And in the dark old lovers feel the pain
Watching young dancers leap ,like statues freeze
Of having lost that power and that control —
Once their own bodies were light as spring rain,
Limber as willow to leap and not to fall to bend with ease
Who have grown heavy and might fear a fall,
That is the actuality, not truth,
For in the dark, motionless as they stare,
The lovers reach new wonders and new answers.
Imagination springs the trap of youth,
For young the soul was awkward, unaware, —
And in their way they join the supple dancers.

For in the flesh those dancers cannot spare
What these old lovers have in ample measure,
The soul itself a lithe and supple athlete,
And how much deepens in the darkening air.
It is not energy, but they light they treasure,
Love-informed passion, love, the paraclete,

Fig. 3. "Old Lovers at the Ballet," draft four. From the files of May Sarton.
Used with permission.

Old Lovers at the Ballet

In the dark theatre lovers sit
Watching the supple dancers weave
A fugue, motion and music melded.
There on the stage below, brilliantly lit
No dancer stumbles or may grieve;
Their very smiles are disciplined and moulded.

And in the dark old lovers feel dismay
Watching the ardent bodies leap and freeze,
Thinking how age has changed them and has mocked.
Once they were very light and bold in lissome play,
Limber as willows that could bend with ease—
But as they watch a vision is unlocked.

Imagination springs the trap of youth.
And in the dark motionless, as they stare,
Old lovers reach new wonders and new answers
As in the mind they leap to catch the truth,
For young the soul was awkward, unaware,
That claps its hands now with the supple dancers.

And in the flesh those dancers cannot spare
What the old lovers have had time to learn,
That the soul is a lithe and serene athlete
That deepens touch upon the darkening air.
It is not energy but light they burn,
The radiant powers of the Paraclete.

May Sarton
Halfway to Silence

Sailing to a Different Shore:
Sarton's Revisioning of Yeats

❦

CATHERINE B. EMANUEL

At eighty, May Sarton still writes poetry and identifies herself first and foremost as a poet. Like Yeats, whom she has cited as a major influence, Sarton usually revises extensively and continues to produce quality work in her "upward years." One poem that has undergone at least eight drafts is "Old Lovers at the Ballet," from Sarton's 1980 collection, *Halfway to Silence*. In this poem Sarton alludes to Yeats's "Sailing to Byzantium," providing the same image of the soul's clapping its hands (an image that Yeats had taken from Blake), but Sarton "revisions" Yeats's journey into old age, landing her boat on a more spiritual shore. As Adrienne Rich points out, women's writings need to "transcend and transform experience; [they have] to question, to challenge, to conceive of alternatives. . . ." ("When We Dead Awaken" 43). By "transforming" Yeats's poem, Sarton provides a subtle but radical change: a shift not only in ideological viewpoint but in class distinction as well. For Yeats, whose vision had aristocratic leanings, leanings that led him to Mussolini and to fascism, the journey culminates in becoming a "hammered gold" figure. For Sarton, however, the journey transcends the physical; Sarton's old lovers merely contemplate the dance, and the moving spectacle of art is enough to move them into a triumphant spiritual realm.

As a lyric poet, Yeats has served as model for Sarton. Both concentrate on sound, combining poetry's rhyme, meter, and alliteration to form music. Each works and reworks form, combining the instruments of poetry to form harmony with meaning. In "Old Lovers at the Ballet," Sarton uses the metaphor of the fugue, music developed in counterpoints, to stage her warring dichotomies, the same contraries around which Yeats structures his poem: youth and age, sickness and health, body and soul. Sarton sets up many of these opposing pairs in her first stanza, a stanza illustrating the darkness and light in which all of the poem's dances occur:

> In the dark theatre lovers sit
> Watching the supple dancers weave
> A fugue, motion and music melded.
> There on the stage below, brilliantly lit
> No dancer stumbles or may grieve;
> Their very smiles are disciplined and moulded. (*HS* 51)

Besides the metaphor of music, Sarton also elaborates on the image of the dance. By the end of her poem, the dance becomes less regimented than the movements she paints in the opening stanza's lines:

> No dancer stumbles or may grieve;
> Their very smiles are disciplined and moulded. (*HS* 51)

By removing the dance from the stage and turning it into the mental choreography of the old lovers, Sarton draws an equation in which contemplation of art and the form itself become inseparable. This joining echoes Yeats's ending of "Among School Children" when his speaker asks, "How can we know the dancer from the dance?" (*The Poems* 217).

Another link between Sarton's "Old Lovers" and Yeats's "Among School Children" is Sarton's reference to the soul. In his two poems, Yeats presents contradictory views. In "Among School Children," the line "The body is not bruised to pleasure soul" expresses a different philosophy from these lines in "Sailing to Byzantium":

> Soul clap its hands and sing, and louder sing
> For every tatter in its mortal dress. (*The Poems* 193)

Though his line in "Sailing" implies that the body is merely the soul's house, and the more ravages the body suffers, the stronger the soul becomes, he does not follow this thought to its logical conclusion. Even though his poem should end as Sarton's does, on the glorification of the spiritual, "The radiant powers of the Paraclete," his speaker prays to the "gold mosaic" on the wall in order that he might maintain a physical presence. His impetus, then, is not spiritual but physical, for in the third stanza, he prays to the figures in the mosaic:

> Come from the holy fire, perne in a gyre,
> And be the singing-masters of my soul.
> Consume my heart away; sick with desire
> And fastened to a dying animal
> It knows not what it is; and gather me
> Into the artifice of eternity. (*The Poems* 193)

Yeats's speaker is blinded by his own desire, not only by sexual desire but by his desire for immortality as well.

While Sarton clearly wants the emphasis of her poem to be spiritual, she does, nonetheless, evoke old "lovers" (whose gender is left ambiguous). Like Yeats, Sarton combines images of sexuality with those of art, and with images of religion as well. Through "Crazy Jane," one of Yeats's many masks, he glorifies physical love and concludes "Love is all / Unsatisfied / That cannot take the whole / Body and Soul" ("Crazy Jane on the Day of Judgment," *The Poems* 257). Since the language of mystics is often wrought with sexual imagery to imply a merging with the divine, the idea of lovers becomes the vehicle for transcendence. Throughout all eight drafts of her poem, Sarton maintains a line equating passion with the spiritual:

> It is not energy but light they burn,
> Love-informed passion, love, the paraclete. (*TS* 1-8)

Her final version's line becomes "The radiant powers of the Paraclete," a change that removes power from the lovers and their love and transfers it to the soul and to Christianity, in the form of a capitalized reference to "Paraclete." Instead of returning to the touching, reinforcing a sexual reference, to include "love-informed passion," Sarton chooses to concentrate on the light, the "radiant" Paraclete. A more direct sexual reference that she also weeded out from the final poem is in the lines:

And as they sigh in their great bed and turn
Go from a long caress to sweeter sleep. (*TS* 3)

Although once again Sarton seems to stress the love more than the lovemaking, she does choose to exclude these lines from the final poem, a change that removes the poem from physical love and takes it into the spiritual realm. Sarton thought carefully about her final version before allowing it to rest, for in the third draft, she appears to have thought about changing the opening stanza to include these two lines. This version would have referred also to dancers in the "flesh," another image that would have emphasized the body, the sexual (*TS* 3).

In beginning with physical love and ending on a spiritual note, Sarton echoes John Donne's Holy Sonnets, which begin with a glorification of physical love and end with a glorification of God and of the spiritual. Like Donne, Sarton's "lovers" move beyond the physical without disregarding its existence or importance, for they have been, in fact, lovers; but for them the soul replaces sexuality with a movement "That deepens touch upon the darkening air." Though they eventually join in a different sort of touch, they are still referred to as lovers.

Even though physical action is removed from the speakers in both poems (Yeats's speaker has already "sailed the seas and come / To the holy city of Byzantium"), Sarton's old lovers do make a Kierkegaardian "great leap of faith," accepting their spirituality in the dark with no witnessed miracles or divine intervention to point conclusively to the soul's ballet. They are in the dark literally, as members of the audience, throughout the poem, yet Sarton, in the last stanza, has their souls "burn" light. By using the word *light* in every stanza except the third, she changes emphasis from the stage to the lovers and from the dancers' physical movement to the lovers' growing spirituality. She then conjures from the word every nuance of meaning. In the first stanza, the light refers to the stage and to the dancers featured there:

There on the stage below, brilliantly lit
No dancer stumbles or may grieve;
Their very smiles are disciplined and moulded. (*HS* 51)

By stanza two, however, light becomes synonymous with youth, as the old lovers reflect upon a time when "they were light and bold in lissome play." Since stanza three supplies no mention of light, it functions as a mystical "dark night of the soul," for in this stanza, the old lovers make a mental "leap to catch the truth." In the concluding stanza, Sarton extends the meaning of the light in these lines:

> That the soul is a lithe and serene athlete
> That deepens touch upon the darkening air.
> It is not energy but light they burn,
> The radiant powers of the Paraclete. (*HS* 51)

Though light still seems equated with youth because they "burn" light in aging, the coupling of energy with light suggests a metamorphosis of sorts, one that results in a brighter light, the spiritual and "radiant" powers of the Paraclete.

Yeats's speaker, on the other hand, observes the "young / In one another's arms" and refers to the "sensual music all neglect," but never pairs with a human lover. While Sarton seems to suggest a completion of sorts in the old lovers, Yeats takes art as his partner. Consequently, he does not use art as a vehicle by which to achieve spirituality as Sarton does; instead, he desires to be figured among the artifacts, locked in a "hammered gold" body. Not quite as egotistical as Shelley's "Ozymandias," Yeats's speaker, nonetheless, desires to be figured among those "Monuments of . . . magnificence," and his wish is to be encased in a physical presence that will never decay.

Though Yeats's and Sarton's craft and gift are the molding of words, the process each employs to form the poem is very different. For Yeats, who once wrote of his revision process, "It is myself that I remake," the end result is often radically different from the first creative bursts (*The Poems* 548). Sarton's process, however, suggests a clearer beginning vision. In a June 1967 article on revision, Sarton says that her early "jottings" for a poem generally contain an image, possibly more than one, around which the poem can be structured. She adds, "The image must be complex enough to carry the weight of complex feeling" (*CEA Critic* 1). For the "Old Lovers," the key image focuses on pairing the physical movement of the dancers with the spiritual process of the lovers, a contrast that appears in every draft of her poem. On the other hand, Yeats's early sketchings of "Sailing to Byzantium" point to no single image; instead, Yeats begins with a concept of Byzantium and of the journey's transformation. In an early draft, he writes: "I fly from things becoming to the thing become" and above it writes, "nature to Byzantium" (Stallworthy 94). Though not clearly evident in all the beginning drafts, the dichotomy that Yeats seems to be working with is Byzantium on one hand and nature on the other, for, like Blake, Yeats thinks that "Without contraries is no progression." Nearly all of his poems are structured on extremes. In this case, though, he has an ideal of Byzantium, which he describes in *A Vision:*

> I think that in early Byzantium, maybe never before or since in recorded history, religious, aesthetic and practical life were one. (279)

Byzantium exemplifies what he terms in *A Vision* as his "Unity of Being," yet throughout the course of his drafts, he finds no solution that would make sexuality and creation choices for him. Instead of becoming the creator and procreator, however, he resolves to become art, a solution not in keeping with the speaker's earlier desires.

In that same 1967 article in the *CEA Critic* on revision, Sarton writes of meter and process in terms that ring true of this poem's progress:

> Among these rough notes I jot down in the moment of inspiration, there is a line which suggests meter, and sometimes I can sense the whole first stanza. (3)

Just as most of the first stanza remains constant throughout the drafts of "Old Lovers," Sarton also provides in her first efforts the line that establishes the meter, iambic pentameter: "Imagination springs the trap of youth." She does, however, alter the first stanza before arriving at the final version. For four drafts, she leaves in two lines that harken back to Yeats's "Sailing":

> As though a sculptor stripped each [dancer] form
> Down to its essence, still alive and warm. (*TS* 4)

In her final version, Sarton provides almost "chiseled" figures, now moulded in discipline rather than marble:

> No dancer stumbles or may grieve;
> Their very smiles are disciplined and moulded. (*HS* 51)

Throughout Yeats's poem are references to the plastic arts forming "Monuments of [their] own magnificence." Even in these two lines that she edited out, Sarton points not to cold statuary but to a Pygmalion-type human sculpture. While Yeats longs for some existence similar to Keats's figures on the urn in that "cold pastoral," Sarton provides not a "hammered gold" body but one very much living, one "alive and warm."

Instead of ensnaring the old lovers in lamentations of lost prowess, as Yeats does in referring to his aged speaker as "A tattered coat upon a stick," Sarton changes the tenor of the dance after the line "Imagination springs the trap of youth." Since the early drafts place this line as fourth, following "The lovers reach new wonders and new answers," Sarton obviously had in mind this line for transition. The change, however, from fourth to first points to a different turning point, one that occurs in the physical darkness. With this line the dance becomes spiritual; the soul becomes for them "a lithe and serene athlete," and what have been the leaps and freezes of the ballet become mental movement as

> Old lovers reach new wonders and new answers
> As in the mind they leap to catch the truth,
> For young the soul was awkward, unaware,
> That claps its hands now with the supple dancers. (*HS* 51)

Sarton then keeps the action of the poem consistent; she merely enlarges the concept of the dance so that the dance becomes a cosmic restoration of harmony, the same sort of imagery that ends Elizabethan comedy. Though Yeats attempts a similar feat by opening with "the sensual music all neglect," his now hammered gold figure, a form not taken "from any natural thing," is perched to sing "Of what is past, or passing, or to come." By the end of the poem, he discards the sensual music and the sexual imagery of the first stanza and replaces them with this golden presence that sings throughout eternity. He again stresses his aristocratic bent in supplying the song to the "lords and ladies" of Byzantium, but nowhere in this final stanza does he suggest the joy and completion that Sarton attributes to her old lovers. Like the old lovers who sit in the audience of Sarton's poem, we as readers become the audience too, widening the democratic reach of the verses.

Unlike Blake, who looked to a future second Eden, Yeats idealizes a past civilization to which he can never belong. "Sailing to Byzantium," written after a long illness, attempts to find a communion between natural and supernatural worlds, between human and divine (Allen 94). Yeats cannot fathom a complete faith, one in which he would have no control. For Sarton's lovers faith is not an intellectual syllogism, not a bargaining for immortality in human form. For three drafts she includes the line "That is the actuality, but not the truth" to begin the pivotal third stanza (*TS* 1, 2, 3). The "truth" for Sarton then revolves around faith, around the unseen, and faith for Sarton's lovers means growing acceptance, the same attitude she writes of in "Gestalt at Sixty":

> I am not ready to die,
> But I am learning to trust death
> As I have trusted life.
> I am moving
> Toward a new freedom
> Born of detachment,
> And a sweeter grace—
> Learning to let go. (*SSE* 200)

This "letting go" of physicality is not without compensation for Sarton's old lovers. In an interesting pirouette that begins the third stanza, Sarton returns the dance to the pair as "Imagination springs the trap of youth."

Much of the difference in tone between Sarton's poem and "Sailing to Byzantium" rests in the attitude that each poet has toward aging. Writing his first poem about old age while still in his twenties, Yeats feared physical change primarily because he could never find a religion that completely satisfied him. His fearful "vision" of afterlife is more apparent in the culmination of the voyage, his poem "Byzantium," which provides a horrific view of "death-in-life and life-in-death" (*The Poems* 248). Sarton, on the other hand, takes the course that she attributes in *At Seventy* to her mother: "to choose and take the path toward elevation rather than despair" (58). Like Sarton's mother, the old lovers choose a transcendence, which takes on a Christian implication, rather than despair. Consequently, Sarton enlarges the idea of the dance not only as art but also as symbol of spiritual celebration.

In a 1990 video production on older poets called *Writing in the Upward Years,* Sarton termed her poetry a "sacramentalization of the ordinary." This idea is perhaps key to Sarton's revision of Yeats's theme. Yeats's speaker must travel to the time that, in his estimation, represents the golden age of art, in order to become a "hammered gold" figure. Though Yeats's speaker has already "sailed the seas," his change still entails a physical repositioning, unlike Sarton's pair, who travel great distances without leaving the theater. They have no need for "gold mosaics" or for any of the goldsmith's wares; instead, they work within the framework of memory:

> And in the dark old lovers feel dismay
> Watching the ardent bodies leap and freeze,
> Thinking how age has changed them and has mocked.
> Once they were light and bold in lissome play
> Limber as willows that could bend with ease—
> But as they watch a vision is unlocked. (*HS* 51)

This "vision" then enables them to see old age differently, to recognize that waning physicality is compensated by a heightened spirituality.

In Sarton's last collection of poems, *The Silence Now,* "The Muse as Donkey" exemplifies the reflection and affirmation suggested by "Old Lovers at the Ballet":

I am a practical person.
Let us believe
That Mystery itself is fulfillment.
It was given to me
To be deeply stirred
To be taken out of myself
By the "evidence of things not seen."
Now the donkey's frail ankles
Absorb my heart,
We are fellow-sufferers,
And we do not despair. (70)

Sarton's personae do not have to see "what is past, or passing or to come"; for them the "mystery" can exist in itself. Though her lovers suffer the ravages of aging, they do not long to be consumed "Into the artifice of eternity."

As lyric poets, Sarton and Yeats both use the musical quality of words to enhance the themes of the poem. Throughout Yeats's multiple drafts, he carefully chooses his words and his pairings; he balances the "Fish, flesh, or foul" in the first stanza with the accompanying "Whatever is begotten, born and dies." Both not only mention music in their respective poems but also support the poetry's music in meter, alliteration, and rhyme. In "Old Lovers at the Ballet," Sarton maintains a specific rhyme scheme, *a-b-c-a-b-c*, with a different beginning rhyme in every stanza except the last. Instead of beginning with a different opening rhyme to start the last stanza, she picks up the rhyme from the preceding stanza (*stare* with *unaware* in the third; *spare* with *air* in the fourth) in order to link the two stanzas. This link between the third and fourth stanzas gives greater weight not only to the old lovers but also to the idea of the spiritual. In a 1966 article titled "The Problems and Delights of Revision," Sarton advises poets to "be sure that your rhyme scheme echoes the mood of the poem, and enhances its *music*" (*The Writer* 22, Sarton's emphasis). In this poem Sarton also points to greater harmony for the old lovers by creating this rhyme. In contrast, the dancers' first stanza contains the slant rhyme of *melded* with *moulded*, a blend that reinforces the idea that "young the soul was awkward, unaware."

Both Yeats and Sarton also employ unusual word use, selecting words not generally associated with the meaning each implies. For Yeats, the line often cited in this regard is: "gather me / Into the artifice of eternity." Since artifice can mean deceit or trickery as well as skill and ingenuity, critics have questioned its use; however, since Yeats's early drafts carry several personal lines, such as "For many lovers have I taken off my clothes" (Stallworthy 89), which he edited out of the final version, he distances himself from the speaker and moves the speaker away from the poem's opening sexual images. Another image that Yeats edited from the final version is that of a fish's carrying souls to paradise (which might possibly foreshadow the dolphin in "Byzantium"). By removing the personal and the natural from the poem, Yeats reinforces "artifice"; a *contrived* heaven fits with the plastic images around which the poem revolves. For Sarton the curious word choice is *melded* in the first stanza. Melded is a term that applies to card games and not to music; Sarton, however, uses the mixing of different suits to equate the countermelodies of the fugue:

> In the dark theatre lovers sit
> Watching the supple dancers weave
> A fugue, motion and music melded. (*HS* 51)

Though not the general use, "melded" fits alliteratively in the line and suggests the poem's disclosure—that the countermelodies and steps will eventually blend.

Another unique effect that Sarton creates comes at the bottom of stanza two. In the line "But as they watch a vision is unlocked," she delivers another slant rhyme—"watch" and "unlocked"—to create an internal rhyme, the same sort of usage that gives Coleridge's *Rime of the Ancient Mariner* its mesmeric effect. Since she places the line before the two stanzas that she joins through rhyme, she creates a dreamy tone for the old lovers. This tone, however, is not in keeping with the negative emotions and images presented earlier in the lines:

> And in the dark old lovers feel dismay
> Watching the ardent bodies leap and freeze
> Thinking how age has changed them and has mocked.

> Once they were light and bold in lissome play,
> Limber as willows that could bend with ease—
> But as they watch a vision is unlocked. (*HS* 51)

This transition from the lament over physical powers' waning to a recognition of the spiritual is followed by the abrupt line "Imagination springs the trap of youth," a line that negates the prowess of the physical dancers and jars the reader into the next phase of the poem. In this last phase, the old lovers transcend earthly aches. And physical movement becomes the action of "the soul [which] is a lithe and serene athlete."

In an early draft, Yeats included "fish, that carry souls to Paradise" (Stallworthy 96). This usage, though edited out, carries the same idea of spiritual intercessor on which Sarton's poem concludes:

> It is not energy but light they burn,
> The radiant powers of the Paraclete. (*HS* 51)

Both poets capitalize their respective references to Paraclete and Paradise, implying a reference to Christian tradition. Instead of a direct communion with the spiritual, however, each relies upon an intermediary. Both Yeats and Sarton envision art as spiritual mediator and inspiration, though Sarton's art leans more toward music and the invisible spirit than toward the plastic arts.

One of the key turns that Sarton takes in her revision of old age and of a soul's clapping its hands is not to drop the reference to the soul. She doesn't exchange it for the immortality of a hammered gold body, of somehow cheating those time cycles that Yeats conjured in the image of conflicting gyres. Instead, she returns to the idea of the phoenix, to old age's being a changing of seasons, bringing with it different sorts of rewards than youth when "they were light and bold in lissome play, / Limber as willows that could bend with ease." In abandoning the physical, they then become spiritual lovers and celestial dancers. In *At Seventy* Sarton writes, "A garden is always a series of losses set against few triumphs, like life itself" (77). In revisioning Yeats's version of old age, Sarton chooses to focus not upon the losses as Yeats does, but upon the triumphs.

In her Christmas 1991 poem titled "Renascence," May Sarton demonstrates that her poetry is still vital, that at eighty she, like the phoenix, rises from the ashes of long illness to rejoice in everyday life:

> After long silence
> An old poet
> Singing again,
> I am a mage myself
> Joy leaps in my throat.
> Glory be to God!

Though "silence" is the word that figures in two of her last poetry collections, Sarton speaks in celebrated vision of the wonders present around her, and through her words we too find the ordinary marvelous.

Works Cited

I would like to thank May Sarton for supplying the draft copies for "Old Lovers at the Ballet" and for granting permission to quote from them and from her 1991 Christmas poem "Renascence."

Allen, James Lovic. "From Puzzle to Paradox: New Light on Yeats's Late Career." *Sewanee Review* 82 (1974): 81–92.

Rich, Adrienne. "When We Dead Awaken: Writing as Revision." *On Lies, Secrets and Silence: Selected Prose 1966–78*. New York: Norton, 1979. 33–49.

Sarton, May. *At Seventy: A Journal*. New York: Norton, 1984.

———. *Halfway to Silence: New Poems*. New York: Norton, 1980.

———. "The Problems and Delights of Revision." *The Writer* 79 (1966): 20–22.

———. "Revision as Creation: The Growth of a Poem." *CEA Critic* 29 (1967): 1, 3, 4.

———. *Sarton Selected: : An Anthology of the Journals, Novels, and Poems of May Sarton*. Ed. Bradford Dudley Daziel. New York: Norton, 1991.

———. *The Silence Now: New and Uncollected Earlier Poems*. New York: Norton, 1988.

————. Typescript drafts of "Old Lovers at the Ballet." Provided by May Sarton.

Yeats, William Butler. *A Vision*. New York: Collier Books, 1937.

————. *W. B. Yeats; The Poems*. Ed. Richard J. Finneran. New York: Macmillan, 1983.

————. *Yeats: Last Poems*. Ed. Jon Stallworthy. Nashville: Aurora P, Inc., 1969.

Video

Robitaille, Stephen, and Bill Suchy, directors and producers. *Writing in the Upward Years*. The Florida Media Arts Center, 1990.

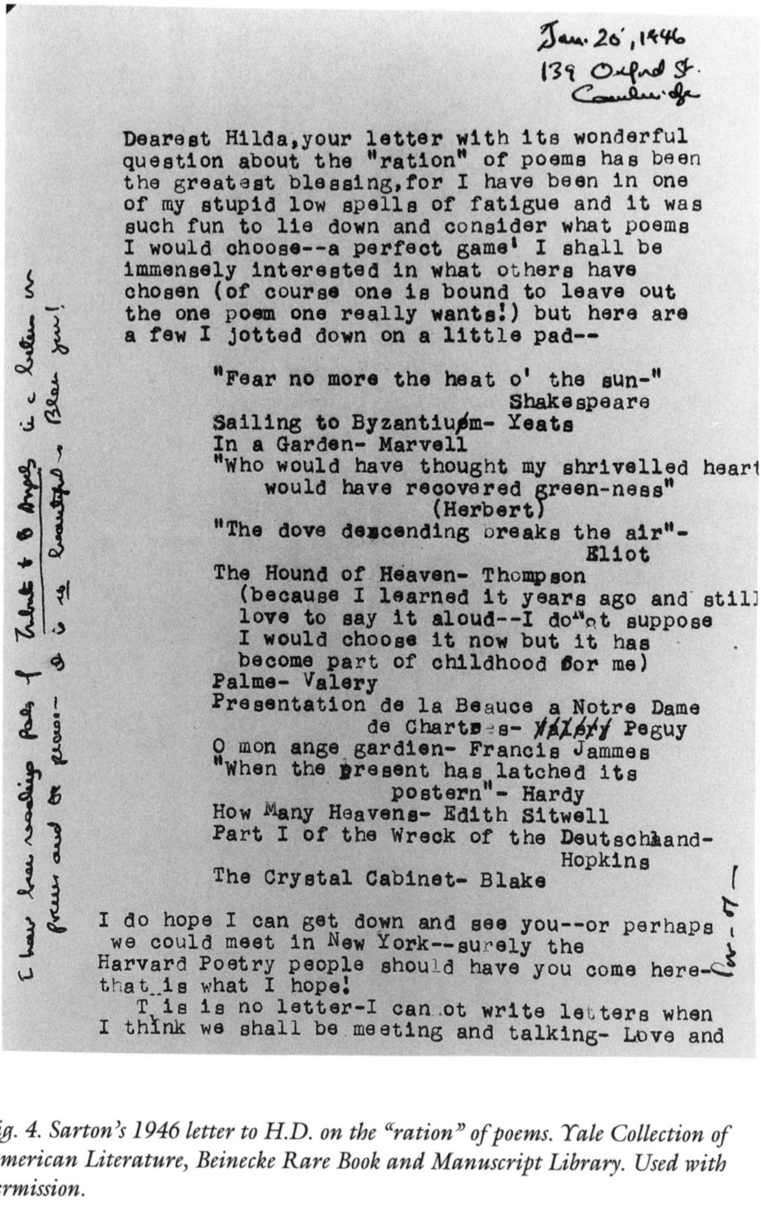

Dearest Hilda, your letter with its wonderful
question about the "ration" of poems has been
the greatest blessing, for I have been in one
of my stupid low spells of fatigue and it was
such fun to lie down and consider what poems
I would choose--a perfect game! I shall be
immensely interested in what others have
chosen (of course one is bound to leave out
the one poem one really wants!) but here are
a few I jotted down on a little pad--

> "Fear no more the heat o' the sun-"
> Shakespeare
> Sailing to Byzantium- Yeats
> In a Garden- Marvell
> "Who would have thought my shrivelled heart
> would have recovered green-ness"
> (Herbert)
> "The dove descending breaks the air"-
> Eliot
> The Hound of Heaven- Thompson
> (because I learned it years ago and still
> love to say it aloud--I do not suppose
> I would choose it now but it has
> become part of childhood for me)
> Palme- Valery
> Presentation de la Beauce a Notre Dame
> de Chartres- Peguy
> O mon ange gardien- Francis Jammes
> "When the present has latched its
> postern"- Hardy
> How Many Heavens- Edith Sitwell
> Part I of the Wreck of the Deutschland-
> Hopkins
> The Crystal Cabinet- Blake

I do hope I can get down and see you--or perhaps
we could meet in New York--surely the
Harvard Poetry people should have you come here--
that is what I hope!
T is is no letter-I can ot write letters when
I think we shall be meeting and talking- Love and

Fig. 4. Sarton's 1946 letter to H.D. on the "ration" of poems. Yale Collection of
American Literature, Beinecke Rare Book and Manuscript Library. Used with
permission.

May Sarton and H.D.: Companions of the Flame, Gardeners of the Spirit

PAT ADAMS FURLONG

Companions of the Flame

According to May Sarton, Hilda Doolittle (H.D.) initiated a correspondence in response to Sarton's first novel, *The Single Hound*, published in 1938. Sarton reminisces:

> I do not believe that I have ever received a letter that meant as much to me as H.D.'s out of the blue in response to my first novel, *The Single Hound*. When I was fourteen and fifteen I had discovered her poems, knew some by heart, had copied them out into notebooks all through the school years. So when I was twenty-six and that first novel came out, it was a miraculous post that brought me a letter from the legendary person whom I had adored. It was the more precious because I had never written to her and I had no thought that she could know I existed!
>
> That was the beginning of our correspondence which flourished during the blitz years in London (H.D. and Bryher stayed all through those war years). And then went on after H.D. was living in Vevey and seemed very much alone.
>
> I met her and Bryher only once after the war, it must have been in 1945, and had tea with them in a rather grand apartment, 49 Lowndes Square, which one approached up stairs carpeted in leopard-spotted

material, very elegant. They peered down at me as I climbed toward them and I heard Bryher say, "She'll do."

The room where we sat was very dark, lit only by what Colette called "un fanal bleu," a round lamp made of blue glass. I could hardly see their faces and felt extremely shy and ill at ease. So our real contact was through letters. (King 49)

Sarton's description of this staircase meeting is evocative of H.D.'s words in *The Walls Do Not Fall*, written in 1942:

> we know each other
> by secret symbols,
>
> though remote, speechless,
> we pass each other on the pavement,
>
> at the turn of the stair;
> though no word pass between us,
>
> there is a subtle appraisement;
> even if we snarl a brief greeting
>
> or do not speak at all,
> we know our Name,
>
> we nameless initiates,
> born of one mother,
>
> companions
> of the flame. (*H.D.* 521)

As women and as poets, "companions of the flame," Sarton and H.D. invite comparisons. Both women inherited sensibilities and talents from artistic, aesthetically attuned mothers. Sarton's mother, Mabel Elwes Sarton, was an artist and designer of furniture and finely embroidered clothing. "Anyone who has seen the exquisitely embroidered dresses and accessories that Mabel Elwes Sarton made for the child May is affected by wonder at the inventiveness of the curving designs of flowers and vines, at the soft, brilliant colors. . . . Each stitch enhances the whole composition" (Hunting 208). H.D.'s mother,

Helen Wolle Doolittle, was an accomplished musician and painter who taught music at her father's Moravian seminary in Bethlehem, Pennsylvania. And as H.D. recalled in her sessions with Freud, "I wanted to paint like my mother. . . . Obviously, this is my inheritance. I derive my imaginative faculties through my musician-artist mother." (*Tribute* 117, 121).

Both Sarton and H.D. have an extensive knowledge and love of flowers and an ability to arrange them, both literally and translated into the imagery of their poems. Their mothers had given them this legacy, a passion and talent for gardening. Sarton has stated in a 1987 interview that she couldn't live without flowers, and when queried further about what the interviewer calls that "pretty heavy statement," she explains, "One, of course, they're so beautiful; it's a tremendous aesthetic pleasure. And secondly, they have the whole sequence of life in them, from the bud to the death. And then, growth, everything about growth is in the flower. In a way, it's all of life" (Goldman 158). Thus she would agree with H.D.'s words in "Eurydice" that flowers, if they could be breathed into oneself, could enable one to dare a great loss:

> if once I could have breathed into myself
> the very golden crocuses
> and the red,
> and the very golden hearts of the first saffron,
> the whole of the golden mass,
> the whole of the great fragrance,
> I could have dared the loss. (*H.D.* 53)

For each poet the loss has often been very great. Both lived and worked in exile. For May Sarton the move from Wondelgem, Belgium, to the United States was forced upon her by the war; she was a child of four when her parents settled for good in Cambridge, Massachusetts, in 1916 (Sarton Interview 99).[1] H.D., although born in Bethlehem, Pennsylvania, chose to live in Europe as an expatriate, automatically becoming a British citizen at the age of twenty-seven upon her marriage to Richard Aldington in 1913 (Silverstein 34).

Sarton is well grounded in the sensory world of physicality and labors in the garden, whereas H.D. was influenced by her Moravian mysticism and drawn by her temperament into a lifelong interest in esotericism and the occult. Yet, as her daughter Perdita Schaffner has written, "H.D. read current best-sellers as well as esoteric tomes. She achieved a perfect balance between anguished sensibility and plain, down-to-earth, everyday life" (6). It is still safe to say that Sarton is more comfortable than H.D. in her relationship to the earth. Sarton writes of "working out [her] anguish in a garden. Without the flowers . . . I might not have survived," she sings in "Gestalt at Sixty" (*CP* 361). Along these lines, Silvia Dobson's firsthand reminiscences of Sarton's and H.D.'s traits and earliest association are enlightening:

> H.D. wrote to May about *The Single Hound* in 1939, when May had come to England to meet authors. She was especially interested in Elizabeth Bowen.
>
> As H.D. lived part of the year in Switzerland, she asked me—in a letter—to invite May to the country cottage we had recently rented. May loves gardens, and thought she was going to see one. We, Londoners, had dug up countless nut trees to make a long vista. Thus our garden looked like the blitzed sites which were soon to appear all over Europe. May Sarton went back to the States on the French liner, *Normandie,* when Nazi U-boats were already sinking Allied shipping. World War II started for us in September 1939, not December 1941. . . .
>
> H.D. spent the whole of the war in London, and suffered a breakdown in 1946. . . .
>
> I don't consider May Sarton's prose or poetry resembles H.D.'s except that they both speak out as concerned women in a man's world. May has always had her "feet on the ground." She is practical, concise, alert, accomplished, in command. Her words—"Critics write that my work is too simple, there's no struggle. That's clarté, complicating element! Deceptive clarity rather than deceptive obscurity—for me that's the ideal" describes her and her work.
>
> H.D., on the other hand, was introverted, psychic, seeing beyond the endings. Talking of Sappho, she wrote:
> "A song, a spirit, a white star that moves across the heavens to mark

the end of a world epoch or to presage some coming glory. Yet she is embodied—terribly—a human being, a woman, a personality as the most impersonal becomes when they confront their fellow beings."

This describes H.D. . . . Thank the Goddess that women writers everywhere are weaving a new feminine web of creativity. . . .

We can admire the "grounding" of May Sarton's images, the characteristic intimacy and directness, in contrast to H.D.'s more remote imagery. In poems like "An Observation," Sarton sings of maternal wisdom about gardening that has been her bequest:

> True gardeners cannot bear a glove
> Between the sure touch and the tender root,
> Must let their hands grow knotted as they move
> With a rough sensitivity about
> Under the earth, between the rock and shoot,
> Never to bruise or wound the hidden fruit.
> And so I watched my mother's hand grow scarred,
> She who could heal the wounded plant or friend
> With the same vulnerable yet rigorous love;
> I minded once to see her beauty gnarled,
> But now her truth is given me to live,
> As I learn for myself we must be hard
> To move among the tender with an open hand. . . .
> (*CP* 271)

In this poem the reader sees the act of cultivation of spirit, the disciplined love and arduous effort required for any artistic creation. "As inheritor of her mother's healing powers, Sarton received a crucial 'truth': vulnerability must be accompanied by rigor, tenderness by toughness, else the 'plant,' the delicate and valuable creation, is unlikely to survive and grow. 'You must remain vulnerable and tough,' Sarton explained during a . . . reading of this poem, 'or else you'll die.'" (DeShazer 355).

Along with bequests from artistic mothers, Sarton and H.D. have also inherited intellectual discipline from their fathers, both of whom were scientists. George Sarton worked daily at the Harvard library on his tomes comprising the new discipline of the history of science. May Sarton has stated that the great thing he gave her was an example of what steady work, disciplined work, can finally produce (Sarton Interview 108). H.D.'s father, Charles Leander Doolittle, was an astronomer and founding director of the Flower Observatory at the University of Pennsylvania. H.D. has characterized him as "Father, aloof, distant, the provider, the protector—but a little un-get-at-able, a little too far away and giant-like in proportion, a little chilly withal" (*Tribute* 38). Perdita Schaffner tells of her mother H.D.'s discipline: "She rose very early, and got straight down to work, filling up the exercise books with tight faint script. She preferred hard pencils; they lasted longer; she didn't have to interrupt herself with the mechanics of sharpening. When she reached a certain point, she closed all the books and put the pencils back in their jar until next morning" (5). Sarton, who has called herself a lark instead of an owl, tells of rising at 5 A.M. to do her creative work before eleven in the morning (Sarton Interview 108).

Sarton's discipline in writing carried over into her use of form. Heavily influenced by Valéry's clarity and precision of form and by the precision of the Baroque music of Mozart, Bach, Albinoni, and Haydn, she exemplifies their classical exactness of form in her poetry, always aiming for the language of precision. Sarton comments on her search for each poem's appropriate form:

> Form is so absolute, as if it had always been there, as if there had been no struggle. The person who sees the lyric poem on the page doesn't realize there may have been sixty drafts to get it to the point where you cannot change a single word. It has been worked for. But something has been given, and that's the difference between the inspired poem and what Louise Bogan calls the imitation poem. In the inspired poem something is given. In the imitation poem you do it alone on will and intelligence. (Sarton Interview 96)

In creating inspired poems, not imitative ones, these workers create from a deep center; from this inner spiraling place H.D. gives birth to Bona Dea and Sophia, the feminine faces of God in *Trilogy*. Indeed, when H.D. wrote her Acceptance Speech to the American Academy of Arts and Letters in 1960, she spoke of this spiral:

> *Wingéd words,* we know make their own spiral—caught up in them, we are lost, or found. It is what a poem does, or can do, timelessly, having no charted orbit, or, if it has, then charted with those space instruments which only the spirit provides.
>
> This winged victory belongs to the poem, not to the poet. But to share in the making of a poem is the privilege of a poet, and so I *can* thank you for measuring in space the whirr of my sometimes over-intense and over-stimulated, breathless meters. . . . (6)

The Jungian analyst Marion Woodman writes of distinctive feminine psychology, that "my central image is a spiral. . . . That center I call Sophia, the feminine Wisdom of God. . . . It is an invisible center encountered only in a creative process, at first not consciously recognized, but gradually revealed as the process unfolds" (72). Sarton lives and works from a hard-won and dynamic center, converting loneliness to the solitude necessary for creation. She writes of how difficult this victory is for the woman to win. "It is harder for women, perhaps, to be 'one-pointed,' much harder for them to clear space around whatever it is they want to do beyond household chores and family life. Their lives are fragmented . . . ; this is the cry I get in so many letters—the cry not so much for 'a room of one's own' as time of one's own. Conflict becomes acute, whatever it may be about, when there is no margin left on any day in which to try at least to resolve it" (*JS* 56).

Sarton's "The Invocation to Kali" deals directly with her primitive center, the dark place of raging demands, in an invocation to the more terrorizing aspect of the Black Goddess. The poem ends with a prayer to this necessary but dark and awesome side of creation:

> Kali, be with us.
> Violence, destruction, receive our homage.
> Help us to bring darkness into the light,
> To lift out the pain, the anger,
> Where it can be seen for what it is—

The balance-wheel for our vulnerable, aching love. . . .
Help us to be the *always hopeful*
Gardeners of the spirit [Ital. mine]
Who know that without darkness
Nothing comes to birth
As without light
Nothing flowers.

Bear the roots in mind,
You, the dark one, Kali,
Awesome power. (*CP* 320)

Sarton has written of H.D. that "around fifteen she was my favorite poet" (letter to author). She was fascinated by H.D. because of the freshness she managed to get into free verse (Sarton Interview 98). Clarity, concreteness, the absence of excess words—these are stylistic techniques that the two poets share. They also share in their poetry their fathers' sense of precision and order, coupled with their mothers' abilities to create finely wrought embroideries. Both Sarton and H.D. are courageous in probing the dark feelings of pain and anger, bringing to them intellectual and lyrical light.

Gardeners of the Spirit

In the H.D. Papers at Beinecke there are four letters from Sarton to H.D., as well as typescripts of Sarton's poems "Return to Chartres," "A Mon Seul Désir: The Cluny 'Dame à la Liconne,'" and "These Images Remain." The letters are dated "October 29, 1944; Jan. 20, 1946—139 Oxford St., Cambridge; June 22, 1947—18 Ave. Lequime Rhodes St., Genese; and April 19, 1949, Patriot's Day," with no address (YCAL).

H.D.'s 7 January 1946, letter to Sarton grew out of H.D.'s 1945 acceptance of Katharine McBride's invitation to give a series of lectures on poetry at Bryn Mawr College in 1946 (Silverstein 43). It reads, in part, as follows:

I am preparing lists of Poet's Poetry, as I call them. I wonder if you would give me a list of from 10 to 12 of your favourite lyrics, short dramatic sections or even prose *bel page*. I want a spontaneous list— what you REALLY do like, or what has stayed with you. I put it this way: suppose you had a RATION of memory, what would you choose to remember. I have lists from various "celebrities" and some outside people. I think this is a good beginning. I want to find out what the Bryn Mawr girls really like, and if I begin telling them what other people like, it will help. I do not want BOOK lists; things that are in your head now—and maybe, not all special or high-brow selections. It is not such an easy matter to select, I find—and several people said it really made them sit up and think about poetry, people who WRITE and LOVE poetry, I mean. I don't think my work will be very arduous—I believe they call it a seminar and it is only one day a week. The girls will be stuffed to the brim—and I will feel shy—but I am sure, with the help of "Poet's Poetry" (a good title, I think) we will break the ice and manage somehow. . . .

Blessings on you for 1946—again—and thanks for all your sustained help and the letters that meant so much during our dark years.

> And Love
> From Hilda.[2] (H.D. 1946)

In Sarton's brief response of only one page torn from a small, casual writing pad (20 January 1946), the poet gladly plays the game that H.D. has invented. Sarton's letter, inserted in the *H.D. Papers*, begins, "Dearest Hilda, your letter with its wonderful question about the 'ration' of poems has been the greatest blessing, for I have been in one of my stupid low spells of fatigue and it was such fun to lie down and consider what poems I would choose—a perfect game." Sarton then goes on to say, "I shall be immensely interested in what others have chosen" before citing the "few [she] jotted down on a little pad" (YCAL). The ensuing section of this essay reflects upon the choices Sarton made in her letter and indicates how those choices represent Sarton's philosophy and/or poetics.

Sarton's list contains the following: first, "Fear no more the heat o' th' sun" (*Cymbeline* 4.2.259); Yeats's "Sailing to Byzantium"; "In a Garden" [*sic*] by Marvell; two lines by George Herbert, "Who would have thought my shrivelled heart / would have recovered green-ness (from "The Flower"); and "The dove descending breaks the air" (from Eliot's *Four Quartets,* "Little Gidding"). Then Sarton mentions "The Hound of Heaven" (by Francis Thompson), and in parentheses under the title, she says she has chosen this poem "because [she] learned it years ago and still loves to say it aloud." She adds, "I don't suppose I would choose it now but it has become part of childhood for me" (YCAL).

Her other citations are Valéry's "Palme," Péguy's "[La] Présentation de la Beauce à Notre-Dame de Chartres," Francis Jammes's "O mon Ange gardien," Thomas Hardy's "When the present has latched its postern" (from "Afterwards"), "How Many Heavens" by Edith Sitwell, Part 1 of "The Wreck of the Deutschland" by Hopkins, and "The Crystal Cabinet" by Blake (YCAL).

In these rich and varied selections, one sees the agile mind and brilliant spirit of a young poet at work (Sarton was not quite thirty-four when she wrote this list of "rations"). In the poems Sarton has chosen, spiritual themes recur; the list presages what Sarton will later write in *Journal of a Solitude* (1973): "The delights of the poet as I jotted them down turned out to be light, solitude, the natural world, love, time, creation itself" (48).

In Sarton's first choice from *Cymbeline,* Guiderius's mourning song to Imogen speaks of time, mortality, love, the natural world, and, as Bevington has said, "the vanity of human striving" (1415). The lyricism of the song also influences the highly lyrical poetry that Sarton will develop:

> Fear no more the heat o' th' sun,
> Nor the furious winter's rages;
> Thou thy worldly task hast done,
> Home art gone, and ta'en thy wages. (4.2.259–62)

In her loyalty to her craft and in her conscious examination of a life lived fully throughout its seasons, Sarton exhibits a heroic attitude to the vicissitudes that Shakespeare cites. The committed artist finds solace in doing (her) "worldly task." "And one element of duration that

[she] *"can* be awake to" is "this moment, this flow of time. . . . One thing that makes growing old lovely," Sarton reveals to her interviewer in 1990, "is that you have more time to look at it" (Robitaille 196).

At least six of the poems Sarton selected for H.D. are particularly overt in their spiritual themes: Péguy's "La Présentation de la Beauce à Notre-Dame de Chartres," Jammes's "O mon Ange gardien," Sitwell's "How Many Heavens," Thompson's "The Hound of Heaven," the lines from Herbert's "The Flower," and Part 1 of Hopkins's "The Wreck of the Deutschland."

Always drawn to Chartres, Sarton has a kinship with Péguy, who vowed to go on foot to Chartres to thank Our Lady after his son's recovery from typhoid:

> J'ai fait un pélerinage à Chartres. Je suis Beauceron. Chartres est ma cathédrale. . . . On voit le clocher de Chartres a 17 kilomètres sur la plaine. De temps en temps, il disparaît derrière une ondulation, une ligne de bois. Dès que je l'ai vu, ça été une extase. . . .[3]

Péguy later writes of his experience of Chartres after making his pilgrimage in 1912. "La Présentation de la Beauce à Notre Dame de Chartres" describes in eighty-nine quatrains of alexandrines his trip across the Beauce, the great plain south and east of Paris in the middle of which rises the cathedral (St. Aubyn 105). Random lines show Péguy's level prosody and his exultation in the mysterious queen:

> Mais vous apparaissez, reine mystérieuse,
> Cette pointe là-bas dans le moutonnement
> Des moissons et des bois et dans le flottement
> De l'extrême horizon ce n'est point une yeuse. . . .[4]

Sarton's poems are briefer than Péguy's, yet they are just as exalted. In their immediacy and intimacy, Sarton's poems celebrate Chartres not so much as Péguy's "mysterious queen," but as a maternal presence or goddess with "the magic spear of grain, the (nourishing) spear of wheat" ("Return to Chartres" 9-10). The draft of "Return to Chartres" in the Beinecke Library is slightly different from the published version (*CP* 90):

> We came to Chartres riding the green plain,
> The spear of hope, the incorruptible towers,
> Stone upon stone, leaf upon leaf,
> The great tree rooted in the heart of France
> Blazing eternally with sacred flowers,
> We came to Chartres, the house without a stain,
> The mastery of passion by belief,
> With all its aspiration held in balance,
> We came to Chartres, the magic spear of grain,
> The spear of wheat forever nourishing,
> One never-wasted stalk, the ever blessing. (YCAL)

Joseph Campbell notes that "you don't have a tradition with the Goddess celebrated any more beautifully and marvelously than in the twelfth- and thirteenth-century French cathedrals, every one of which is called Notre Dame" (Flowers 170). Similarly, Rachel Blau duPlessis posits, "The 'thing' held in the arms of Bona Dea at the end of H.D.'s *Trilogy* is not the 'Mosaic' male baby but the flower or sheath of wheat that particular fertility goddess carries; in this case [the bundle of] myrrh [in Bona Dea's bosom]. . . ." (97). In "Once More at Chartres" Sarton speaks of Chartres as the Mother:

> A desperate child, I run up to this gate
> With all my fears withheld and all my dark
> Contained . . .
> . . . .
> A child, I rest in your maternal gaze,
> That which encompasses and shelters, yet,
> Lifting so gently, still demands rebirth,
> Breaks open toward sky the dark of earth,
> And proves unyielding where the rose is set,
> Where Love is light itself and severe praise.
> . . . .
> I stand within your arduous embrace.
> This is pure majesty, there is no other.
> I suffer all beginnings and all ends.
> Here this enclosure opens and transcends
> All weaker hopes under your tragic face—
> The suffering child here must become the mother. (*CP* 349)

The poet's efforts at rejuvenation provide the central theme of this poem, in which Sarton celebrates the maternal presence of the great cathedral at Chartres as a living testimony to the power of the mother in life and art. As the "patient recreator of creation" (*CP* 349), Chartres becomes at once a mother, a lover, and a muse for the poet-daughter. Most importantly, however, the cathedral awakens in the poet a realization of her own creative capacity (DeShazer 353). "The suffering child here must become the mother," must become the creator herself.

In another celebration of Chartres, "At Chartres," Sarton writes of paradox as she moves into the cathedral's world of spiritual images and brings them into palpable form:

> Perhaps there is no smallest consolation,
> No help, no saving grace, no little ease;
> Only the presence of this pure compassion
> We lifted up, who fall upon our knees.
> Nothing we have to give it or implore.
> It does not speak to us. It has no face,
> And is itself only an open door—
> Forever open, that will never close. (*CP* 348)

"Here," the poet tells us, "we are measured by our own creation. . . . / Here we are measured against the perfect love, . . . / The door is open, but we cannot move, / Nor be consoled or saved. But only see" (*CP* 348).

In this state of contemplation or receptivity, there is no desire to "re-arrange the spiritual furniture"; "we cannot move / Nor be consoled or saved. But only see" (*CP* 348). Here is a desire to be alive to the present moment, attentive to the poetic vision, so that the epiphany becomes its own way of seeing through the open door of revelation.

This transparency opens into that same place of radiant light which Sarton has spoken of as one of the "delights of the poet" (*JS* 48). It is the light of the angelic kingdom which Jammes invokes in "O mon Ange gardien" (cf. Sarton's "rations"). In this poem the stabilizing spiritual presence throughout the exigencies of life is sustained by the closed *a* in the repetition of *ange* and by each stanza's tender yet incantatory plea to the angel of comfort: "O mon Ange gardien . . .

Tiens ma main dans ta main" (Jammes). The stabilizing presence of the guardian angel will also be a source of comfort for Sarton throughout the exigencies of her life. She, too, invokes angelic helpers in poems such as "The Beautiful Pauses":

> Angels, beautiful pauses in the whirlwind,
> Be with us through the seasons of unease; . . .
> Remind us of your great unclouded ways.
>
> . . . .
>
> Angels, who can surprise us with a lucky chance,
> Be with us in this year; give us to dance. . . . (*CP* 223)

Sarton, who was reading H.D.'s *Tribute to the Angels* at the time of the 20 January 1946, correspondence, will also employ myriads of angels from different kingdoms. Like Rilke, who writes in *Duino Elegies* that "every angel is terrible" (29), Sarton will write of "fierce angels (who) come— / Not gentle and not kind" ("A Storm of Angels," *CP* 378). Their wings are "harsh," she tells us. And in "The Smile" Sarton will write, candidly and paradoxically, of "angels [that] are grave if they exist at all / Lifted above the gritty frustration." Yet, in the same poem she writes of "an angel of the earth secretly smiling" (*SN* 75); the angel, in its contradictory aspects, blesses creation.

Edith Sitwell, also on Sarton's list of wartime "rations," invokes an angelic presence in "How Many Heavens." Like Sarton's "angel of the earth," Sitwell's "angel [pierces] through the earth to sing / 'God is everything!'" In another parallel with Sarton's work, Sitwell's lines about "emeralds like the spears / Of grass" and "green shade" evoke a unified consciousness that greenness creates for Sarton:

> The emeralds are singing on the grasses
> And in the trees the bells of the long cold are ringing, —
> My blood seems changed to emeralds like the spears
> Of grass beneath the earth piercing and singing.
> (Sitwell 306)

If God, as Sitwell concludes, is "the core of the heart of love" and "our ultimate shore," he is also the Divine Lover as the Seeker in Francis Thompson's "The Hound of Heaven." Although Sarton has told H.D. that she chose this poem as one of her "rations" only because of what it meant to her childhood, this lyric has the same quick tempo and eloquent style that characterize Sarton's poetry. Sarton speaks of the (lyric) poem as being "like lightning—like a streak of lightning . . . something that you're shocked into by joy or grief . . ." (Bonetti 89). "The Hound of Heaven" moves at this lightning-swift pace. It also reaches the rapture and energy of flight that are inherent in Sarton's poetics. In "Elegy for Meta" Sarton's movements are lightning-swift:

> Fiery, the tender child
> From the beginning burned,
> And that beginning hard.
> She raced like a young colt,
> Spirit no man could tame,
> And yet so warm and wild
> All nature toward her turned,
> Came to her hand and word—
> Extravagance, revolt:
>   The signature was flame. (CP 287)

Sarton had memorized "The Hound of Heaven"; its cadence and rhythm stayed with her as a model for her own lyrical poetry.

All her life Sarton has striven through faithfulness to her craft to reach that place of purpose and blessing from the "Austere, great one" in "Prayer Before Work" (CP 31). In her poem "Of Prayer," she tells God:

> It is a mistake, perhaps, to believe
> That religion concerns you at all;
> That is our own invention,
> Longing for formal acceptance
> To a formal invitation.
> But yours to be the anarchist,
> The thrust of growth,
> And to be present only in the
> Prayer that is creation. . . . (CP 133)

Faithfulness through the prayer of her work characterizes the life of May Sarton. Like Sarton, H.D. believed that she finally reached a place of ultimate commitment to her craft as she said in a letter to Norman Holmes Pearson from Küsnacht a few years before her death, "I think I did get what I was looking for from life and art" (Guest 333). The demands of the creative daimon are great, but finally, as in "The Hound of Heaven," a place of restoration is reached.

Thompson was primarily a childhood influence on May Sarton; George Herbert has been an enduring influence on her poetics. The influence of his imagery of greenness in lines such as these from "The Flower," "Who would have thought my shrivel'd heart / Could have recover'd greennesse?" (1.8–9), pervades Sarton's work (166). Herbert's unity of purpose, balanced style, absence of excess words, and delicacy of technique, as well as what Helen Vendler has called his "provisional quality of being ready at any moment to change direction or to modify attitudes" (19), have formed a lasting model for Sarton's style. Moreover, greenness is one of Sarton's richest images throughout her poetry. This "resonance of emerald" serves at many levels to bring rejuvenation and vitality to the poet, especially after intervals of spiritual aridity not unlike those times of despair that Herbert undergoes in "The Flower." Sarton admits to periods of despondency, just as she has spoken of being in one of her "stupid low spells of fatigue" in her letter to H.D. (20 January 1946, YCAL). Nonetheless, as one studies greenness in Sarton's poems, it becomes apparent that the image embodies vibrancy and eventually attains the same healing virtue that H.D.'s "Eurydice" has attributed to flowers.

In "Summer Music" Sarton sings, "Summer is all a green air," and "Summer is all a green sound" (CP 117). Greenness appears elsewhere in Sarton's work as hopeful imagery, as the green plain in "Return to Chartres." Other phrases reinforcing hopefulness include: "cherishing green hope" ("Song"), "At the bottom of the green field she lies" ("The Second Spring"), and "The growing tree is green and musical" ("The Work of Happiness"). In "Boy by the Waterfall," a poem of only thirty-one lines, Sarton uses the image of green four times: "in the dappled green light . . . like a god suspended in green air . . . Under the green wave smiling . . . suspended for a second in green air" (CP 109). Sarton does not employ colors for their own sake. Instead, she merges her identity with the image of life-giving greenness, making a union that rises from its earthly source toward the Absolute. In "Green Song" this consummation of color and image melds into a nurturing intake of greenness:

> Here where nothing passes,
> Where centuries have stayed
> Alive under the grasses,
> Gently the heart is laid.
>
> Oh, breathe these meadows in
> Till you are filled with green,
> A drunkard of the scene
> Your dreams will wander in. . . .
>
> And sleep away all care,
> Lay rushing time to rest,
> And rise up light as air,
> Green-fed and meadow-blessed. (*CP* 170)

Another of Sarton's poetic "rations" for H.D., Part 1 of "The Wreck of the Deutschland," is a sustained and personal prayer that begins with "Thou mastering me / God!" and ends with "Make mercy in all of us, out of us all / Mastery, but be adored, but be adored King." Between these Alpha and Omega points of mastery and adoration lies the first part of Hopkins's most difficult poem, an ode in the spirit of Pindar. Regardless of H.D.'s suggestion that May Sarton's choices for her "Poet's Poetry" need not be "special or high-brow selections" (H.D. letter), this particular choice is one that challenges and must be studied closely.

The metaphysical melding of diverse images and ideas in Part 1 of "The Wreck of the Deutschland" invokes for Sarton the delights of the poet. The primary images of Hopkins's invocation are the hour-glass and the well, which substantiate the idea that as the temporal life wanes, the spiritual life grows stronger:

> I am soft sift
> In an hourglass—at the wall
> Fast, but mined with a motion, a drift,
> And it crowds and it combs to the fall;
> I steady as a water in a well, to a poise, to a pane,
> But roped with, always, all the way down from the tall
> Fells or flanks of the voel, a vein
> Of the gospel proffer, a pressure, a principle, Christ's gift.
> (Hopkins 52)

Throughout Part 1 runs a lovely thread of the beauty and mystery of creation. The pinnacle of paradox and mystery is reached in stanza 5:

> I kiss my hand
> To the stars, lovely-asunder
> Starlight, wafting him out of it; and
> Glow, glory in thunder;
> Kiss my hand to the dappled-with-damson west:
> Since, tho' he is under the world's splendour and wonder,
> His mystery must be instressed, stressed;
> For I greet him the days I meet him, and bless when I
> understand. (Hopkins 53)

Like Hopkins, who makes a direct mystical connection with God in these lines, Sarton "thinks [she's] certainly a mystic, if being a mystic is being very aware of something that's back of ordinary life all the time" (Robitaille 198). She, too, stresses God's mystery, "greet[s] him the days [she] meets him" and even on the days she appears not to meet him. Lines from her poetry and from *Journal of a Solitude* show her heroic sense of God's omnipresence in times of joy *and* times of spiritual darkness. "Gestalt at Sixty" ends with prayerful thanks in all circumstances:

> Praise God for His mercies,
> For His austere demands,
> For His light
> And for His darkness. (*CP* 364)

In *Journal of a Solitude* Sarton writes eloquently of what she calls the "only one possible prayer: Give me to do everything I do in the day with a sense of the sacredness of life. Give me to be in Your presence, God, even though I know it only as absence" (58).

As "The Wreck of the Deutschland" deals in stanza 5 with God's mystery at the macrocosmic level of creation, Hardy's "When the Present has latched its postern behind my tremulous stay" ("Afterwards") speaks to Sarton's "sense of the sacredness of life," her love of particularity. Hardy longs to be remembered as one who used to notice "the May month [that] flaps its glad green leaves like wings / Delicate filmed as new-spun silk" (Hardy 553). Whether he is speaking of the "dewfall hawk" or "the hedgehog (that) travels furtively over the lawn," Hardy yearns to live on in memory as one who "strove that such innocent creatures should come to / no harm," as "one who had an eye for such mysteries" (553). Sarton, too, conveys the sacred nature of the ordinary. She also has the ability to stand before the mystery of life, to view its natural phenomena with "absolutely pure attention" (Weil 71)—which *is* prayer—and thus to make each creation a holy act.

Whether Sarton declares in her crystalline observance of the particular that "Sometimes two poppies can compose a world" ("A Flower-Arranging Summer") or "That saving the world / May be a matter / Of sowing a seed / Not overturning a tyrant" ("The House of Gathering"), she consistently honors small beginnings that require patient germination and inner cultivation. No creature is too small for a song or poem: "The twittering flight of goldfinches" ("The Silence Now"), elegiac verses for Bramble, Sarton's beloved cat ("Wilderness Lost"), the innocent cosset lamb ("The Cosset Lamb"). Like Hardy, Sarton feels tenderness for "such innocent creatures" and "strives," through prayer, "that they should come to no harm":

> For all that is so dear
> And may be mauled,
> For terror and despair
> And for help near,
> I weep, I am undone.
> For all that can be healed,

> The cosset lamb you hold,
> And what cannot be healed,
> The mother in the field,
> I pray now I'm alone. (*SN* 35)

With Sarton's connection to the ordinary world as a sacrament, it is natural that she would choose this Hardy poem as one of her "rations."

Sarton's choice of Blake's "The Crystal Cabinet" is also portentous; she will develop its themes of love and sexual awakening throughout her opus. Less apparent than the themes of love and sexual awakening in "Blake's enigmatic setting, is the youth's striving to seize the inmost Form," the form of art. "Achieved art for Blake is a harmony of the fourfold man, in whom the living creatures of imagination, wisdom, love, and power have found again their human form" (Bloom 54). Through her frequent alchemical magic of merging the spiritual with the physical, Sarton also achieves such harmony in her poetics.

In another "ration," "The dove descending breaks the air" ("Little Gidding" IV), Eliot creates the paradox of the fiery descent of the dove, which is usually the symbol of spiritual peace and the Holy Spirit. Yet in the setting of World War II, the dove becomes the symbol of intensified light: of either fire of German bombers or pentecostal fire (Milward 212). "We only live / only suspire / Consumed by either fire or fire," Eliot asserts in this choice of Sarton's to H.D. (Eliot 57). Indeed, the paradox of fire that consumes yet purifies, coupled with the paradox of poetic survivorship despite war, storm, and tumult, is analogous to Sarton's and H.D.'s privations and struggles during World War II. We cannot help thinking of the phoenix in Sarton's poetry and in H.D.'s *Trilogy*. Out of initiation by fire and apparent destruction emerge the poetic spirit and ultimate triumph.

Certainly, Yeats's "Sailing to Byzantium" deals with the paradox of "flux and energy of the natural world" versus "the cyclical processes of birth, growth, reproduction, and decay" (Mack 7):

> The salmon-falls, the mackerel-crowded seas,
> Fish, flesh, or fowl, commend all summer long
> Whatever is begotten, born, and dies. (Yeats 193)

Like George Herbert, Yeats has been a primary mentor for May Sarton. The choice of "Sailing to Byzantium" in Sarton's "rations" of poems is appropriate for many reasons. Although the poem deals with Sarton's delights of the poet (*JS* 48)—"the natural world, time, and creation itself"—its perfect golden bird, set upon a "golden bough," is a symbol for the alchemy of poetry.

Valéry's "Palme," first published in *Charmes* in 1922, also meets Sarton's criteria for poetic delight. In its imagery from nature it speaks metaphorically about patient ripening of spirit, which is a major theme in Sarton's poetics. *Charmes* means "songs" or "incantations"; there is charm in the poems, a grace coupled with the precision of form and content that is characteristic of Valéry's poetics. Valéry's crystalline style is of major importance to Sarton who, in collaboration with Louise Bogan, translated his poems from the French. However, "Palme" was translated solely by Sarton, whose knowledge of French surpassed Bogan's expertise.[5]

"Palme" calls on our intellectual, emotional, and sensory abilities. The "organicity of the tree" is integral to "Palme"; indeed, "The whole of the poem is a hymn to invisible growth" (Hytier 158):

> Par la sève solennelle
> Une espérance éternelle
> Monte à la maturité! . . .
> . . . .
>
> Patience, patience,
> Patience dans l'azur!
> Chaque atome de silence
> Est la chance d'un fruit mûr! (Valéry 282)

Sarton's translation of these lines reads smoothly:

> Gravely the rising sap
> And the eternal hope
> Grow to maturity. . . .
> . . . .
>
> Patience, and patience,
> Patience across the blue.
> Each atom of your silence
> Ripens the fruit in you.

This imagery speaks to Sarton's patience with her growth as an artist in silence and solitude. Whether singing in "Hawaiian Palm,"

> . . . The tree is separated essence,
> First rooted, then fruitful, standing
> Unmoved, it would seem, and tense.
> We do not catch the subtle blending
> Until we are bored, half in trance,
> Able to sense the ever-spending
> Rich presence as a dance . . . (*AG* 53),

or speaking of "ripening to a greater ease" (*SN* 26), Sarton is arbiter between Valéry's world of flight toward the absolute and the inward, organic, human growth of the poet.

Herbert's greenness in "The Flower," the greenness, solitude, and sundial of temporality in Marvell's "The Garden," Hardy's and Sitwell's green and emerald, and Valéry's ripening palm all serve as important images for Sarton's many poems about the garden of life and the garden of spirit where "the thinking one / spends his spirit on / The gifts of his own growing" ("Palme," Sarton's translation). Throughout her career Sarton will continue to enlarge upon the garden and flowers as a metaphor for unfailing variety, color, plenitude, growth, and change throughout the seasons. Thus in choosing her thirteen particular "rations" for H.D.'s "Poet's Poetry" as "hopeful Gardeners of the spirit," Sarton has chosen a path on which she "spends (her) spirit on / The gifts of (her) own growing."

Between the time of that first correspondence initiated by H.D. in 1938 and the time of their continuing correspondence and poetry "rations" in 1946, a bond had grown between May Sarton and H.D. Sadly, however, H.D. never made her 1946 trip to America to teach the Bryn Mawr seminar on "Poet's Poetry"; instead, soon after her January 1946 letter to Sarton, she suffered a breakdown and had to be flown to Privat Klinik Brunner, Küsnacht, for psychiatric treatment (Silverstein 43). Sarton's final letter to H.D. in the Beinecke collection (19 April 1949) begins with the rose and the rose's "falling" into her week. "Dearest Hilda," she writes, "it was lovely to have a rose fall into one day last week and at last to hear again from you." At the end of this letter, Sarton concludes with these words, "With much love and blessings on you and your work. Have you been writing poems?" (YCAL).

The final typescript in the Sarton correspondence at Beinecke is a draft of Sarton's poem "These Images Remain," dated July-August 1948, in Sarton's hand. The last section of this version of the poem is a consummation of Sarton's poetics. "Light, solitude, the natural world, love, time, creation itself" (*JS* 48)—they are all here—along with the eternal rose; the annual seasons of growth, flowering, death; and all-consuming spiritual fire:

> The rose has opened and is all accomplished,
> The inner violence of its growing done;
> The petals, fashioned as the center wished,
> Rest on the air in silent consummation,
> Still held but all unfolded and resolved,
> And still contained but with its falling near.
> It is immense and quiet. It is solved.
> Saint at the fire's centre with no fear,
> And like the saint detached from its own fall,
> A rose of blood, a central seeing rose,
> The legendary rose of the cathedral,
> Transparent to the light that does enclose,
> Holy and wholly indivisible,
> The heart of love and keeps it visible. (YCAL)

May Sarton and H.D. share an inward incandescence, an *épanouissement,* that inner expansion of dazzling flowers, a blossoming of light. This is the place of the inviolable self, an eternal stillpoint of creativity. The final section of H.D.'s "Eurydice" also expresses the beauty and strength of this flame:

> At least I have the flowers of myself,
> and my thoughts, no god
> can take that;
> I have the fervour of myself for a presence
> and my own spirit for light. . . . (*H.D.* 55)

The fire and the rose of the inward garden are one in the poetry and spirits of May Sarton and H.D. Like H.D.'s "flowers of herself," Sarton's recurring image of the phoenix celebrates art's power over death:

> After the flame, a pause,
> After the pain, rebirth.
> Obeying nature's laws
> The phoenix goes to earth.
>
> . . . .
>
> To sing her thrilling song
> To stars and waves and sky
> For neither old nor young
> The phoenix does not die. (*SN* 76)

Acknowledgments

Quotations from the Hilda Doolittle Papers and the facsimile of the May Sarton letter to H.D. are reprinted by permission of Perdita Schaffner, H.D.'s daughter and literary executor, and the Yale Collection of American Literature, Beinecke Rare Book and Manuscript Library, Yale University. Patricia Willis, Curator of the American Literature Collection at the Beinecke Rare Book and Manuscript Library, Yale University, facilitated my work. Special gratitude is extended to Perdita Schaffner for permission to photocopy all of H.D.'s letters to May Sarton in the Henry W. and Albert A. Berg Collection of the New York Public Library, Astor, Lenox and Tilden Foundations, and to Francis O. Mattson, Curator of the Berg Collection, for providing me with photocopies of H.D.'s letters to May Sarton and for granting permission to quote from this correspondence in my study. Quotations from H.D.'s poetry are taken from *H.D. Collected Poems: 1912–1944*, copyright 1982 by the Estate of Hilda Doolittle. Reprinted by permission of New Directions Pub. Corp. Permission to quote from Edith Sitwell's *Collected Poems* has been kindly granted by David Higham Associates.

I am also grateful for the encouraging correspondence from Susan Stanford Friedman during the course of my study and for her putting me in touch with Silvia Dobson, who graciously provided me with firsthand insights of May Sarton's earliest meeting with H.D. I thank Louis H. Silverstein, cataloguer of the *H.D. Papers* and principal catalog librarian on the Yale University Library's Rare Book Team at Beinecke for his invaluable assistance and for his depth of knowledge. I also thank Georgia Hooks Shurr with whom I consulted about Francis Jammes's "O mon Ange gardien." Finally, I am grateful for the generous spirit of May Sarton, for her permission to quote from correspondence to me.

Notes

1. Although I have used the original Saum interview, it also now appears in the 1991 *Conversations with May Sarton,* ed. Earl G. Ingersoll (Jackson: UP of Mississippi), 108–29.

2. Misspellings from the original typescript have been corrected, where H.D. wrote "lyrices" for "lyrics," "gilrs" for "girls," and "prepairing" for "preparing."

3. "I made a pilgrimage to Chartres. I'm a Beauce man. Chartres is my cathedral. . . . You see the spires of Chartres seventeen kilometers away across the plain. Occasionally it disappears behind a fold in the ground or a line of wood. As soon as I saw it, it was absolute ecstasy . . ." (trans. Halévy 217).

4. "At last you have appeared, mysterious queen, / The tip seen yonder in the creamy surge / Of harvest fields and woods and on the verge / Of trembling distance is no evergreen . . ." (trans. Halévy 218–19).

5. See Sarton's portrait of Louise Bogan in *A World of Light,* especially pages 223–24. In August of 1955, Sarton reminisces, Bogan copied out Sarton's rough draft of Valéry's "Palme"; Jackson Mathews, editor of the complete Valéry in translation for the Bollingen Foundation, later saw Sarton's translation and apparently misunderstood and thought Louise Bogan had done the version of "Palme" herself (223). Also see Elizabeth Frank's *Louise Bogan: A Portrait* (356–57) for further insight on the Valéry work between the two women.

Works Cited

Bender, Todd K. *Gerard Manley Hopkins: The Classical Background and Critical Reception of His Work*. Baltimore: Johns Hopkins UP, 1966.

Bloom, Harold. *The Visionary Company: A Reading of English Romantic Poetry*. New York: Doubleday, 1961.

Bonetti, Kay. "An Interview with May Sarton" (1982), transcription edited by Elizabeth Meyer from an interview for American Audiotape Library, *Conversations with May Sarton*. Ed. Earl G. Ingersoll. Jackson: UP of Mississippi, 1991, 85–107.

DeShazer, Mary Kirk. *The Woman Poet and Her Muse: Sources and Images of Female Creativity in the Poetry of H.D., Louise Bogan, May Sarton, and Adrienne Rich*. Diss. U. of Oregon, 1982. Ann Arbor: UMI, 1982. 8224831.

Dobson, Silvia. Personal correspondence to Pat Adams Furlong, 13 July 1991. Quoted with the permission of Silvia Dobson.

DuPlessis, Rachel Blau. *H.D.: The Career of That Struggle*. Brighton, Sussex: The Harvester Press, 1986.

Eliot, T. S. *Four Quartets*. New York and London: Harcourt, 1971.

Flowers, Betty Sue, ed. *The Power of Myth*. New York: Doubleday, 1988.

Frank, Elizabeth. *Louise Bogan: A Portrait*. New York: Knopf, 1985.

Goldman, Connie. "A Conversation with May Sarton" (1987), transcription edited from the series "I'm Too Busy to Talk Now: Conversations with Creative People Over 70," *Conversations with May Sarton*. Ed. Earl G. Ingersoll. Jackson: UP of Mississippi, 1991. 150–59.

Guest, Barbara. *Herself Defined: The Poet H.D. and Her World*. New York: Doubleday, 1984.

Halévy, Daniel, ed. *Péguy et Les Cahiers de la Quinzaine*. Paris: Grasset, 1941.

———, ed. and trans. *Péguy and Les Cahiers de la Quinzaine*. New York, Toronto: Longmans, Green & Co., 1947.

Hardy, Thomas. *The Complete Poems of Thomas Hardy*. Ed. James Gibson. New York: Macmillan, 1978.

H.D. *H.D.: Collected Poems, 1912–1944*. Ed. Louis Martz. New York: New Directions Books, 1983.

———. "Speech of Acceptance to the American Academy of Arts and Letters." *H.D. Newsletter* 3.1 (1990): 4–6.

——. *Tribute to Freud*. Boston: David R. Godine, 1974.

——. Excerpt from letter of 7 January 1946 to May Sarton. Henry W. and Albert A. Berg Collection. New York Public Library. Astor, Lenox and Tilden Foundations.

Herbert, George. *The Works of George Herbert*. Ed. F. E. Hutchinson. Oxford: Clarendon P, 1959.

Hopkins, Gerard Manley. *The Poems of Gerard Manley Hopkins*. Ed. W. H. Gardner and N. H. MacKenzie. New York: Oxford UP, 1967.

Hunting, Constance, ed. *May Sarton: Woman and Poet*. Orono, Maine: National Poetry Foundation, University of Maine, 1982.

Hytier, Jean. *The Poetics of Paul Valéry*. Trans. Richard Howard. New York: Doubleday, 1953.

Ingersoll, Earl G., ed. *Conversations with May Sarton*. Jackson: U Press of Mississippi, 1991.

Jammes, Francis. *Clairières dans le Ciel. 1902–1906*. Paris: Gallimard, 1906.

King, Michael, ed. *H.D.: Woman and Poet*. Orono, Maine: National Poetry Foundation, University of Maine, 1986.

Mack, Maynard, Leonard Dean, and William Frost, eds. *Modern Poetry*. New York: Prentice, 1950.

Milward, Peter, S. J. *A Commentary on T. S. Eliot's Four Quartets*. Tokyo: The Hokuseido Press, 1968.

Robitaille, Stephen. "Writing in the Upward Years: May Sarton" (1990), transcription edited from an interview in conjunction with "Writing in the Upward Years," *Conversations with May Sarton*. Ed. Earl G. Ingersoll. Jackson: UP of Mississippi, 1991. 193–99.

Rilke, Rainer Marie. *Duino Elegies*. Ed. J. B. Leishman and Stephen Spender. New York: Norton, 1967.

St. Aubyn, F. C. *Charles Péguy*. Boston: G. K. Hall, 1977.

Sarton, May. *Collected Poems, 1930–1973*. New York: Norton, 1974.

——. *A Grain of Mustard Seed*. New York: Norton, 1971.

——. Interview. "The Art of Poetry XXXII: May Sarton." With Karen Saum. *Paris Review* 89 (1983): 81–110.

——. *Journal of a Solitude*. New York: Norton, 1973.

——. Letters to H.D. In H.D. Papers. No. 24:1 Box 14:501. Yale Collection of American Literature. Beinecke Rare Book and Manuscript Library.

——. Letter to the author. 4 May 1991. Quoted with the permission of May Sarton.

————. *The Silence Now: New and Uncollected Earlier Poems.* New York: Norton, 1988.

————. *A World of Light.* New York: Norton, 1976.

Schaffner, Perdita. "A Sketch of H.D.: The Egyptian Cat." *Signets: Reading H.D.* Ed. Susan Stanford Friedman and Rachel Blau DuPlessis. Madison: U of Wisconsin P, 1990, 3–6.

Shakespeare, William. *The Complete Works of Shakespeare.* Ed. David Bevington. Glenview, Ill.: Scott, 1980.

Silverstein, Louis H. "Herself Delineated: Chronological Highlights of H.D." *Signets: Reading H.D.* Ed. Susan Stanford Friedman and Rachel Blau DuPlessis. Madison: U of Wisconsin P, 1990, 32–45.

Sitwell, Edith. *Collected Poems.* London: Macmillan Ltd., 1957.

Valéry, Paul. *Paul Valéry: An Anthology.* Ed. Jackson Mathews. Princeton: Princeton UP, 1977.

Vendler, Helen. "The Re-Invented Poem: George Herbert's Alternatives." *Forms of Lyric: Selected Papers from the English Institute.* Ed. Reuben A. Brower. New York: Columbia UP, 1970. 19–45.

Weil, Simone. *Waiting for God.* Trans. Emma Craufurd. New York: Capricorn Books, 1951.

Woodman, Marion. *Addiction to Perfection: The Still Unravished Bride.* Toronto: Inner City Books, 1982.

Yeats, William Butler. "Sailing to Byzantium." *W. B. Yeats: The Poems Revised.* Ed. Richard J. Finneran. New York: Macmillan 1983, London 1984.

The Cusp of Stillness and Motion:
The Art Image in May Sarton's Poems

KAREN OHNESORGE-FICK

In "Airs Above the Ground" May Sarton acknowledges the artist as one who has mapped on canvas the scene at hand, improbable lightness and mass juxtaposed in the figures of horses:

> The white horse floats above the field,
> Pegasus in a child's dream by Chagall
> Where gravity itself is forced to yield—
> Oh marvelous beast who cannot ever fall! (*HS* 13)

Often Sarton's words invoke the visual arts. She may refer to particular paintings and drawings, as a witness to their forms; or she may act to create some part of art's universe, empowered by her imagination. In these poems the plastic arts coexist with poetry. And this symbiosis occurs not only at the level of image, as in her lyric description of Lippizan horses, but also in the technique and artistry of her verse, where there is often a correlation between the form of her language and the methods of the art.

Sarton's explorations of art image and word emerge from a history of dialogue on the two. In his *Laocoön*, Gotthold Ephraim Lessing argues the distinctions between poetry and the plastic arts, concluding that poetry portrays actions, using "single properties" to indicate "bodies," and the plastic arts portray "bodies," using the most pregnant single moment to indicate actions (55). In his discussion Lessing cites an inherent stasis in the art image, an intrinsic flux in language. As stasis and flux form an important polarity for Sarton, it is natural that her poems on artworks, artists, and creativity would reflect this dualism.

In the framework of her work, the blend of poet and artist follows from the bare fact that she has written these poems into being, that they are intrinsically art objects, beyond their referents in art or in the natural world. The translations from the visual to the verbal image forge new experience, interpret, focus the gaze, praise, or reinvent. This phenomenon bridges the space between the actively imagining eye of the audience and the energetic creativity of the artist or poet.

In Lessing's notes on imitation, where motifs and stories set down in one art form find their way into another, he differentiates between art that "makes the work of the other the actual subject of his [*sic*] imitation" and art that has "the same subject and the one borrows from the other the style and fashion of the imitation" (33). Lessing's point here is that there are imitations that till new ground by encountering the previous work, and there are imitations that merely mimic the original—to provide "cold recollections of features from another's genius in place of original features of his [*sic*] own" (33). These are important distinctions, for art *about* other art is clearly superior to art *like* other art—the former results from powerful creativity, while the latter results from weak imitativeness.

According to Lessing's formulations, May Sarton's poetry on the plastic arts asserts her originality. These are evocations of art history as a continuing dialogue among creative powers. References to the visual arts in Sarton's poetry encompass many artists, Chagall, Rousseau, and Piero della Francesca among them. The poems often refer to particular works, artists or eras in art history, as well as reflecting the subtleties of artistic envisionment. In their totality these poems convey the complex matrix of creative power where its potency is strongest, in the crux of order and chaos, stillness and fluidity; the poems form an ongoing body of writings that begin in some of Sarton's earliest books and extend into *The Silence Now* with poems such as "Invocation." Her *Collected Poems (1930–1973)* demonstrates that Sarton's interest in art images dates back to her earliest collections, notably *Inner Landscape* (1936–1938) with "Architectural Image"; *The Lion and the Rose* (1938–1948) with "The Lady and the Unicorn"; and *In Time Like Air* (1953–1958) with "Nativity." By the time *A Private Mythology* (1961–1966) appears, with its series of lyrics on Japanese prints, art references have become integral to the collections (*CP* 5–13).

Sarton's *Selected Poems* includes poems inspired by works of visual art or by the art-making process, along with others inspired by music, in "The Composed Imagination," the book's opening section. Together these poems document the multifaceted creative process. They enumerate ways the eye has of seeing—they take long glances at particular pieces; and even when they make no direct reference to the visual arts, many poems dramatize the processes—composition, detailing, modulation of forms—inherent in painting, sculpture, and drawing, as in "Baroque Image," "Portrait by Holbein," and "Nursery Rhyme."

Poems integrating techniques and images from art also appear in more recent volumes. "For Monet" (*LM* 37) claims from the outset a kinship between the impulse to write and the impulse to paint. "Poets, too," she begins, "are crazed by light," a natural form whose complexities artists and writers are driven to translate: "Light through a petal, / Iridescence of clouds before sunrise." Sarton refers to the unexpected "vermilion under the haystack" of Monet's series, focusing on the process of forming the image, a primary concern for the Impressionists. She notes the problem of laying hold of objects in time: "To hold the fleeting still / In a design—." In the second of three stanzas, Sarton lets her eye fall on her own house in the present moment, "Today," where she finds vision inadequate under the circumstances, with a blizzard equalizing light and dark beneath "milky veils." Without shadows definitions fail. In the final stanza light is the substance of mystery, and Monet's lifetime is a long attempt to "undazzle the light / And pin it down." By ending with this last phrase, Sarton emphasizes the struggle to hold "illuminated transience" in stasis on the canvas or page.

In many respects "For Monet" exemplifies Sarton's poems on art. It presents the elements of artist, artwork, and natural world, as well as the problems of representation: reference to the object, time within the frame, and liaison between image and artist, among them. It outlines parallels: author becomes artist's eye, attempting "to see what one sees" (*LM* 37); artist becomes subject of scrutiny, Sarton examining Monet's endeavors; and nature becomes a contrary force beneath "milky veils," resisting formulation.

Even in her journals, the arts of drawing, painting, and sculpture sometimes become central metaphors for her thinking, maps for sorting out, for contextualizing. In *Recovering*, Sarton speculates about the parallels between sketching with words versus sketching in drawn lines, especially regarding how the world receives the hidden efforts of the writer and the painter: "The sketches that we see later on paper are visible, the problem as it is solved is visible; whereas most of the writer's 'sketches' are in his mind, like terrible knots to be unraveled, and the concentration required is of a different order, partly because there is so little 'métier,' such as brushes to be washed, a canvas to be stretched, and actual semi-mechanical tasks such as filling in background" (44).

For Sarton the visual arts provide fertile ground for her poetry to take root in image and concept. This interest in art as metaphor for the creative being leads her to explore the complex and interconnected arenas of audience, artist, and artwork. These are the basic elements of art, and they form a vital triangle whose nuances Sarton's poems explore.

Take, for example, her treatment of *The Nativity* by Piero della Francesca, which hangs in London's National Gallery (Clark 62, pl. 119). The painting features geometrically arranged figures posed in the foreground: a rectangular grouping of angels to the left, three stern shepherds to the right, and beside them Mary kneeling at the feet of the infant Jesus, who—as Zbigniew Herbert writes—"rests on a grass-patch worn like an old rug" (8). The figure of the infant is Sarton's focus at the opening of her poem "Nativity" (*SP* 17). The barren sky and ground she sees seem a hazardous environment for new life, and the restorative power of the painting is therefore a challenge to the emotions, a paradox.

"Why do we feel restored," she asks, "As in a sacramental place?" (*SP* 17). The emerging answer is that "artifice" formulates the healing. The geometry is "distilled and spare," unlike stereotypically overwrought encounters with "Mystery" or holiness. Still, this painting praises, and Sarton, in her turn, pays tribute to the "serene glory" that radiates from the piece, a living aurora paradoxically present in the static composition. In the final stanza she returns to the figure of Christ, "love, naked, lying in great state / On the bare ground, as in all human faces." The universality of della Francesca's aphoristic representation creates for Sarton a gracious similitude between Christ and all humans. Further, her poised, precise language forges an empathic interpretation of the painting, poem and painting both formed with elemental spareness.

Sarton's voice as poet-observer is an active recipient of the visual arts, one who transmits observations to readers through language, acting as a translator of the aesthetic experience. In "These Images Remain," Sarton approaches the initial art process, the mind's original conception of idea, as a constant in the matrix of time, "Enlarged by love to think only in shapes / That compass time and frame the changing skies" (*SP* 40). The paradox of change and stasis emerges in a setting like Olympus, filled with the elements of infinity—arches, fountains, open squares— but inhabited by the moving deity of imagination, the Eye that holds stillness and life, and an entity that doubles as the active receiver who encounters art itself. The poem affirms the permanence of art in the face of mortality, "Though we are caught by time, by time estranged."

The clear argument of the poem is reinforced by sound patterns and enjambments that work together to incorporate this contrast of flux and stillness in the language fabric of the poem. To begin, the "classic landscapes" here find articulation in the immediately recognizable form of the Shakespearean sonnet, implying the stability of long tradition. The rhymes emerge formally to delineate a pattern along the right margin, a pattern lightly reflected also at the left margin, where many words connect through alliteration ("these," "that," "though"). The containment of the poem is further intensified by the repetition of the comma-halved line structure that opens and closes the poem: "These images remain, these classic landscapes," Sarton writes, going on to explain the existence of these images in the fluidity of time. She concludes with another caesura: "Though we are caught by time, by time estranged." The paradox convinces, that we might be entrapped and excluded simultaneously, where imagination enforces our mortality as we must know death, yet where imagination makes death seem cruelly improbable.

Meanwhile, these sound patterns play against a temporarily conflicting current of enjambment: line breaks occur at syntactical moments that deny end-stopped phrasing: When Sarton writes of ". . . these classic landscapes / That lie" (*SP* 40), the enjambment places the noun on one line and its dependent descriptive phrase on the next. The same type of break appears in the next line, where the "eyes" are separated from their description, "Enlarged by love . . .":

> . . . these classic landscapes
> That lie, immense and quiet, behind eyes
> Enlarged by love to think only in shapes
> That compass time and frame the changing skies. . . .
> (*SP* 40)

Instead of reflecting stability through end-stops in these first lines, logic and grammar more comfortably find the natural pause in the midst of a line, marked by a comma—especially as the poem opens. Progressively, until the ending couplet, confluence emerges between rhymed line-ends and end-stopped syntax. As a result, the poem moves from flux to stability in terms of its enjambments, so that agreement increases between the regular sound patterns throughout and the line breaks that eventually imply stasis.

The eye in "These Images Remain," or perception, doubles as a force that creates design by understanding the world as pattern, as image. In the artist Sarton sees a conjoining of powers: observation and formulation. The artist is also the poet, also the divine force that creates what is seen. Sometimes, as in "Composition" (*CP* 393), the creator is implied, becoming the force that imbues the landscape with coherence—blending with the poet herself, who charts nature in a poem, declaring objects to be "here" or "there." In a line such as "Take a huge sky above a steadfast land," (*CP* 393) Sarton, with conciseness and assurance, formulates landscape, the sky and earth, each in its own realm, swept into being by the preposition "above," which economically governs the relationship between the two.

Other poems describe particular works of art and praise the artist's habit of looking searchingly, as in the poem "Nativity," after della

Francesca's painting (*SP* 17). Sarton observes the artist forming image in paint or threads or stone, rather than in words. Sometimes the image itself attains a measure of life. In "The Lady and the Unicorn" (*SP* 16), self, or poet's voice, crosses over to the image, so that the voice of the poem *is* the unicorn, mourning the displacement of its emotion by the ulterior concerns of the beautiful woman. Throughout the poem, repetitions of phrases, redesigned in new contexts, form a pattern of moving across, then back across an idea. The unicorn's thoughts repeat like an incantation, reflecting the back-and-forth motion in the act of weaving, and emphasizing the mythical beast's submission by linking its refrain to the highly patterned and predetermined format of tapestry:

> I am the unicorn and bow my head
> You are the lady woven into history
> And here forever we are bound in mystery
> Our wine, Imagination, and our bread,
> And I the unicorn who bows his head.
>
> You are all interwoven in my history
> And you and I have been most strangely wed
> I am the unicorn and bow my head
> And lay my wildness down upon your knee
> You are the lady woven into history. . . . (*SP* 16)

Nine stanzas comprise "The Lady and the Unicorn," four stanzas of five lines to begin, and five stanzas of two lines to conclude. These last consist of three couplets and then two stanzas whose rhymes alternate. The longer stanzas at the top of the poem form a sense of mass or weight, as well as emphasizing the geometry of the rectangle (the stanzas are block-shaped) or of the cross (the four stanzas form four arms). In the first two stanzas—shown above—first and last lines of each stanza are nearly perfect reflections of one another, congruent with their content about submissiveness and fate: "I am the unicorn and bow my head / . . . And I the unicorn who bows his head" (lines 1 and 5); and "You are all interwoven in my history / . . . You are the lady woven into history" (6 and 10).

Individual words also invite comparisons between the method of the poem and the method of tapestry. The lady is "woven," and they both are "bound" in the first stanza. The voice of the unicorn consistently refers to the enforced stasis of being an element of the tapestry, his "wild love chastened to this history." In the eighth stanza the proximity of the words "wound" and "woven" elicits connection and comparison between the two, so the "woven" fate of the lady and the unicorn is parallel to the "wound" of love forsaken (*SP* 16).

But the conjoining of tapestry and text is most thoroughly explored in the final five stanzas:

> I am the unicorn and bow my head
> To one so sweetly lost, so strangely wed:
>
> You sit forever under a small formal tree
> Where I forever search for your eyes to be
>
> Rewarded with this shining tragedy
> And know your beauty was not cast for me,
>
> Know we are woven all in mystery,
> The wound imagined where no one has bled,
>
> My wild love chastened to this history
> Where I before your eyes, bow down my head. (*SP* 16)

The expectation for rhymed couplets set up in the first three of these is violated in the last two stanzas, which are set up with an *a-b-a-b* rhyme scheme, so that the two stanzas interchange their sounds emphatically. This emphasis points out the intent of the poem to respond in kind to the woven pattern of the tapestry. These final stanzas also clarify the pairings in the poem, reflective of the warp and woof of the fabric, and including the "I" and "you" of the unicorn and the lady, delineated as intersecting forces.

Formally, Sarton's poems often reflect the materials and compositions of the works they refer to. While "The Lady and the Unicorn" is woven like tapestry, the unresolved, "free verse" structure of "Portrait by Holbein" (*SP* 19) is appropriate to discourse on a drawing, since drawing is an art form that permits the artist to explore rather than rigidly formulate. The lines of the poem, like the lines of Holbein, are crisp—the diction clear, precise—but they are uncompleted wisps of thought—they barely touch on noun-verb-object before they enjamb toward appositives and adjectives, stacking and perfecting to explore the shape of the human, moving toward the likeness, but never creating an image in perfected stasis:

> Your face is drawn in pencil,
> startling the sense
> with its perfected shape,
> the tension of the outline,
> the curious created purity—
> (*SP* 19)

In these lines the poet does not describe any specific facial features; instead, she makes generalizations about the process of implying form with abstracted elements of shape and outline. In the line "the tension of the outline," the repeating *n* sound creates an auditory image of tension, of stretching linearly along a narrow band of sound. From its accuracy of description to the lyricism of its individual lines, the poem as a whole is a sensitive and masterful response to Holbein's drawing.

For Sarton selection and imagining are the markers of artistic creation. The particularizing or selective mind causes detail and precision to emerge from the vagaries of experience. In "Journey toward Poetry" (*SP* 26) Sarton spins a mental landscape that refuses to solidify because it is entirely composed by undifferentiated expanses—field, sky, sea. The scene emerges from a background of off-rhymes and rhythms that syncopate and vary:

> First that beautiful mad exploration
> Through a multiple legend of landscape
> When all roads open and then close again
> Behind a car that rushes toward escape. . . . (*SP* 26)

Early in the poem color and form congeal momentarily as a "pink geranium standing on the wall," but even that image explodes into vastness of reference. The flower "Rests there a second, still, and then breaks open / To show far off the huge blood-red cathedral / Looming like magic against a bright blue sky . . ." (26). The pink deepens as the blood-red of a cathedral, distant, outlined on a blue expanse, much like the vigorous landscapes of Impressionists, and just as tensely maintained in one human fragment of time as any canvas by Monet. Finally in this poem, the mind—or the car, or sensation—rests on singularity of vision: "All landscapes crystallize and focus here— / And in the distance stand five copper beeches" (26).

Always between the viewer and the natural landscape or artwork is observation, a privilege Sarton blesses and whose healing power she describes in "Nursery Rhyme" (*SP* 23–24): "Shut your eyes then / And let us slip / Out of the city rain. . . ." Sarton grants the weary vision its rest, while treating the inner eye to a guided image of a jungle's enfolding vegetation and iconic inhabitants in the spirit of Rousseau, with the same brilliance of color and simple placement of stylized objects: the "crimson sun / In a pale milky sky / With a vermilion / Lizard near by . . ." (*SP* 24). The brief lines and defined rhythms reflect with remarkable accuracy the geometry of Rousseau's work, his childlike imaging of edges and shapes as idealized, truer to the tropical exotica of the mind than photographically accurate renderings could hope to be. To go further, Sarton invokes the claustrophobia of these works, their seeming airlessness, the forests of repeating shapes without currents of air or action to influence their design:

> . . . The strangeness that hovers
> Like a green pall,
> Envelopes and covers
> In a warm still suspense
> All of the landscape. . . . (*SP* 24)

They only hang where they grow, those leaves, and the figures are stoic idols without motion or emotion. To recreate the environment in language, Sarton refers to a "strangeness," "a sixth sense" that compels the image to stasis (*SP* 24). The relentless rhythm of the poem, the feeling that it turns upon itself and will go on endlessly, reinforces this sense of "no escape."

In this meditative context, the self and other emerge in response to borders and frames so that the observer and observed appear. Pronouns provide the initial boundaries: "I" has invited "you" to travel briefly to the stillness of image, where a central calm accompanies the lapse of time. A disassociation from the "city rain" takes the reader with the voice across a border to Rousseau's jungle, his timeless, unmoving vegetation. Here the artist captures them on the canvas, seen through the frames of his glasses. This journey requires observer and observed; it relies for its essence on divisions between subject and object, between motion and stillness, between consciousness and dream; and this journey traverses the common ground of art and writing. Finally, with words that imply the framed edge of the canvas, "Nursery Rhyme" returns to consciousness: "Open your eyes again" (line 52). This last line represents the border between the art image and the world.

In "A Parrot" (*SP* 31), another poem owing to Rousseau, the singsong quality of the brief lines and strong, end-stopped rhymes invoke the regularly patterned and symmetrical compositions of Rousseau; and Sarton's plain-spoken, vivid yet flattened, portrait of the bird figures in language Rousseau's bright colors and sharp edges: "My parrot is emerald green, / His tail feathers, marine" (lines 1-2). Rhythmically, the whole poem waltzes along three-beat lines.

This parrot becomes the center of a singsong discussion about truth, virtue, and belief. In his color and behavior, "He must be believed to be seen" (31), reversing the assumption that belief follows observation, and defining vision as a function of the imagination. With this reversal Sarton asserts the vitality of the artist. In the geometry formed among artist, audience, and artwork, the artist has the power to invoke worlds and realities, via the artwork, in the mind of the audience. The artist separates void and matter, flux and stasis; the creator modulates form, imposes order; Sarton's parrot "becomes too true to be good" (31) when he speaks his uncensored repetitions. The inversions of adages produce a topsy-turvy environment, governed by imagination.

In the end Sarton's parrot, like her poem, takes its long glance at the context in which, seemingly incongruously, it finds itself—the fallen leaves have left a visually impoverished landscape, a gray scene that evokes murmured "muffled words," a sudden loss of clarity from a being so recently confused with a witch in its bright screech. Sarton writes, "That stuttered staccato scream / Must be believed not to seem / The shriek of a witch in the room" (*SP* 31). But on looking at the dim day outside the window, he mutters "Like someone who talks through a dream" (line 21).

This gray ground parallels the canvas's or lake's surface—the blank arena that invites a wild call or broad brush stroke, that demands fulfillment, allows meaning to exercise its force. The artist mythologized becomes creator, sculptor of world, separating light and darkness to impose a living geometry to compose motion and calm, stasis and flux. "Under the wave," writes May Sarton in "The Return of Aphrodite," it is altogether still" (*SP* 169). The artist and poet emerge empowered from the deep, from the dark openness, where the imagination works its spell on the framable spaces of canvas, poem, loom, or natural vista.

Works Cited

Clark, Kenneth. *Piero della Francesca*. London: Phaidon, 1969.

Herbert, Zbigniew. "Piero della Francesca." *Writers on Artists*. Ed. Daniel Halpern. San Francisco: North Point, 1988. 7–20.

Lessing, Gotthold Ephraim. "Laocoön." 1766. Trans. W. A. Steel. *Laocoön, Nathan the Wise, Minna Von Barnhelm*. New York: Dutton, 1949. 1–101.

Sarton, May. *Collected Poems (1930–1973)*. New York: Norton, 1974.

———. *Halfway to Silence*. New York: Norton, 1980.

———. *Letters from Maine*. New York: Norton, 1984.

———. *Recovering*. New York: Norton, 1980.

———. *Selected Poems of May Sarton*. New York: Norton, 1978.

———. *The Silence Now*. New York: Norton, 1988.

IV

Approaching Silence

In the Simple Day:
A Foray into May Sarton's Poetry

JANE MILLER

One reads *into* poetry not only for information and essences about the world, but also for the obvious personal reason of finding something out about herself. We have all suffered, as May Sarton's "Contemplation of Poussin" says: "Romantic impulse turned against itself, / Snake biting its tail. I'm torn in half." The poem also tells us, "No sanctity within my mind to bless / or to redeem a cannibal distress—" (*LM* 13). Base human emotion, here anguished, is overpowering. This poem is prelude to the volume *Letters from Maine;* in it, she asks that question the book will go on to answer: "Without the mask what art could learn to show / A naked heart alive, fire under the snow?" (*LM* 13). Immediately, the first poem, "A Farewell," responds:

> I must not go back to the murderous past
> Nor force a passage through to some safe landing,
> But float upon this moment of communion
> Entranced, astonished by pure understanding. . . . (*LM* 17)

Clearly a mask, a silence, a distance, a contemplative experience, an internal transformation is required, demanded, to break pain's back. It is an aesthetic experience for Sarton which proves remedial, investigating primordial activity. This is not very far from Wordsworth or Keats, except that I get the impression that Sarton accepts, even has come to love ("float . . . entranced"), to receive power from, the silence itself. This, it seems to me, is a much more interesting model than the nineteenth century's, where the Romantic moment, induced by fantasy, phantasm, and the like, seals off the transcendent experience and emphasizes the resultant (indulgent) knowledge gained, rather than the process itself. It is not only that something might be understood by Sarton in the Romantic expansion, but also that the moment itself satisfies. This relationship to silence—it is in her book titles *The Land of Silence, Halfway to Silence, Journal of a Solitude,* all over *Letters from Maine* ("After a Winter's Silence," etc.)—shapes Sarton's otherwise traditionally Romantic, studied poetry into space that is sometimes uncontrollable, for, in fact, something has crept in, beyond measure and content, that positions the subject, and hence the reader, in a postapocalyptic blankness, a white space.

This existential space is familiar, but in Sarton's case there is a particular resoluteness, a power responding to it. From someone with one leg in the old world and one in the new such as May Sarton, whose writing spans over fifty years, it is an enterprising and difficult position. One finds a description of the location in "History," from Jorie Graham's *Region of Unlikeness:*

> Where we are now she's done the bright swift part, the coil has long since sprung.
> She's deep into the lateness now,
> undressing.
> She's standing in the open ringed with photographs of what took place. (35)

Later in Graham's poem,

> The mystery of *interval,*—her push, his refusal—what we call love.

Finally, near the end of this poem, we are addressed:

> Out there: look up into the evening surrounding
> us,
> what can you see, what does she have to show
> for all the centuries of this undress? patience? desire? the thing called form? (Graham 36)

Here, Graham has described, in wholly different form from Sarton's, and with profoundly different, twenty-first-century intentions that acknowledge a fractured universal time, Sarton's fecund silence. For all the natural description that we get in Sarton of her beloved New England, "But in the time of splendor was alone / in a strange land of fire and broken stone" ("The Cold Night," *LM* 38), it is finally a metaphysical place she inhabits. The style of this habitation, vigorous, dignified, is poignant and, it seems to me, inspiring.

Indeed, one of the most inspiring aspects of May Sarton's poetry is its very existence: fifty years of poetry, an extraordinary effort for anyone, but—say it—for a woman in this culture speaking from a sensuous, private, formal place, particularly extraordinary, since she wasn't embraced (i.e., controlled) by canonists. Compare Sarton, for example, with the poet Elizabeth Bishop, whose long career was encouraged by praises and rewards. Of course the issue is complicated: Bishop's self-imposed exile in South America had to have been induced, at least in part, by her decision to live a private life with another woman; whether intended or not, this had the obvious effect of separating the public poet, who "lived" in the U.S. through her published work, from the woman who lived in Brazil. Distance from one's native scene naturally can be sought for many reasons; Bishop's decision, though, together with her decision to suppress her lesbian love poetry, only now surfacing thanks to Lorrie Goldensohn's efforts in unearthing and publishing Bishop's erotica (see her *Elizabeth Bishop: The Biography of a Poet*), gives an impression of hiding. Sarton knows and describes her contrasting situation:

> I hold fast to the little I can hold,
> Along continuum so like the play
> Of the incessant waves, unbroken theme
> Of love, love without a fold
> Murmuring under silence like the sea. ("Seascape," *LM* 39)

This must refer to something specific, but there is the sense it is an obvious metaphor for her relationship to the public, where she is consigned to this "Murmuring under silence." Although Sarton often lapses into banalities or sentimentalities (in "Snowfall," "A tenderness of snowing"), or tonal anachronisms (in the title poem, "Letters from Maine," "The muse of course airs out the inner world"(*LM* 26), such murmurings are part of a deep internal commitment to love and to language, to openness.

Such marginalized language, by definition uttered against the predominating force, is innately rebellious (even when it uses mainstream forms, as in Sarton's case), and confronts issues of power and interpretations of reality. It is a problem very much in the forefront of the consciousness of the contemporary woman writer, even if such a writer steps forward, undaunted, or more formally politicizes that engagement, making an aesthetic issue of that encounter, as Rachel Blau DuPlessis describes it regarding her contemporary Susan Howe:

> Howe speaks of her own fear of being an artist based on her apprehension that madness and breakdown [Plath's suicide, Sexton's, Woolf's, Stein's disenfranchisement (to this day)] were the retributive punishment for ambition. Tremendous psychic struggles are revealed in Howe's persistent linkage of "the bond between mad and made." The apparent insanity of other women artists blocked her from her own declarations; to struggle against such received interpretations of other women artists by analyses of their intellectual breadth was to struggle for one's own ambition and achievement, at once an act of cultural criticism and of personal necessity. (DuPlessis 161)

In Sarton's case, this struggle appears obliquely; significantly, the struggle is turned inward, toward self, toward relationship, toward landscape, where the territory (metaphor) is delimited and the demons are pure, psychic. In other words, Sarton inherited the nearly insurmountable circumstance of the woman writer with her borders cordoned off—the entire twentieth century, in the midst of being deranged by unfathomable speeds, seemingly unavailable to her, happening elsewhere—and she has made of this "elsewhere" (the term is deconstructionist and feminist, a place of non-dichotomous activity) a viable place from which to broadcast.

What makes the achievement intense and lasting is its chafing motion against those borders of the ordinary and the accepted. Because she was so personal in her work she needed something to contain it. I have the sense that Sarton's reliance on and love of formal structures has been her way to have her female companions, her female muses; these strategies of containment and refinement are a means for her, in effect, to have her *nature*. From "The Image Is a Garden":

> My image is this garden in the autumn
> A tangle of late asters, unpruned roses,
> Some to be frost-killed, others still to open,

Some failures visible, some wild successes. . . .

We have what was planned, and something more,
We have what was planned and something less. (*LM* 59)

At the end of her essay on Susan Howe, Rachel Blau DuPlessis sets forth the perennial situation of the marginalized writer. She describes it as

The taxing struggle to assemble and maintain a self-questioning (who? how?) cultural position: anti-authoritarian, yet authoritatively provoked by one's female identity. . . . (DuPlessis 164)

Eventually, I feel, this chafing, this quarrel loses its meaning; one goes off, wounded and/or triumphant, to write less self-consciously. Otherwise the art is reactionary, and we know how easy it is to become enamored of the conflict, to get used to participating in our own catastrophe. Hence Sarton's various uses of silence; her constant references to solitude, silence, blankness, the invisible, that which cannot speak—"Without the wine, without the wild-eyed goat / Where would creation start, or generate?" she asks in "Contemplation of Poussin"— amount to such a crescendo that it can no longer be adversarial, but is aggressive, a silence that opens into recognition, cognition, and excavation (*LM* 13). It is a gestating thing of beauty in itself. The style, however, meticulous, simple, is hers. She knows her way on her own territory: "I know my way on barren islands," she tells us in *Letters from Maine,* a world of climate, music, action, wickedness, grace.

"Every style is a means of insisting on something," Susan Sontag reminds us in her classic 1965 essay "On Style." She elaborates:

Style is the principle of decision in a work of art, the signature of the artist's will. . . . And the rules are always, finally, artificial and [they] arbitrarily limit, whether they are rules of form (like *terza rima* or the twelve-tone row or frontality) or the presence of a certain "content." (33)

There is something beyond subject, beyond the awkward and necessary balancing of diction and music, beyond the sensuality of the composition. Sontag illumines this expression at some length:

> The role of the arbitrary and unjustifiable in art has never been suffi-
> ciently acknowledged. . . . Usually critics who want to praise a work of
> art feel compelled to demonstrate that each part is justified, that it
> could not be other than it is. And every artist, when it comes to his [*sic*]
> own work, remembering the role of chance, fatigue, external distrac-
> tions, knows what the critic says to be a lie, knows that it could well
> have been otherwise. The sense of inevitability that a great work of art
> projects is not made up of the inevitability or necessity of its parts, but
> of the whole. (33)

Sarton's obsession with silences extends from the content of the poetry, with references to the unknown and unspoken, as in "Contemplation of Poussin": "Uprooted love, contempt (that dirtied snow) /
Struggle to deal with the unspoken curse," into the presence of that
which is omitted, avoided, assumed (*LM* 13). The struggles/struc-
tures of a Romantic platform, including her use of landscape as extended metaphor, evaporate suddenly, the artifice crumbling, and
there is silence and solitude, insisted upon and therefore become a
style in itself—devilish, familiar, inexplicable. Silence—place of refusal
and gestation.

We out here who have been in a much more privileged position to
resist either obliteration or victimization must acknowledge the work,
the difficult dig of one consistently forced to be internal, sentimental,
single-minded. Sarton structures a life; she insists on that paradigm,
as she tells us in her typically self-reflexive way (title and all), in "Letters to Myself":

> Who tells the poet, "silence, danger here!"
> God knows I live each day in greater fear
> And out of agony structure my face
> To sustain tension, yet discover poise,
> For this Magnificat of severe joys. (*LM* 56)

If the places where Sarton comes to rest—in form, in the natural
world—seem irrevocably decentered given the eruption/correction/
conception of space and time, they remind us of the value of engagement. As the present crystallizes and dematerializes, we learn relation-

ship to it and to ourselves. We have, in fact, been hoisted up here, capitalized, raised (like a voice), have been given the opportunity to participate:

> There on your bed lay poetry alive
> With all that it can ever hope to give,
> And there at last for one transcendent hour
> You gave yourself into its gentle power.
> Now the long tension slowly falls away
> And we may be together in the simple day. . . .
> ("The Consummation," *LM* 58)

What world is this? A world in which to hear not simply that we are mere shape, emblem, larger than life, but that life itself is large. For her dedication to this world, I have May Sarton to thank in this public place.

Works Cited

DuPlessis. Rachel Blau. "Whowe: An Essay on Work by Susan Howe." *Sulfur* 20 (1987): 157–65.

Goldensohn, Lorrie. *Elizabeth Bishop: The Biography of a Poet.* New York: Columbia UP, 1991.

Graham, Jorie. *Region of Unlikeness.* New York: Ecco Press, 1991.

Sarton, May. *Letters from Maine: New Poems.* New York: Norton, 1984.

Sontag, Susan. "On Style." *Against Interpretation.* New York: Doubleday, 1990. 15–36.

Desiring Silence:
"Halfway" as Lyric Mediation
in the Postmodern World

KEITH S. NORRIS

In the mid-to-late twentieth century, with its distinct turning away from conventional ideas of meaning, including our conventional ways of understanding human feeling in terms of idealized absolutes, we hesitate to denote the lyric as a viable form for expressing "postmodern" thought. Old forms don't apply in understanding the new disjointed world: this is part of the story we've been told and are telling about the postmodern world. However, some of May Sarton's late poetry, particularly that of *Halfway to Silence* (1980), represents a kind of lyric poetry being written in the late twentieth century that *uses* the lyric to bring together divers elements of contemporary life, to provide both a means of understanding and political escape, to engage and understand an expanding world.

Historically, the lyric has been concerned with perception and the poet's judgments of those perceptions, with the emotion of the poet toward his or her own way of seeing. Whether in the pastoral setting of sixteenth-century poets, in Wordsworth's Romanticism, or Baudelaire's inner searching, the lyric concerns *how* the poet feels, how he or she responds to the physical or psychological situation at hand. The lyric becomes a record of the process of the poet's imaginings. May Sarton's lyrics of the 1980s are at times beautifully ambiguous, many of them attempting to make no judgment past *now;* indeed they seem to seek an almost Archimedean point best defined by the term Sarton uses in the titles of two of her most recent books of poetry— "silence." There is a danger, a reductive movement toward establishing the objective correlative (a single meaning for the term *silence*) if we acknowledge that she ever attains complete silence.

The title poem of her 1988 collection, *The Silence Now,* may lure the reader to attempt such a reductive reading. Sarton begins the poem by addressing the silence, by giving it objective qualities:

> These days the silence is immense.
> It is there deep down, not to be escaped. (*SN* 16)

Here, the idea of silence is presented as image, something to be seen, perceived as real. But it is real only as image; it is not to be taken as conceptual truth. Terry Eagleton's discussion of the Kantian Aesthetic is helpful here:

> Aesthetic judgement is then a kind of pleasurable free-wheeling of our faculties, a kind of parody of conceptual understanding, non-referential pseudo-cognition which does not nail down the object to an identifiable thing. . . . (85)

"Silence" strives to be a concept here, to become completely objective—a knowable thing. But it is not object, nor is it correlative to any one meaning. Silence is an aesthetic image for the poet—something that she can even speak to, or perhaps name, but not know, only speculate about.

Such speculation is a good thing, a political release, a possibility of aesthetics that frees the poet to conceive a world where thoughts of criticism, infirmity, and abandonment are stilled: "silence." This kind of aesthetic movement is "a kind of dream or fantasy which displays its own curious lawfulness" (Eagleton 85–86). In "The Silence Now," Sarton is bound to a discipline, a form holding to the middle road between "the uniform laws of understanding and some utter chaotic indeterminacy" (Eagleton 85). The law of pursuing silence is that it must only go "halfway," as Sarton terms it, *Halfway to Silence.* This is the political possibility of a lyric aesthetics in our age—halfway takes us to the brink of considering the limits of silence, a desirable but final option (the extreme of silence is the death of the poetic voice); it forces us to realize that the extremes of postmodernism—complete abstraction, absence of form and music, the death of the poetic voice— are too far removed from the moment to actualize, to poetically conceptualize.

At the center of "The Silence Now" Sarton poses a stanza of questions:

> At the bottom of the silence what lies in wait?
> Is it love? Is it death? Too early or too late?
> What is it I can have that I still want? (16)

These questions form the parameters for Sarton's interaction with "silence." Silence is necessary as image to question, as the necessary attempt of the aesthetic to bring back a knowledge of the object. But the means is the end here; the asking of the questions, the *movement* toward silence, is what the postmodern lyric seeks as its end. It doesn't seek arrival but perpetual motion toward, constantly creating a new "halfway there." Each question in this series moves us closer, culminating in the avatar of postmodern questions: "What is it I can have that I still want?" It's a short move from this question—what is still desirable? what is aesthetically pleasing enough to satisfy the postmodern imagination, done in with excess, with *having*?—to the end of desire in silence.

Sarton moves away from the desire for silence to the romanticism of "Now." She responds with a glance toward what cannot stay, the flowers of mid-spring, the moment when both daffodil and iris are open in the garden, the moment of blooming and fading, the halfway point that is constantly moving. The poem ends with a glance back at what silence "is":

> At the bottom of the silence it is she
> Who speaks of an eternal Now to me. (16)

The poet's Now is the counterpoint to silence, the other voice in a dialectic of poetics that Sarton uses to create her "halfway."

Such an aesthetic has an "implicit materialism," but this kind of materialism, of Now, one caught up in the fading moment, may be "redeemable" if the "burden of idealism" is removed (Eagleton 196). In lyric poetry, the ideal is usually a conceptual utopia where the human condition is somehow fixed, or where the individual can go to gain enough knowledge to survive or even overcome earthbound situations: certain Romantic lyrics, like some of the *Lyrical Ballads,* or perhaps longer Romantic poems, like Shelley's "Mont Blanc" come to mind. Sarton's evocation of silence works against this; the material of Now is mediated by the desire for silence. A convincing critique of aesthetic materialism requires "a revolution in thought which takes its starting-point from the body itself, rather than from a reason which struggles to make room for it" (Eagleton 196–97). Sarton's mediated materialism is a politically viable "halfway" located in the body of the poet.

This mediation, the political viability of the lyric poem in the postmodern world, is most clearly visible in *Halfway to Silence.* For example, the poem "At the Black Rock" has two wonderful final stanzas—this is the last:

> Can I do it? Can you?
> It means yielding all.
> It means going naked
> No refuge but rue,
> Admitting stark need—
> Eden after the fall. (*HS* 37)

The poem ends with a necessary tension, the poet preparing, like Kinnell's speaker in *The Book of Nightmares,* to expose herself to the elemental to achieve truth, to risk death in the hopes of ending halfway. What the poet desires to "do" is to,

> . . . go to the rock
> Where the beasts hide
> And kneeling there, pray
> For some heart-cracking shock
> To set us both free
> From anger and pride. (*HS* 37)

This, the third stanza of the poem, is almost too much; it gets too close to claiming an objective answer and is only redeemed by the final stanza. Indeed, the poem would be stronger without the overt definition of "anger" and "pride," which stanzas one and two have already evoked. The poem goes beyond halfway and achieves not silence, but hyperbole. Elsewhere in the book, the tension between aggressive emotions and a loving, generous approach to life and art works well for the poet, and leads to the politics of "halfway." In "Mal du Départ," Sarton writes of the moment of absence after the departure of a companion.

> Another day a letter
> Might tell you I am better,
> The invalid has taken
> Some food, is less forlorn and shaken.

> But for today it's true
> That I can hardly draw
> A solitary breath
> that does not hurt me like a little death. (*HS* 28)

The purposeful ambiguity of the final line leaves us in the tension. The possibility of "better" is left open, but not fulfilled; the "little death" hurts, but its implications are hardly fatal.

In looking at the title poem, "Halfway to Silence," "halfway" is, in a sense, *entropy*—"Is there a choice?" means there is *every* choice— there is more to the action of choosing here than to what is being chosen.

> I was halfway to silence
> Halfway to land's end
> When I heard your voice.

> Shall I take you with me?
> Shall we go together
> All the way to silence,
> All the way to land's end?

> Is there a choice? (*HS* 5)

The answer to the last line's question doesn't present itself as a foregone conclusion. The asking of the question is the movement itself of the lyric. Some questions are intentionally omitted, but are an absent cause that drives the poem forward: Can we get to silence? Why do we desire silence? This poem negotiates between an individualism (it's certainly easier to get to silence without the *other* voice) and an inclusive humanitarianism that can stop along the way, perhaps change the route, allow for the unforeseen, perhaps not make it to silence at all, for absolute silence *is* death. Sarton's use of "silence" is revolutionary, as Julia Kristeva defines the term in *Revolution and Poetic Language* (1984): "The text is a practice that could be compared to political revolution: the one brings about in the subject what the other introduces into society" (17). The subject speaking of "silence" here in Sarton's poetry is attempting to create a viable political space, one where her voice is valid, where it won't go unheard or be purposefully ignored, where it will be completely understood.

Silence can work as desired political space for the poetic imagination to free itself of material constraint. Silence is real to the desire of the poet, but not an objective truth, not a final destination for the lyric; silence becomes an imaged end that works as Kristeva's "*chora,* a nonexpressive totality formed by the drives and their stases in a motility that is as full of movement as it is regulated" (25).

Sarton's *choratic* silence is regulated by the constant movement of the lyric poet toward the material world—to stop, see, taste, touch— the very desires that won't allow the descent into silence. This creates a dialectic of political safety for the postmodern lyric poet and parallels Eagleton's description of the failures of the avant-garde: "Truth, morality and beauty are too important to be handed contemptuously over to the political enemy" (372). By retaining elements of the lyric, the postmodern poet can keep the end of postmodernism, silence at its most desirable and deadly, as *chora,* with the poet living and writing at the halfway.

In "Halfway to Silence," the poet, "halfway to land's end," is drawn by another voice from the material world. The poem moves constantly toward and away from the *chora.* Similarly, in "Two Songs," from the *Halfway to Silence* collection, the silence exists and is imaged as a place invented by the hand of the poet as a fertile place in an otherwise dry country:

Give me a love
That has never been,
Deeper than thought.
Bring earth alive,
The desert green
After long drought.

In the flesh, leaf,
In the bones, root,
The gardener's hand
Untangles grief,
Invents a land. (*HS* 18)

The poet wants to touch the totality beyond her own thought, to find a land that expresses all that this "desert . . . / After long drought" cannot. Here the *chora* is given form, a landscape, a "topology" according to Kristeva, who goes on to say that though the poet can "lend it [the *chora*] a topology, . . . one can never give it axiomatic form" (26). In this poem, the *choratic* silence takes on a form but does not become self-evident; the desire for the *chora* creates its temporary form.

So in the most interesting of Sarton's late poems, we see a revolutionary struggle of the subject toward a totality, roughly akin to Kristeva's *chora*, that we can also regard as a revolutionary struggle of the aesthetic judgment of the poet to negotiate some sort of inhabitable middle ground between "understanding" and "chaos."

All of this works toward the political end of finding in this middle ground, this "halfway," a safe place for the lyric poet to survive in an environment distinctly not given to lyricism. The use of mini-narratives works as a strategy for survival in *Halfway to Silence;* narrative can create a "local place" for political freedom, where the individual can return to a world that isn't "compartmentalized" (Jameson 40). Sarton's striving toward silence works as a kind of narrative in lyric poetry to create a mediated world where the poet can speak in relative safety.

The poem from *Halfway to Silence* that most clearly works out this lyric mediation is the longest, "Winter Notebook." In it, Sarton hints at a meaning that she doesn't quite let us in on. She breaks the poem into brief lyric moments that work together as a narrative of poetic freedom. This poem fights with form; it fights with the idea of meaning something by its progression to silence; it finds joy in the solitude of winter and regrets the coming of community.

The poem begins at low tide, set on the Maine shore, with a three-line reading of the motion of the sea: "The surge and slur / Over rocky shingle." Other items in our sight are a "blurred gray sky" and a field that "shines white." This is the landscape of silence, its topology in *this* poem, the visual manifestation of what the poet wants. Sarton introduces her speaker in the second section of the poem:

> I am not available
> At the moment
> Except to myself.
>
> Downstairs the plumber
> Is emptying the big tank,
> Water-logged.
> The pump pumped on and on
> And might have worn out.
>
> So many lives pour into this house,
> Sometimes I get too full;
> The pump wears out.
>
> So now I am emptying the tank.
> It is not an illness
> That keeps me from writing.
> I am simply staying alive
> As one does
> At times by taking in,
> At times by shutting out. (*HS* 57)

The subject, the poet, is not particularly ungrateful toward community, but makes a necessary move toward a totality of solitude, the balance of the last two lines—taking in and shutting out.

The poem continues without a distinct narrative structure or controlling metaphor save the winter solitude itself, the *chora* the poet leans toward, but is pulled back from, again by the flowers, which in their immediacy must be tended to and in turn give back the material thrill of green life:

> After breakfast
> I tend to all their needs,
> These extravagant joys,
> Become a little drunk on green
> And the smell of earth. (*HS* 58)

This is aesthetic taste mitigated, redeemed even, by the chill and "shiver" of the winter air. The last two lines of this fourth section portray life in the political halfway of the poet: "We have lived through another / Bitter cold night" (*HS* 58).

The poem progresses into the day, and illustrates the mysteries of natural life despite the winter weather. Pheasant, ornamental cherry, cedar waxwings are all lyric moments against the bleak landscape, "the waste of dirty snow." But the dreary winter topography isn't a villain here—it becomes a desirable backdrop for the moments of material life, a necessary designation of silence for the poet's imagination.

The final stanza, the eighth, returns to the poet's vision:

> The dark islands
> Float on a silvery sea.
> I see them like a mirage
> Through the branches of the great oak.
> After the leaves come out
> They will be gone—
> These winter joys
>
> And snow coming tonight. (*HS* 59–60)

This poem represents a tension within the book—speaking about silence is strange, wonderful, and disturbing. The brief lyrics move us into a desire for silence, too, thus allowing us to at least partially answer the questions of the opening poem. Yes, there is a choice about silence. Both Sarton and her readers are making it here. Silence *is* desirable. But it is only successful in negation, when vocalized, when struggled with—*silence spoken* becomes our desired political end.

Works Cited

Eagleton, Terry. *The Ideology of the Aesthetic*. Cambridge, Mass.: Basil Blackwell, 1990.

Jameson, Fredric. *The Political Unconscious: Narrative as a Socially Symbolic Act*. Ithaca, N.Y.: Cornell UP, 1981.

Kristeva, Julia. *Revolution and Poetic Language*. New York: Columbia UP, 1984.

Sarton, May. *Halfway to Silence*. New York: Norton, 1980.

———. *The Silence Now*. New York: Norton, 1988.

Fig. 5. Stone sculpture of "the phoenix" in May Sarton's garden, York, Maine, 1991. Photograph by Susan Sherman. Used with permission.

Fig. 6. May Sarton with tulips in winter, sun room of her home in York, Maine. Photograph by Susan Sherman. Used with permission.

The Light That Stayed On:
Imagery of Silence and Light in
Halfway to Silence, Letters from Maine,
and The Silence Now

KENNETH G. POBO

E. M. Forster's famous epigraph at the beginning of *Howard's End*—
"only connect"—could serve as an epigraph to many of May Sarton's
poems. Sarton is eighty and has published three books of poetry during the last twelve years. These three books strongly connect to her
earlier works; however, they also show a poet continuously challenged
by the discipline of verse itself, by the way the line shapes rhythm, by
sound (as the Maine shoreline is revised by the endless push of the
cold water), and by imagery.

The dance of silence and light comes to mind when we consider
Sarton's later work. Silence and light are closely related throughout
the body of her work, and in the later poems they are inextricably
linked. Although both are difficult terms, abstractions, Sarton does
not leave them to dampen in such a cerebral place. Instead, she gives
them color, winds them up, and invites us to smell them as we would
the shirley poppies in her poem of the same name.

Light has always been a crucial image for poets. Revelation is light's
"goal," what light must do. Nevertheless, even in the light most of us
miss much. We see selectively. Sarton's poems give the focus that we
would probably miss. The "small" detail of a Christmas tree observed
by one human being suddenly becomes an intersection of silence and
light in "Christmas Light." Here the speaker is alone with the Christmas tree. In the silence that tree and speaker share, the speaker says
she is "reborn again." As she enjoys the solitude ("When everyone

had gone"), she finds that "the garland of pure light / Stayed on, stayed on" (*SN* 27). The purity of the light sharpens the revelatory nature of the moment. That the light stays on suggests its eternal quality, something from which the speaker will continue to take hope.

Moreover, that this light "stayed on" is an evocative image, a small sun in her home, a life-sustaining force. Sarton writes often in both her poems and in her journals about her garden; in the garden the colors of silence blend with those of light. A gardener knows how important it is to make good use of the light—the time for work, the latch against chaos. Because the light does not always stay on, we feel all the more illuminated by it when it does. We revel in it. Those isolated moments when the light remains with us become defining. They are roadmaps into those deepest and most inaccessible parts of ourselves. This poem ends not only with the sense of revelation but also with a triumphant gratitude so much in evidence in Sarton's poetry. In "Winter Night" from *As Does New Hampshire*, Sarton's poetry collection from 1967, even night has a "radiance" (18). Darkness must bring forth light.

Light not only reveals; it highlights the shades and subtleties in nature, in our lives. In "Autumn Sonnets," the speaker questions why we call autumn "fall," a season of "elevation" through its changes and an "ascent / From dawn to dawn." The poem celebrates this paradox; fall doesn't fall so much as we rise up to meet it. She sees "skies more huge and luminous at dusk, / Till we are strained by light and still more light" (*HS* 49). The paradox of one twenty-four-hour period that includes both a night and a day matches the paradox of a single year in which opposites connect and require each other—winter needs summer, fall, spring.

We live ("strain") within those opposites. We are attracted to them, and they help us to discover our own life rhythms and patterns. In the second sonnet in "Autumn Sonnets" the earth itself reveals paradox. The speaker notices that her "gentle earth is barren now, or nearly" (*HS* 49). Earth itself is "strained" in the light of its own changes. What is "gentle" in the garden—the tender shoot, the seed nudging the soil apart so it can enter the light—fades, as daylight fades, as seasons fade.

Autumn's colors become barren ground. We know, as the speaker

knows in autumn, that "the worst is still to come." To endure the
sharpening days of late autumn and the harsh settling in of winter, we
must learn how to "Withstand, endure." The speaker says she contains "love as if it were a warhead." Love is anything but taciturn here.
As earth hugs the underground warhead, enclosing it from the elements and winter's bite, so the speaker must have love in the deepest
part of herself, far from the cold that threatens to stretch and deepen
in the coming months. The speaker compares herself with a wild fox
that "burns his brightness for mere food or bed." Only this brightness can save the fox in the fierce winter.

The warhead image startles and awakens. One remembers George
Herbert, a favorite poet of Sarton's, or Donne—in Sarton's work we
often find the kind of illumination resulting from the juxtaposition of
dissimilar images. In this odd fusing together, we are once again
"strained by light," by paradox itself. "Strain" also suggests a pouring
of a liquid substance through some kind of filter; we are the liquid
and we are refined by the light.

Light heightens our awareness of the landscape and of those things
nearest to us which we often ignore. Light can be, for a poet or any
creative artist, a strong connection with the muse. Sarton has often
referred in her journals to her necessity of having a muse. She claims
that for her the muse is always a woman. "I am glad of her / As one is
glad of the light" sings the poet (*HS* 61). This gladness, this gratitude, is a light Sarton gives her reader as she celebrates it herself—the
gift is also the giver. To be "glad" of this kind of light is to be glad of
creativity, of words that demand a place on the page.

Sarton consistently uses diction that reflects a grounding in Christian metaphor. Her "rejoice" and her phrasing, which often sounds
biblical, are central to her poetic expression—not as the missionary
but as the humanist, the observer and enjoyer of the light. Still, if
light is not an explicitly "Christian" image, it is nonetheless a humanistic image. The New Testament suggests that "the Word" and light
are synonymous in the figure of Christ. In Sarton's poetry, light and
word meet in song. Rhythm becomes revelation.

Sarton's claims that she is not a Christian are not inconsistent with
her world view, which emerges from her poetry and journals. She
wants the widest possible scope, the lens through which the light gets

the widest exposure. Yet she is hardly antireligious; she celebrates the paths on which a religion, as opposed to dogma, can take any individual. Religion is not the "bad guy" as much as it is a path many travel without a knowledge of the rocks. Stumbling is the human way.

Sarton is more than aware of those who would interpret her vision as flawed, as unfortunate, as if to suggest that if she were only straight, how great she'd be. Yet as the work of her last three poetry books suggests, she is able to affect both gay and straight readers. She gives no apologies for her life, for her spirit. These volumes suggest a poet who is at ease with her history. The muse is not merely a sexual light; the muse is female, is nurture, is the intersection where silence and light meet in the imagination, expanding the poems beyond Nelson or York and into those distant places where many live—she becomes as much a resident of Butte, Montana, as she is a resident of Maine. The poet is a resident of a particular location, but she also resides in the imagination, the birthplace of her poems. The poet journeys out alone, in silence, into unmapped places. Silence is the poet's natural condition; what breaks this silence can lead to the creation of a new poem. In "The Geese" the speaker runs to see some geese after hearing them honk; the geese break the silence.

Although the nurturing muse sheds light on the poet, connecting the poet with the necessary imagery to create this female center is difficult and can unexpectedly leave the poet—as light can fade.

In *At Seventy,* Sarton expresses gratitude for a particular muse— and her awareness of how quickly that muse can remove itself. The muse is a form of light; the poet writes not so much under its spell as under its illumination, as the moon illumines our path in the dark. The muse is a giver—and poetry for Sarton is a great gift—and the poet must receive the gift and respond in gratitude. This gratitude is the poem itself, which restores order. In "Letters from Maine," the speaker considers "The long silence of winter when I shall / Make poems out of nothing, out of loss" (*LM* 18). During the act of writing, the poet meets the muse; the exchange of gifts becomes complete. And that gift, ultimately, is given to the readers.

This kind of gift can often occur only through some sort of poise between tensions. Sarton says:

. . . I jotted down some of the tensions I experience in the process of writing a poem, tensions which discharge a load of experience in a most beneficent and exciting way when the piece of weaving on the loom turns out to be a real poem:

1) The tension between past and present,
2) between idea and image,
3) between music and meaning,
4) between particular and universal,
5) between creator and critic,
6) between silence and words. (*WW* 7)

The word "between" acts to create a litany, a credo that suggests where the muse appears—between poet and page, between writer and reader. Her last "between" is that of silence and words. This, too, is a paradox. As silence takes shape, words are born; as words are born, they lead us back into silence. The silence changes and it is a place we seek more so than a destination. Sarton's book titles suggest as much: *Halfway to Silence, The Silence Now.*

This silence is light and solitude, for only in solitude can we ready ourselves for what the light may reveal. Reading itself is usually a solitary experience. In her poem "On Sark" the speaker says in stanza 3: "Islands are for people who are islands, / Who have always detached from the main / For a purpose, or because they crave / The free within the framed as poets do" (*HS* 55). Poets crave "the free within"—perhaps readers, or at least those readers who are somehow "detached from the main," crave this same freedom. As the poem gives the a frame, (a sonnet, rhymed quatrains) the poet has the necessary structure in which she can fully explore her own imagination, to find connections between images.

In "For Monet" the opening line is "Poets, too, are crazed by light" (*LM* 37). Like Monet, who investigated crannies of light and shade, the poet tries "To hold the fleeting still / In a design—." The poem's conclusion suggests that Monet "spent a lifetime / Trying to undazzle the light / And pin it down." Poets do the same—but they have no pins, only words, and words are great escape artists. "Trying" is a key word here; there are no guarantees that, even with his enormous gifts, Monet really could "undazzle the light / And pin it down."

This "trying" is the poet's quest too—the light is larger than anyone's command of language. Language shakes and cracks along the edges, the way light fades at dusk on a water lily. However, in the trying comes the creation, the joining of creativity and vision.

While light is a central element of Sarton's later work, an image that persists from her earliest poems, loss of light is also a compelling metaphor. One of the most poignant poems in *Letters from Maine* is "Mourning to Do." In this expressive and personal poem, the speaker mourns over the loss of "Judy" who was "For years lost in the darkness of her mind." The speaker says that she herself "cannot fathom that darkness" (*LM* 48). Light, then, has limitations; some places are so dark and sturdy that no light can break through—we cannot "fathom" such a darkness. The speaker says she is "Alone here in the lovely silent house." The silence, which is usually lovely, now becomes a place of grief: "Judy is gone forever" (*LM* 48).

Just as the muse does not always stay, although the poem given by the muse remains, light, too, can be ephemeral. "Mourning to Do" ends with an image of light, perhaps suggesting that light can somehow ultimately survive even the most intense darkness: "Happy the dawn of memory and the sunrise." The cycles of night and day mirror our own here—the *night* of mourning is followed by dawn. Memory becomes a place of light, a place where the mourner can go for healing.

Memory is also often a painful place; to become healed often requires pain, a facing of the loss. In *The Silence Now* Sarton's poem "The Muse as Donkey" claims that "Illumination costs" (68).

The poem echoes one of her most charming tales, *The Poet and the Donkey,* from 1969. In that tale, an older poet named Andy recovers his muse through taking care of a donkey (Whiffenpoof) who usually resides on a local farm. Andy finds his own stubbornness (and tenacity) in the donkey's. Andy's last name is *Light*foot. At the end the narrator calls him "a boy"—the donkey has restored the youthful wonder necessary for creation, has renewed "the old man," who comes to understand why this donkey is necessary for his own spiritual journey and his writing. He thinks to himself, "who wants to live outside pain, outside joy?" (*P&D* 126). In "The Muse as Donkey," the speaker says she has "grown a third ear / Listening / Keeping the silence alive" (*SN* 68).

That connection between pain and joy is also evident in "The Muse as Donkey." The poem's resolution comes when the speaker says, "Unable to heal myself, / I shall spend the summer / Healing the donkey. . . ." Later the speaker says that "Mystery itself is fulfillment" (*SN* 70). Perhaps light can only brighten after we spend time in the darkness, especially that of mourning. Then the muse can come to the poet as both comfort and spur. Light needs darkness as poet needs donkey: "We are fellow sufferers / And we do not despair" (*SN* 70). The donkey suffers from frail ankles; the poet from a loss of creative spark.

The last poem in *The Silence Now*, "The Phoenix Again," is central to all of Sarton's poetry. Here the paradoxes she has worked with throughout her career are not resolved or explained; rather, they are put in the perspective of the bird that will not die, the bird that will not decline into darkness only. Fire (light) brings the bird back. The phoenix itself is an image we can trust; she will "take flight / Over the seas of grief" (*SN* 76).

This rebirthing process, this refining and re-seeing of light, is both the struggle of the individual and that of the poet. The muse must leave the poet in darkness to allow the poems a chance to be born. The poet, like the phoenix, is looking for that which does not die, something stronger than the bone cage in which we live. This transcends aging and the inevitable confrontation with death: "For neither old nor young / The phoenix does not die" (*SN* 76).

The poem survives her creator, flies to a place where the muse may be surprised by what it reveals in a light that is both words and wordless. The reader must bring a silence to the poem to see the bird resurrect. The bird rises because it can sing "her thrilling song." *We* are the phoenix and we are reborn in the experience of reading the poem; our lives gather clarity, light, sound, as we contemplate (preferably in solitude as Sarton's journals and poems suggest) the bird that *must* fall in order to survive.

These three books of May Sarton's later years are phoenixes; each shows a spirit that has gone down into darkness, so that it can rise again and fly into light. As the poet, once again, rediscovers her wings, we soar with her. We "only connect" as light keeps a step ahead of darkness. We walk in its trail; an iridescent shirley poppy gives us courage. Petals require of us our eyes. The silent flower opens as "an explosion, / And so silent!" (*SN* 18).

Of these three books, *The Silence Now* (the latest) is in some ways the one most connected with Sarton's past work. The third section is called "Earlier Poems," and the style is often more formal than the rest of the collection. Still, these poems prepare us for our climb with the phoenix. In "Over Troubled Water" the speaker says that "The poet dances on a rope held taut / Between reality and his desire" (*SN* 56). Reality and desire resemble each other as the dance continues.

In the following poem, "The Muse as Donkey," the poet examines those sources from which inspiration, suddenly and often inexplicably, appears. There too "reality" is no more or no less a darkness than desire. The poet "wants" to create; the reality is a painful aridity that, thankfully, a donkey ends.

About writing poetry, Sarton says,

> Poetry is a dangerous profession because it demands a very delicate and exhausting balance between conflict and resolution, between feeling and thought, between becoming and being, between the ultra-personal and the universal—and these balances are shifting all the time (*WW* 69).

Danger. This is what the phoenix learns—and what the bird can help us to survive. "The balances" Sarton suggests are those of day and night, light and darkness—they shift all the time, as do our feelings and fears. Moreover, "the balances" between silence and sound keep shifting. Silence prepares us for the spoken word. In this balancing act we live, and here poetry, especially Sarton's, says "I'm here!"

Works Cited

Sarton, May. *As Does New Hampshire*. Dublin, N.H.: William L. Bauhan, 1967.

———. *At Seventy*. New York: Norton, 1984.

———. *Halfway to Silence*. New York: Norton, 1980.

———. *Letters from Maine*. New York: Norton, 1984.

———. *The Poet and the Donkey*. 1969. New York: Norton, 1984.

———. *The Silence Now*. 1988. New York: Norton, 1990.

———. *Writings on Writing*. Orono, Maine: Puckerbrush Press, 1980.

The Music of Happiness: Form and Freedom in the Poetry of May Sarton

SUSAN FACKNITZ

The movement of the poem into voice in the work of May Sarton is a movement into loss, a movement toward inhabiting that solitude, that space that places us outside of the temporal world, that offers us a vantage point from which we can view our lives. The moment out of which her poems sing, woven of solitude and sensibility, is a moment of heightened awareness that finds expression in the tension "between music and meaning, between silence and words" (*WW 7*). It is a moment of yearning toward the spirit within the conflicting emotions of pain, anger, loss, and exaltation. As *Journal of a Solitude* and her poems (especially those in *Halfway to Silence, Letters from Maine,* and *The Silence Now*) show, the sense of form and music that dominates her work lies outside of the mainstream of twentieth-century formalism in America. Instead of a desire to exploit the complexities of form, Sarton seeks to lend a spiritual music to the struggles with the mundane and temporal through which we all live in her carefully woven music. She seeks, not an architecture for her vision, but a voice for her song.

Sarton's music is not esoteric, and her poetry has suffered much in its critical reception on this account. She writes in *Journal of a Solitude,* "The moderate human voice, what might be called 'the human milieu'—this is supremely unfashionable and appears even to be irrelevant" (68). Her sense of craft is not, as it has been for so many of the canonical poets of our century, a sense of building difficulty into the poem. Instead, the music of her work seeks to express the moment of joining, the act of linking ourselves to time, for time is the framework in which music happens. In this the music of her work is generous. The poet is "The acrobat of feeling trained by thought" (*SN* 56), but it is the feeling that dominates and the thought is at its service. As she says in *Journal of a Solitude,* "I have written novels to find out what I *thought* about something and poems to find out what I *felt* about something" (41).

The challenges facing the poet of feeling are many. First, she must find a way of expression that is not self-indulgent. Second, the poet must find a release or catalyst for the voice which will allow an authentic poetry to take place. Finally the poet must do the work of creation in making the poem real, not facile. All of this work takes place to some degree in the music of her poems, for Sarton does not celebrate the poet as one whose griefs are beyond the capacity of others, but as one who does the work of poetry, which is the finding of a voice, a music in which these griefs can be both sung as themselves and transformed into acts of love.

In her best poems, the catalyst for Sarton's voice is her contemplation of the issues in our lives, perhaps most clearly of the possibilities of living with loss. She asks us in "Letters from Maine" to "meet me in the silence, if you can, / . . . when I shall / Make poems out of nothing, out of loss" (18). At times she celebrates those who are unaware of loss or those who have the courage to persevere in the face of it. Her love for plants and animals is, to some degree rooted not only in their transience ("It is the transient that touches me, old") but also "because they live / In the present and cannot drag us down / Into those caverns of memory full of loss." These creatures live in an "eternal Now" (*SN* 16), outside of history and human life. But the poet is human and must assert this humanity in that place of the awareness of loss where "The poet lives on peril and to give / Joy from his pain, a curious kind of love" (56).

In "Two Birthdays," Sarton offers us two models of dealing with the losses made inevitable by long life, and in this finds a way of avoiding self-indulgence. In this celebration of others, in her gesture of looking outwards, she is able to find ways of learning and celebrating "the spirit springing fresh and ever agile / To balance what is lost and what will keep" (24). In this balance, in these exemplary characters, Sarton finds a way of expressing the central concerns of her work, with loss and diminution, which offers a hope less provisional than that often expressed in the journal. For it is in the making of the poem, finding the expressive shape of experience in the form of the poem, that redemption or recompense is found, "For courage keeps and love is still newborn" (24). As Robert Hass writes in "One Body: Some Notes on Form," "It seems to me . . . we make our forms because there is no absolute continuity, because the first assurances are broken. The mind in the act of recovery creates" (63). Or as May Sarton herself writes, "The prayer is in the looking; the answer to the prayer is the poem" (*WW* 42). In her journal she hopes "the fact that a middle-aged single woman, without any vestige of family left, lives in this house in a silent village and is responsible only to her own soul means something" (*JS* 40). The way that this meaning is made is through the poems, which are "whittled and willed" (*SN* 74) out of this context.

Another stay that Sarton finds against self-indulgence in the poems is her sense of form. As she writes in "Revision as Creation,"

> The form itself creates intensity. You can't wallow—you have to *control.* I have said that form is earned. What I mean by that is that the music of a poem does not show itself unless one's whole being is at a high pitch of concentration. . . . The trouble with free verse is that very rarely . . . does the intensity seem great enough; the danger is the diffuse, self-indulgent, not closely enough examined content. (*WW* 62)

The creation of a form becomes a way of looking, an ordering of perceptions. As Robert Hass writes, "The form of a poem exists in the relation between its seeing and its music" (65).

In her awareness of silence as a source of her work, we can begin to sense the importance of the elements in her poetry which might be called musical. This emphasis on silence, in fact, calls attention to the analogies with music that Sarton so often uses when discussing poetry, for silence is not a formal element of poetry. It cannot exist on the page. It is, however, an essential element of music in performance, and it is the field out of which all music rises. It also creates the context out of which Sarton believes poems are written, and which the poems oppose. The poems represent moments rescued from the annihilation that time imposes, for the poem "rises / In an unbroken

wave and topples to silence" (*LM* 26). And in the celebration the
poem offers, Sarton finds "in the music of the poem . . . the greatest
mystery lies" (*WW* 63). There is a strong sense in Sarton's work of
celebrating the human, and this is evident in the music of her poems.
In her strongest poems she presents our struggles to deal with or open
ourselves to mystery, in music that is measured, formal, and humane.

The attempt to create, to hear this music, dominates her methods
of composition. Such listening creates the need for solitude and the
silence that accompanies it, broken most often by the music she plays
as she awaits the "musical stir," the "spell" (*WW* 44) that brings the
poem into voice. This sense of music dominates her attitude toward
form as well as toward the composition of each poem: "Routine is
not a prison, but the way into freedom from time. The apparently
measured time has immeasurable space within it, and in this it re-
sembles music" (*PD* 56). This space within the music of the poem,
this place that both the reader and writer can inhabit, becomes a focus of her poetry.

In "The Work of Happiness" (*CP* 66), we can hear and experience
her music and come to understand the role it plays in her poetry. In
the poem, Sarton celebrates the fact that happiness is a made thing,
not granted but constructed, and therefore available to us all in some
measure. She writes often of her own life in this way, not only in terms
of happiness, but of "my life waiting for me somewhere, asking to be
created" (*JS* 32), and she celebrates poetry as "the soul-making tool"
(*JS* 36). The formal elements of poetry are traces, too, of the poem's
having been made, and they communicate their power by their du-
plicity, alternately drawing attention to their effort and fading into
the natural voice of the poem. But the music of the poem is its "inward work," which lifts the poem from struggle into blessing.

The idea of happiness presented in the poem is characteristic of
Sarton's work in that it is hard won and it resides in deep pleasure
rather than in flashes of excess. Her poems end in the triumph of joy
and blessing rather than in personal ecstasy, and the structures of her
poems reflect this. The use of alliteration and assonance in "The Work
of Happiness" is typical of the formal values in her work. In the opening lines she sets up a rhythm and sense of sound that continue through-

out the poem. The rhythms are slow, steady, and quiet, and the sounds reinforce the pleasure and beauty the poem celebrates through their long vowels and soft consonants. Throughout the poem, these sounds will appear in different combinations, moving from "woven" to "growth" to "growing," for example, with "how" and its off-rhyme with "house" interspersed. The sounds are woven into the poem, offering connections and comforts through the formal elements of the poem which complement the content.

The poem begins, "I thought of happiness, how it is woven / Out of the silence in the empty house each day" (CP 66), introducing a sense of happiness as created and as a stay against the empty house. The music is solemn at this point, but pleasurable, the long vowels comforting with a sense of stately beauty. The second line emphasizes the provisional nature of happiness, however, and the fact that such construction is a daily task. The poem then goes on to define by negation and introduce the simile of the tree. In the simile, Sarton emphasizes the unself-conscious music she seeks in her work, saying, "No one has heard the root go deeper in the dark, / But the tree is lifted by this inward work." The effect of the formal elements of a poem should be a natural complement to the content. The rhythms here are unaffected, and the assonance and alliteration recall the opening metaphor of weaving.

The second stanza of the poem ends, "The growing tree is green and musical," allying music and growth and vitality. Such harmony is central to the growth of the poem, "For what is happiness but growth in peace, / The timeless sense of time." Once again we are caught in the eternity of music, and the eternity the music resists. For while the spaces within the music may be eternal, music itself is entirely temporal; it takes place within the passage of time, and it is this tension that the music of a poem must express and surmount. The union of the silence and the sounds that reveal it creates music.

In the final stanza of the poem, Sarton again emphasizes the emotional over the rational in the creation of poetry. She points out that

> No one has heard thought or listened to a mind,
> But where people have lived in inwardness
> The air is charged with blessing and does bless. (CP 66)

204 🐾 Susan Facknitz

The source of the poem is life, and the movement of the poem is from the mind through the life into the spirit. The act of making the poem makes happiness, but also makes a soul. Here the weaving of sound is less pronounced, and the language is direct and relaxed. The content may be revelatory, but the language emphasizes that such revelations are made rather then given, and are, finally, lived. The artifice of the poem becomes subdued and focuses on the world around the speaker in the last line, emphasizing its contrast with the opening line, "I thought of happiness. . . ." Here, the speaker is unself-conscious, is almost gone, absorbed into the world that surrounds her with blessings, for "Windows look out on mountains and the walls are kind." We may not have (or even wished to have) "heard thought or listened to a mind," but we have all seen and felt and been able to respond. This is the work of happiness, finally. It lies not in complexity or difficulty but in speaking out of the lived life.

Even the formal elements Sarton values in her work appear in the poems because of the ways in which they link us to life rather than the ways they emphasize artifice. While Sarton often writes poems in free verse, she is perhaps best in her skillful use of meter. What she values here is the "free within the framed" (*HS* 55) and the sense of meter as reflecting something real within our bodies and our lives. As Robert Hass writes: "Rhythmic repetition initiates a sense of order. The feeling of magic comes from the way it puts us in touch with the promise of a deep sympathetic power in things: heartbeat, sunrise, summer solstice. This can be hypnotically peaceful; it can also be terrifying, to come so near self abandonment . . ."(116). Sarton knows the terror and indulgence solitude can inspire, but recognizes that formal control may help the poems resist. The making of a poem is an act opposing self abandonment, "For poetry is, I believe, always an act of the spirit" (*WW* 49). In giving shape to the poem, however, Sarton does not value the difficulty or the exacting craft of fixed forms. Instead, she values them as "device[s] for discharging tensions and apprehensions which we might not otherwise have strength to bear, and which as it is, become simply transposable *energy*. So grief itself is transformed into a curious joy" (*WW* 21). The transformation the poem offers must not be a simplification or only a distillation of experience or feeling, for "Somewhere between the minute particular and the essence lies the land of poetry" (*JS* 97). Her models of formal control are the Flemish painters who were able to capture the texture of reality in their art and who were able to "compose the world without ever imposing a rigid schema upon it" (*JS* 111). Instead, the formal elements of their work help the viewer enter the work and find the connections the act of painting was able to reveal.

The importance of connection is apparent in her use of rhyme in her poetry. While she uses off-rhyme and buried rhyme, she also uses end-rhyme and exact rhyme, often in combination. In her work, rhyme becomes, as Robert Penn Warren was fond of saying in conversation, an essential way of making connections, a way of moving toward the truth through the words rather than through thought. While at times the rhyme is too simple, too direct, and undercuts our sense of coming upon something new or newly said, at other times the connections are expressions of fresh perceptions and hit us with a sense of recognition or identification, which means we have entered the poem and come away renewed. As Sarton herself has said, "Rhyme in English is a hard master. The obstacles it raises in the current of our thought slow us down, make us think, and of course also sometimes (there is a saving grace!) bring us the lucky chance that may enrich meaning in unexpected ways" (*WW* 18).

Most often enrichment comes at the ends of poems, where she uses rhyme to create closure. The combination of rhyme and content is often startling, as at the end of "The Cold Night" (*LM* 38), where the speaker stands in the wash of feeling left after the retreat of vision. The poem breaks after fourteen lines and closes with a couplet that entreats us "Listen, listen! The wild foxes bark. / Venus is rising, tranquil, through the dark." In the couplet, she recapitulates the movement of the poem, from the frenzy of the speaker in the throes of vision to the silence that overtakes her. The frenzy, however, is not stilled. Instead, the silence contains it, and we hear the wild foxes barking as we watch the planet ascend. These simultaneous acts are captured in rhymes that emphasize the clamor of the foxes and the surrounding darkness in which their voices are heard. In this, the end of the poem captures the mixed sense of poetry which holds both terror and beauty poised, the geography of "peril" which the poet explores.

In content and form, Sarton's work is concerned most often with recurrence or its absence. Rhyme functions in her work in this way, as well, emphasizing the sense of sounds returning. There is a comfort in the way these words and sounds punctuate the poems, much as there is a deep sense of personal renewal in her experience of spring and the regeneration it offers. Even in a poem like "AIDS" (*SN* 36–37), which confronts a difficult subject, there is an edgy comfort to the rhyme. This formal element helps keep the poem as a whole from seeming self-indulgent. It helps convince us of the formal truth of the connections made in the poem and offers us a voice whose revelations have been given up to language so that they exist on a plane where writer and reader can meet. In a poem thus charged, the formal quality of the rhyme allows a space for the reader to participate and to feel the strain that the poem is about, for the rhyme here seems hard won, as have been the accommodations the content reveals.

In the first stanza of the poem, most of the rhymes are masculine and the lines are rough, lending a kind of awkwardness to the poem as "we are stretched to meet a new dimension." It's as if the poet has not quite found the words for the experience that will lend it grace. The challenge to the value of speech seems evident:

> . . . Intention
> Here can neither move or change
> The raw truth. Death is on the line. (*SN* 36–37)

But when the poet does, after nine lines, find the right word, she drives it home: "Fear. Fear. Fear. Fear." After, this, we spend four lines in the place that such overwhelming emotions and our capitulation to them makes. Here the rhymes are exact and simple. The writing seems pitiful, intentionally so. Such simplicity is "Lonely and sterile." But with a "simple turn of the head," a human gesture of looking, of acknowledgment, we return in the next stanza to the humane world of complexity, and the poetry resumes its profound music. The exact rhymes mix with off-rhyme ("morphine," "discipline"); the lines, while not jagged as in the opening stanzas, contain caesuras and are more often enjambed. They break "across the rhythms of speech," as Frost recommended, and supplant the sterility of self-indulgence with the central music of Sarton's work, the music of communion.

But "Where do we go from here?" as Sarton says earlier in the poem. What follows is dangerous territory, for Sarton continues with a series of straightforward declarative sentences, like "We are forging a new union. We are blest," which could easily degenerate into propaganda or self-righteous or self-congratulatory diatribe. Instead, Sarton marshals the formal elements of the poem to preserve the sense of this as knowledge or belief achieved through experience and held against the onslaught of time: "The word is not fear, the word we live." These are not ringing statements of triumph. Instead they are what we can say now out of loss. She emphasizes the difficulty of this *"strange* tenderness" (emphasis mine) through the caesuras that occur in the majority of the lines: "As we learn it again, as we bring it alive." We cannot build up any momentum toward finality in these statements. Each is provisional and builds upon the others. We accumulate comfort and a kind of surety, but we never arrive at it. This is made clear in the last line, which simply repeats the word *love*. In the typical dramatic poem the final line would simply be the one instance of the word, having arrived at this conclusion, being the point of the poem. Instead, Sarton writes "Love. Love. Love. Love," insisting in this form that each instance of this emotion is distinct and that love is not an eternal thing, but a human quality manifested in individual acts as the rest of the poem demonstrates, something that must not only be emphasized, but also reiterated.

In "AIDS" Sarton counterpoints the effects of free verse with the punctuation that rhyme can offer, to give us a poem on a difficult subject which mirrors the humane difficulty Sarton values in her work. The formal elements of the poem are meant to be expressive; thought remains at the service of feeling. This is the sense of form present in her strongest poems. Sarton's subjects are most often familiar, her language is direct, and her images accessible. The danger for her work comes when all of this matches with a music too closely linked to abstraction and too little joined to the verities of experience. As she says, "We must labor . . . to deepen, and even sometimes roughen, the too facile music that floats about on the surface of consciousness" (*WW* 17). This takes place through her exploration of the tensions that construct and propel experience. The tension, once found, shapes the poem: "A high tension, a delightful inner humming is set up between the apparently innocuous rhyme, the image back of it, and my own response, both conscious and unconscious, to what is going on in my head" (13). This "musical stir'" is a "tension of phrasing asking to be musically resolved" (12) and is the moving principle behind the poem.

But the issue of music, of the manipulation of the elements of sound and form in the poem, is not easy to resolve on any level, for ideas of form and the execution of form, the creation of a music, engages the writer in issues beyond those of the individual poem at hand. For T. S. Eliot, form is the bone the burglar throws to the dog. For Robert Creeley, it is nothing more than an extension of content. For Robert Hass, "rhythm is always revolutionary ground. It is always the place where the organic rises to abolish the mechanical and where energy announces the abolition of tradition" (108). For Sarton, though, form expresses our existence in history, our relationship to our past and to ourselves and our time. It is the ground out of which we rise. "Each new poem is partly propelled by the formal energies of all the poems that have preceded it in the history of literature," she writes in "The School of Babylon" (*WW* 8). And in each poem, "The dynamics of form have to do with our intimate relation with the past" (9).

If this relationship is, at times, too accepting or unquestioning, sometimes offering us poems weighted toward simplicity rather than clarity, more often the poems invigorate the forms, investing them with vitality and voice. She does not value form for its own sake. In "Pruning the Orchard" (*HS* 50) the workers are, like the poet, "Shaping the formless back to symmetry," but

> They do not work for beauty's sake
> But to improve the harvest some next year.
> Each tough lopsided branch they choose to break
> Is broken toward fruit more crisp and rare. (*HS* 50)

She wants forms that are expressive and generative. The writing of poems is deeply personal work, being "open from the inside out," (*JS* 22), and the discovery of form is as much a part of the process of the poem as the delineation of content. She seeks "The blessings of pure form that opens space / And makes us stop and look in sudden peace" (*HS* 46). These blessings are mixed, however, for her poems must also make "space for that intense, hungry face at the window, starved cat, starved person. It is making space to *be there*." (*JS* 57). Through her poems that capture the "perilous equilibrium between music and speech" (*WW* 18), Sarton makes a place for us to be there as well. Through her use of rhythms in the poems that capture speech or that provide a more measured, formal music, Sarton calls us awake. She draws on rhythmic resources that capture and hold our attention and that involve us in the poem, body and spirit.

In the act of crafting the poem, the poet defines her ambiguous relationship with time:

> What is released by concentrated hours,
> The long dressage to catch a chancy rhyme,
> And craft that may sometimes harness strange powers,
> Those airs above the ground that banish time. (*HS* 13)

Yet the relationship between time and rhythm parallels that between silence and music. Rhythm can only be experienced in time. To banish time is to banish rhythm, and to banish silence is to silence music. The horse may be suspended for an instant, but it is the knowledge that true permanence is impossible, in this movement or any other, that makes the feat majestic.

The poem itself cannot banish time or silence. But "It's possible that what humans want from works of art are shapes of time in which the sense of coming to an end is also, as it very seldom is in the rest of life, a resolution" (Hass 120). Through its form and content the poem can provide this. What is resolved in Sarton's best work is complex and emotional. Her poems capture the intensity of experience through a process she herself prescribes: "Work, love, be silent. / Speak" (*SN* 26). While this is the prescription for the poet, while it defines the sources of poetry for Sarton, she offers another avenue for those seeking, not to make art out of their lives, but simply trying to live with loss. In this, we see that she is "a practical person" (65) and that her poems are aimed at our hearts and lives. In these three lines we see her control of the formal elements of the poem in her creation of an expressive music. The lines are broken by caesuras at first, the sounds uncoordinated and conversational. But the last line, the moment of transparency in the poem when we see, not the poet, but ourselves doing as the poem suggests, becomes a presence rhythmically smooth and musically rich. It provides a "shape of time" and a "resolution." It asks us to come out of ourselves as May Sarton's best poems always do, and offers us a music in which we can meet the world.

> So deal with absence. Survivors learn it.
> Eat grass. I know my way on barren islands.
> Lie down on rock at night and read the stars. (*LM* 27)

Works Cited

Hass, Robert. *Twentieth Century Pleasures.* New York: Ecco Press, 1984.

Sarton , May. *Collected Poems (1930–1973).* New York: Norton, 1974.

———. *Halfway to Silence.* Norton, 1980.

———. *Journal of a Solitude.* Norton, 1973.

———. *Letters from Maine: New Poems.* Norton, 1984.

———. *Plant Dreaming Deep.* Norton, 1968.

———. *The Silence Now.* Norton, 1988.

———. *Writings on Writing.* Orono, Maine: Puckerbrush Press, 1980.

May Sarton and the Muse: Lovers, Water, and Leaves

BETH CASEY

The mysterious muse, the source of poetic vision, has been the central focus of May Sarton's poetry and poetics for over sixty years. For Sarton, the muse opens the poetic dialogue with the self, confirming and releasing that poetic identity necessary to the creative act and to participation in the experience we have called the sublime. In two of her fables, *Joanna and Ulysses* and *The Poet and the Donkey,* she depicts the essential relationship of the muse to nature and to human care and compassion; and in her novel *Mrs. Stevens Hears the Mermaids Singing,* she explores the psychological origins of poetic inspiration in human love. The unique achievement of Sarton's poetry, as well as her successful revisions of the American tradition of the sublime, are best revealed through an understanding of her mythologizing of the muse and her representation of this crucial life experience over time. The muse allows her to mediate what she has termed "the daily conflict between art and life" (*AS* 132). As she writes in *Recovering,* "I reach and have reached the timeless movement, the pure suspension within time, only through love" (*RE* 188).

The muse, for Sarton, is always a woman. "The seizure," she writes, "when it came, was so commanding I could not doubt its value. I could not believe I was wrong or aberrant. It gave me courage to be myself and not to allow the ethos of the times to blur my vision" (*AS* 91). The fact confirmed her belief that women must understand themselves "as central, not peripheral" before anything real can happen (*TH* 224). William Drake, in his study of modern women poets writing between 1915 and 1945—a revolutionary period that includes

Teasdale, Wylie, Moore, Bogan, and St. Vincent Millay—declares Sarton's work "a kind of watershed in women's poetry in its deliberate avoidance of indirection and artistic gameplaying in order to overcome the incapacitating effects of gender delimitation" (261). Sarton was the first of the modern women poets to acknowledge the sources of her strength with emotional candor and forthrightness. Drake quotes Sarton's unpublished letter to Louise Bogan in which she notes that the relationship to "the muse" is a breaking out of yourself to find yourself and is not to be confused with sex. She writes, "One never reaches the deepest place of feeling part of the almost unconscious universe, of being lost. Instead one reaches a place of extreme consciousness; one is found as an individual" (Drake 264). Sarton's changing relationship to the muse constructs the path to individuation which parallels her successful poetic achievement.

In her journals and memoirs, Sarton explores the sources of the sustaining mythologies of her work, including her meditations on the muse. In *A World of Light,* she narrates an unusual encounter with a family friend, Edith Forbes Kennedy, who once rescued her when she was very young from a difficult personal situation and whom she also credits with being the first to teach her to think clearly and hard about feelings. Sarton writes that this encounter may serve as "a perfect example of a seizure by the muse" (*AW* 91). The event involved an extraordinary coincidence. Sarton returned from Europe to visit Edith with a story about a man who turned out to have been Edith's lover at an earlier time. The tumult of emotion which seized Edith at the time catalyzed the young Sarton and resulted in an outpouring of poems, which she later published as *Inner Landscape,* her second book. The writing of these poems was a joyous release into gift giving; the virtues of a strong muse she details as "contemplative, listening with great attention, critical yet completely detached" (*AW* 99). It is, thus, not surprising to discover Sarton's fictional character Hilary, in Sarton's novel *Mrs. Stevens Hears the Mermaids Singing,* relating the same anecdote about being brought to an outpouring of poems by her friend Willa, who succeeds in "making Hilary accept that the poem itself was the reality, accept, at least at first, that together, for some mysterious reason, they made possible the act of creation" (*MS* 141). For Sarton, the source of creation or transcendence lies within the nexus of human relationship but does not involve possession or internalization of the other, whether the other is nature or human nature. This stance allows her to confront the transcendental sublime, creatively, in her identity as a woman and thus opens the door to a different point of origin, a nonpatriarchal line of descent.

Mary K. DeShazer, in her study *Inspiring Women: Reimagining the Muse*, examines the frequent tendency of women poets to construct "a revised and revitalized female muse," "a mother-goddess-sister-self of her own invention and design" (6). Margaret Homans, in her study of women writers and poetic identity, also concurs that a recovery of maternal origins not only supports creativity and reestablishes genealogy but acknowledges that the rest of the world is not to be possessed and, thus, encourages a different relationship to otherness (Homans 17). A redefinition of her relationship to the source of imagination, however, does not simultaneously redefine a woman's relationship with her poetic precursors. As Joanne Feit Diehl notes in her work on women poets and the American Sublime, women poets most often perceive themselves as "exceptions, as isolates, departing from, rather than building upon, a tradition" (2). In contrast, the male poet aligns himself with the patriarchal voices of his progenitors, assumes his superiority to them, and simultaneously accesses his muse, his source of a relationship to nature and imagination, at his will.

In "My Sisters, O My Sisters," an early poem, Sarton expresses this sense of isolation and exception and seeks both to create an alternative line of descent, a matriarchal genealogy, and to deliver a critique of female precursors (*CP* 74). Part 1 of the poem, written in five-stress couplets playing against the rhythms of speech, describes women poets as "strange monsters who renounce the treasure / Of their silence for a curious devouring pleasure" (*CP* 74). Sarton finds in Dickinson, Rosetti, and Sappho the need to build "inward in fearful isolation," the renunciation of sexuality, the awareness of something "lost, strained, unforgiven" in the poet. She looks forward to a fuller release of personhood for the woman poet:

To be through what we make more simply human
To come to the deep place where poet becomes woman,

Where nothing has to be renounced or given over
In the pure light that shines out from the lover,

In the pure light that brings forth fruit and flower
And that great sanity, that sun, the feminine power. (*CP* 75)

In the last line of this poetic invocation of her precursors, Sarton metaphorically seizes the sun, boldly renaming the feminine power with the dominant masculine image in Western poetry for the logos, centrality, or Reason.

In Part 3 of the poem, she quests for the source of "the fertile feminine goddess, double river," the origin of woman's double nature, to create a new genealogy for the necessity "To be Eve, the giver of knowledge, the lover; / To be Mary, the shield, the healer and the mother" (*CP* 76-77). In conclusion, in Part 4, she mourns how far from home, "how parted from / The earth, my sisters, O my sisters, we have come!" (*CP* 77); and she seeks for the liberation of passion "from deep in the earth" and for that free expression of joy and anger necessary for fully human creation. In the controversial final stanza of the poem, Sarton is forced to name the joy of creation "a masculine and violent joy," as her quest is not yet concluded. In a later journal she notes that Sappho should have been brought into the conclusion of "Sisters, O My Sisters!," as the true precursor of those in the light of "that sun, the feminine power" (*AS* 91).

It is the muse who accompanies Sarton's journey to a fully human poetry and to an imagination faithful to the earth. In an early poem, "The Lady and the Unicorn," she invokes the pathos and irony of the legend of the unicorn and his virgin consort, in this instance the version depicted on the Cluny tapestries. The sad unicorn and lady constitute a still life "woven into history," as the mythical beast bows his head, recognizing one whose beauty was not cast for him, "so sweetly lost, so strangely wed" (*CP* 78). "You are the lady woven into history / Imagination is our bridal bed: / We lie ghostly upon it, no word said." (*CP* 78). The unicorn is rewarded forever with "this shining tragedy," as Sarton critiques the curious worship of the virgin in a powerful couplet: "Know we are woven all in mystery, / The wound imagined where no one has bled" (*CP* 78). Sarton presents in "The Lady and the Unicorn" an ironic inversion of Keats's "Ode on a Grecian Urn." Recall Keats's "She cannot fade, though thou hast not thy bliss, / Forever wilt thou love, and she be fair!" Sarton's realistic portrayal does not celebrate the "still unravished bride," "forever panting and forever young." The union of virgin and unicorn produces no creative joy. It begins instead to deconstruct the mystery of this cold pastoral.

In all her early work, Sarton strives to articúlate a relationship between the flesh and the spirit, between the lion and the rose, which will be productive of poetry and, concomitantly, of a human life and a kinship with nature. In "The Sacred Order," a poem for her father, she writes, "Never forget this when the talk is clever: / Wisdom must be born in the flesh or wither" (*CP* 86). But the quest is arduous. In the dreamlike atmosphere of "The Second Spring," the muse is a woman embodying nature lying at the bottom of a green field. Birds' wings flash in her open eyes. She is a plant, a stream, a source, a mysterious flow, forever rooted and forever passing:

> When will the diviner be sent for, to strike
> The hidden source with his wand, and there the wand
> Leap out of his hands as the waters wake,
> She wake from her dream, alive and stunned. . . . (*CP* 102)

In "Because What I Want Most Is Permanence," she strives to articulate a relationship with the muse which will "free the complicated act of will," and produce "The long unwinding and continuous flow / Of subterranean rivers out of sense,"—a permanent stream of poetry. Deliberately in this poem, however, she moves away from a vision of a sexual union with the muse, which she associates with the "blue Atlantic where the sailors dream/ Their girls under the waves and in the foam—" (*CP* 137). Instead she writes:

> I set my mind to artful work and craft,
> I set my heart on friendship, hard and fast
> Against the wild inflaming wink of chance
> And all sensations opened in a glance. (*CP* 137)

The poet "banks the blaze within," bringing her muse "years of praise" instead of "hours of fire." The sailors' vision may be suggestive of possession, a relationship to be eschewed in Sarton's work.

In "Binding the Dragon," Proteus is the mythical name of transcendent being, the dragon of reality, which the poet wants alive in his fist, but neither possessed nor killed. The poet's analyst suggests he sublimate, but desire must somehow be released in the poet's work. "And so he wept and cursed the analyst." (*CP* 187). Again in "The Action of the Beautiful," Sarton presents the image of the beloved's face, poised between silence and speech, suggesting an "inward music" and uniting multiple and fragmented images, "the broken radiance of reality." Thus, she concludes, "And I, the stranger, centered in your presence, / Come home and walk into the heart of peace." (*CP* 163).

This vision of detachment *with* relationship—an "essence" of reality—is vividly depicted in another poem from the late fifties: "In Time Like Air," a metaphysical lyric, comparing the self in love's "early transformation" to a mysterious salt that dissolves in water and yet is present—both lost and found at last. "Without a future or a past, / And a whole life suspended in it" (*CP* 182). In the last stanza Sarton finds in an extended conceit a way of describing the newly emerging and transformed self as a salt crystallizing out of water into air—out of its loving union into detachment.

> The faultless crystal of detachment
> Comes after, cannot be created
> Without the first intense attachment.
> Even the saints achieve this slowly;
> For us, more human and less holy,
> In time like air is essence stated. (*CP* 182)

But the process of individuation accompanying the growth of a poet's imagination cannot be entirely smooth. As Paula Bennett argues in her study of women's creativity, *My Life a Loaded Gun,* women's inability to access anger can make it all but impossible for them to develop the ego strength necessary for them to become artists or perhaps even to survive (263). In the late 1960s the anger generated during the social protest movements pushed many women poets toward a renewed confrontation with their inner feelings. Dominant among the images women poets chose to express their newly discovered sense of self is the figure of the Medusa. Bennett cites immediately Sarton's poem "The Muse as Medusa" as a primary example of this new symbol for the woman poet's "liberated self" (Bennett 245). The poem marks a turning in Sarton's work, perhaps first initiated by the sonnet sequence "A Divorce of Lovers," in which the traditional theme, a lover's celebration of a muse who represents her idealized self, is replaced by a difficult struggle between two lovers who cannot reconcile. "The Muse as Medusa" appears in *A Grain of Mustard Seed,* a volume published in the late sixties, which includes several poems of protest as well as meditations on the violence of modern war. The volume ends with such poems as "The Godhead as Lynx," "The Waves," and "Beyond the Question," in which Sarton begins to establish a new relationship to nature, both autonomous and correspondent, which emerges directly from her ability to deal with the rage at times encountered even in loving relationships.

In "The Muse as Medusa" Sarton depicts herself and her thoughts and wishes as fish swimming in the ocean of Medusa's silence: the cold lover. Medusa was loved by Poseidon, god of the ocean, the source and mother of our lives. Perseus, who does not appear in the poem, slew her, and from her blood emerged Pegasus, the winged horse of poetry, presumably in recognition of the mediating power of Perseus's shield. Sarton's psyche, her "fish," has been bold and venturesome in love, often encountering powerful emotions.

> The fish escaped to many a magic reef;
> The fish explored many a dangerous sea—
> The fish, Medusa, did not come to grief,
> But swims still in a fluid mystery. (*CP* 332)

She finds useless Medusa's "abdication by total lack of motion," for the world of feeling is "fluid still," and " love is healing, even rootless love." The final stanza boldly reveals Sarton's representation of the psychological truth of the myth:

> I turn your face around. It is my face.
> That frozen rage is what I must explore—
> Oh secret, self-enclosed, and ravaged place!
> This is the gift I thank Medusa for. (*CP* 332)

Sarton has written of her own worst angers, which occur when she is unjustly criticized or attacked or prevented from leading her "real life," i.e., having to break chosen solitude because of too many external demands (*AS* 196). She also links personal rage to national violence and argues for the necessity of nations as well as people to detach themselves—to turn the image of violence around—in order to look hard at the cause for violent behavior. She writes:

> How can we deal with it, the violence in ourselves? Somehow or other we have to find a way, religious or not, of sanctifying life again, for only if we can do that will it be possible to face the worst, and still bear with it in ourselves and heal it in ourselves, because we have again become part of the mystery, given up some primary need to terrorize and subdue, and quite literally fallen on our knees. (*AS* 196)

It is the last passage concerning the surrender of domination necessary to become part of the mystery that is most important for a clear understanding of Sarton's later poetry.

In "The Invocation to Kali" Sarton seeks to overcome rage by understanding it, though she acknowledges that at times she thinks "only of killing / "The voracious animal / Who is my perpetual shame," Kali is the terrible goddess of both creation and destruction:

> I am the cage where poetry
> Paces and roars. The beast
> Is the god. How murder the god?
> How live with the terrible god? (*CP* 316)

At times, "The Invocation to Kali" becomes prosaic as Sarton struggles to illuminate the subject, but the language of the poem itself argues the difficulty of expression:

> Every creation is born out of the dark.
> Every birth is bloody. Something gets torn.
> Kali is there to do her sovereign work
> Or else the living child will be stillborn. (*CP* 317)

Violence is within us, "the kingdom of Kali," "the built-in destroyer" and cannot be overthrown. Until "the destroyer, has been blest, / There will be no child, no flower, and no wine" (*CP* 317). In Part 3, she turns to the horror of the concentration camps, and in the fourth section, "The Time of Burning," she recognizes the need to pray for self-knowledge:

> But she must have her dreadful empire first
> Until the prisons of the mind are broken free
> And every suffering center at its worst
> Can be appealed to her dark mystery. (*CP* 319)

The poem concludes with a realization of pain, anger, and subsequent violence as "the balance-wheel for our vulnerable, aching love" (*CP* 320).

Such deepening understanding results, in *A Grain of Mustard Seed*, in some of Sarton's finest poems. A new humility allows her to separate from nature while simultaneously voicing, as if from within, its wisdom and will. "The boom, the constant cannonade" of ocean and "the turning back of tides and their returning" in "The Waves," Sarton's courageous swerve from Matthew Arnold's "Dover Beach," is representative of this new understanding. The lover addresses her beloved not as Arnold does, "Ah, love, let us be true / To one another!" in a world that lies before us without joy, love, or light, without certitude, peace or help for pain, but in a different context.

> Oh love, let us be true then to this will—
> Not to each other, human and defeated,
> But to great power, our Heaven and our Hell,
> That thunders out its triumph unabated,
> And is never still.

For we are married to this rocky coast,
To the charge of huge waves upon it,
The ceaseless war, the tide gained and then lost,
And ledges worn down smooth but not downcast—
Wild rose and granite. (*CP* 354)

Arnold finds his lovers on "the darkling plain" from which the Sea of
Faith on which he depends has been withdrawn. Sarton finds a will in
nature itself, directly related to a will found in the lovers themselves:

Here in the darkness of the stillest wood,
Absence, the ocean, tires us with its roar;
We bear love's thundering rumor in the blood
Beyond our understanding, ill or good—
Listen, once more! (*CP* 354)

Sarton's lovers cannot construct a dyadic unit separated from the
earth, but are natural inhabitants of the world regardless of loss or
"distant wars." In "Beyond the Question," she writes,

Voices do not speak
From a cloud,
But we are inhabited. (*CP* 357)

But in "The Godhead as Lynx," though she feels a longing "To sub-
merge self in that essential fur, / And sleep close to this ancient world
of grace, / As if there could be healing next to her," she nevertheless
indicates her necessary human separation from this godhead, as an
emergent, compassionate, though guilt-ridden, being who "groans
and thinks" (*CP* 353).

Sarton's last three volumes, published in the eighties, manifest an in-
creasingly intense recognition of the mystery and necessity of the human muse. It is not surprising that they contain her most successful
poems. *Halfway to Silence* is a frank celebration of sensuosity leavened
by the wisdom of older years. The title poem reveals immediately the
pressure of approaching death. "Halfway to silence," "halfway to land's

end," the poet hears the voice of her muse and asks, "Shall I take you with me?" (*HS* 5). There is, she reveals, no choice. Without the muse, no poetry exists. But this muse is neither Petrarch's Laura who *is* poetry, and, therefore, cannot be a poet, nor Dante's dead Beatrice, whose spiritual image leads him to the divine. As Lawrence Lipking notes, for Dante, poetry stands at the center of existence, not love, which appears only by poetic license (21). Philosophical truth reigns, as Dante records his growth as a poet, and not on a mortal but on a spiritual plane.

It is the separation of such planes which Sarton resists in her late poetry, though mysteries are manifold, and the encounter with them once again revises the poet's relationship to nature and newly challenges her. In "Three Things," for example, she strives to express the transformation she experiences during a walk in the woods when the force of love which she carries in her head encounters "the shiver of poplar leaves," "the threshing of water over stone."

> Three things for which no one has found a word—
> Wind in the poplar, tremor under the skin
> Deep in the flesh, a shiver of more than blood
> When lovers, water, and leaves are wholly one. (*HS* 25)

"Three Things," however, remains a simple record of a suspended movement in time. "After the Storm" reveals the evidence of the transformation and renewal inherent in love, as the poet senses the same experience in nature in the song of the "peepers singing out so sweet and frail" above the pounding roar of surf, suggesting "something is going right." "Whatever locked love cannot bear to do, / The tree frogs can and spring is breaking through" (*HS* 42).

In "In Suffolk" the poet mourns the lost sequence of lovers: "To what have I been faithful in the end?" And yet she recalls the faithfulness inherent in changes and transformations, in falling in love and detaching, and she acknowledges herself:

> . . . faithful only to these,
> To earth itself turning toward the fall,
> To earth's relentless changing mysteries. (*HS* 56)

Only the earth itself consoles "the many times bereaved."

> The poem, life itself, labor of birth
> Has been forced back again and again
> To find renewal in the fertile earth. (*HS* 56)

Sarton's ability to identify herself with the earth as maternal matrix results in a celebration of the harvest "so rich it fills my bin. / What had to grow has been allowed to grow" (*HS* 56).

A new and elegant transparency, poetry standing naked in its bare bones, marks Sarton's late work. We look through the poetry to the experience itself as in "The Summer Tree."

> In all the summer glut of green,
> Serrated leaves, a dark and shifty screen,
>
> Catalpa flowers, unseasonal surprise,
> To tense the landscape up for drowsy eyes.
>
> We come alive beholding points of white,
> Among the leaves, immense rosettes alight.
>
> The blessing of pure form that open space
> And makes us stop and look in sudden peace. (*HS* 46)

The four and five stress lines emphasize the rhythms of natural speech as the rhymed couplets remind us of "the blessing of pure form that opens space," and the final unrhymed couplet enhances and focuses our stopping and looking at "space" in "peace."

Celebrating this transparency Sarton "prunes the orchard," in a poem of that title, cutting overgrowth to improve her harvest of poems with fruit "more crisp and rare":

> Muse, pour strength into my pruning wrist
> That I may cut the way toward open space,
> A timeless orchard, poetry-possessed,
> There without guilt to contemplate your face. (*HS* 50)

In "A Voice," she depicts the mysterious experience of the inner music liberated by the muse. In powerful four-stressed rhymed tetrameters, reminiscent of Coleridge's depiction in "Kubla Khan" of Alph the sacred river, it appears:

> Blurred as though it has been woken
> From an underground and secret river,
> This voice itself and not the language spoken
> Has made the air around me shiver. (*HS* 21)

The poet's destiny is a journey in quest of the mysterious source to "bless the magic throat (*HS* 21). The drumbeat returns in the poem "Control," which, like an earlier poem acknowledging being as an ungraspable protean god, portrays possession by the muse as a wild proud tiger who can be blessed but not seized or captured.

> You may have complete control.
> There will be no roar or growl.
> But can you look into those eyes
> Where the smothered fire lies?
>
> Tame the tiger. Break his pride.
> You will find yourself outside
> With all those who can destroy
> Tiger love and tiger joy. (*HS* 32)

It is essential to realize that Sarton's "seeing" constitutes her own unique version of the American sublime. This is not Emerson's direction to his American poet: "Thou shalt leave the world, and know the muse only. Thou shalt not know any longer the times, customs, graces, politics or opinions of men, but shalt take all from the muse" (Emerson 326). For the mysterious experience of Sarton's muse lies within human relationship itself. Nor is Sarton's "art" either man's or woman's will applied to nature for purposes of possession and domination. Sarton writes in "Blizzard," a poem making a swerve from Frost's "Stopping by Woods": "New Englanders are skeptical / Of what cannot depend on will" (*SN* 17). Nor is the self lost to transcendent spirit in Sarton's work as it is in Emerson. The father of the American sublime merges with his deity on a simple walk in the woods:

> I become a transparent eyeball; I am nothing; I see all: the currents of
> the Universal Being circulate through me; I am part and particle of
> God. The name of the nearest friend sounds then foreign and acciden-
> tal. (Emerson 189)

As Harold Bloom notes, "The final price paid for the extreme discontinuities of Emersonian vision is that we are left with a simple, chilling formula: the American sublime equals *'I am the Abyss,'* "—the abyss being tradition, history, or any other (Bloom 255). For Emerson, even nature vanishes as he becomes one with the world and assumes its authority. Bloom also observes that Wallace Stevens, in the last poem of his collected work, "Of Mere Being," presents a sense of being beyond "human feeling or meaning" (Bloom 292–93).

Sarton's revisions of the sublime in such late poems as "Moose in the Morning" retain both the natural and the human and provide the reader with "seeing" itself. The freshly enabling vision she experiences in her encounter with the moose is depicted in the phrase "When all I can is *see*." This extraordinary linguistic maneuver creates a verbal naming; and the moose, the wild and gentle beast, emerges as a promise kept, something "ancient" both lost and found at once. Sarton invokes the moose like a muse:

> Oh wild and gentle beast,
> Immense antlered shape,
> This morning in the meadow! (*LM* 41)

Her joy is experienced as "Wilderness and escape!" simultaneously retaining and escaping the natural. The guilt so often experienced at the appearance of a muse disappears.

> You make a truant of me
> This moose-enchanted day
> When all I can is *see*,
> When all I am is this
> Astonishment and bliss. (*LM* 41)

The poet observer experiences an intensification of human experience in the poem, the seeing self both lost and newly found in this enraptured experience. The supernatural is here experienced in the true meaning of the word, as an intensification of the natural.

In the elliptical poem "Shell," Sarton paratactically places the sound of the "sea's susurration" alongside the "terrible silence" of a loveless house, transforming that house itself to a shell "Abandoned by the creature / Who lived there once / And opened to the tide." In this meeting of the human and the natural an understanding is whispered in the silence of the shell-like house:

> The rumor of a wave
> Long ago broken
> And drawn back
> Into the ocean—
> And so, with love. (*LM* 33)

The lighted Christmas tree in "Christmas Light" is personified and feminized for the intimate encounter of human and nature: "She and I alone. / How softly she shone!"; and the solitary spectator experiences true presence, "Love distant, love detached / And strangely without weight." Even absence itself, "the abyss," is made almost familial in Sarton's poem of that title as she creates again the great white pine whose ample green branches she watched from her upstairs window, home for red squirrels and nuthatches:

> Until a winter hurricane
> Brought it, shuddering,
> Down against the house,
> Until that quiet strength
> Was broken by force. (*SN* 31)

Now she sees "Ragged firs / And formless bits of sky," an "irritation," and perceives "The air is silent." The last phrase makes absence itself palpable, implying presence.

The masterful balance of nature and mystery is noted in the "The Muse as Donkey" as a conflict between the highway to the White

Goddess and the omen provided by the presence "Within an island of trees" of a Great White Owl. Here, indeed, is the American side of Sarton. On the way to meet with the White Goddess she has a significant encounter:

> A dead owl lay on the road,
> Still warm.
> I could lift the great soft wing
> To its full span,
> Brown and white.
> I saw strong yellow legs
> And a terrible beak. (*SN* 67)

As she carries her "broken friend" to shelter she weeps, knowing there is "hard news ahead." The human poet cannot leave nature entirely for the house of the White Goddess nor can she deny her vision. For she has seen signs and "crude omens":

> My clouded eyes have seen
> The head of Medusa
> Calm in sleep.
> Not all dreams are lies. (*SN* 68)

Sarton's vision of the sublime is founded on the experience she depicts in "Of the Muse." (*HS* 61)

> Today, I have learned
> That to become
> A great, cracked,
> Wide-open door
> Into nowhere
> Is wisdom.
>
> When I was young,
> I misunderstood
> The Muse.
> Now I am older and wiser,

I can be glad of her
As one is glad of the light.
We do not thank the light,
But rejoice in what we see
Because of it.
What I see today
Is the snow falling:
All things are made new. (*HS* 61)

This "breaking open" unites self and nature, reality and imagination. The light comes and, naturally, goes, and in Sarton's vision is her joy. In "Salt Lick" this new freedom allows her to perceive her words as a dissolving salt, as she once perceived her psyche in the earlier poem "In Time Like Air." The readers who journey to talk with her mistake her personhood for the poem, like deer coming to a salt lick:

The salt, a mystery,
The written word,
Not me. (*SN* 23)

Their confusion is the reverse of the deer, who cannot realize that it is she who is being used to fill their need for the salt lick. The poet perceives both her natural mortality and the immortality of poetry, with a witty aside to the traveling readers who cannot know her simply through the poem and wear her out with visits to "lick and lick."

On some cold winter day
I shall be licked away
Through no deer's fault,
There will be no more salt. (*SN* 23)

Sarton's achievement in such late poems as "The Silence Now," "The Cosset Lamb," "Absence," or "New Year Resolve," manifests a psychological strength and maturity as well as a superb aesthetic accomplishment. In "Letters from Maine" she celebrates the mystery of human love, whether lost or found.

Let the muse bury the dead. For that she came.
Who walks the earth in joy and poverty?
Who then has risen? The tomb is empty. (*LM* 27)

It is the spirit of Sarton's poetry that is alive for us and continuing. It is difficult to imagine a more humanistic vision for poetry.

Works Cited

Bennett, Paula. *My Life a Loaded Gun*. Champaign: U of Illinois P, 1990.

Bloom, Harold. *Poetry and Repression*. New Haven, Conn.: Yale UP, 1976.

Derrida, Jacques. "White Mythology: Metaphor in the Text of Philosophy." *New Literary History* 6.1 (1974), 5–75.

DeShazer, Mary K. *Inspiring Women: Reimagining the Muse*. Elmsford, N.Y.: Pergamon, 1986.

Diehl, Joanne Feit. *Women Poets and the American Sublime*. Bloomington: Indiana UP, 1990.

Drake, William. *The First Wave: Women Poets in America 1915–1945*. New York: Macmillan, 1987.

Emerson, Ralph Waldo. *Selected Writings*. Ed. William Gilman. New York: New American Library, 1965.

Homans, Margaret. *The Woman Writer and Poetic Identity: Dorothy Wordsworth, Emily Brontë, Emily Dickinson*. Princeton: Princeton UP.

Lipking, Lawrence. *The Life of the Poet*. Chicago: U of Chicago P, 1981.

Sarton, May. *At Seventy*. New York: Norton, 1984.

———. *Collected Poems (1930-73)*. New York: Norton, 1974.

———. *Halfway to Silence*. New York: Norton, 1980.

———. *The House by the Sea*. New York: Norton, 1977.

———. *Letters from Maine: New Poems*. New York: Norton, 1984.

———. *Mrs. Stevens Hears the Mermaids Singing*. New York: Norton, 1965.

———. *Recovering*. New York: Norton, 1984.

———. *The Silence Now: New and Uncollected Earlier Poems*. New York: Norton, 1988.

———. *A World of Light*. New York: Norton, 1976.

Chronology

1912   Eléanore Marie Sarton born 3 May in Wondelgem, Belgium, daughter of Mabel Elwes Sarton and George Sarton. In same year, George Sarton begins famous journal *Isis*, a review devoted to the history of science and civilization.

1914   At outbreak of World War I, family flees Belgium, passing through advancing army to reach England.

1916-18   Sartons immigrate to United States, living in New York and Washington. Family settles in Cambridge, Massachusetts. George Sarton begins *Introduction to the History of Science* with the help of Carnegie Institute, also teaching at Harvard in exchange for Widener Library privileges. Mabel Sarton becomes successful clothing designer and designer of fine furniture.

1917   Brother Alfred Sarton dies five days after his birth. MS enrolls in Shady Hill School, where she meets Agnes Hocking (founder and poetry teacher), Katharine Taylor, and Anne Thorp, all of whom become influential figures.

1924   Sarton family becomes naturalized citizens. Mabel Sarton wins gold medal at the International Exhibition of Decorative Arts, Paris.

1925   MS attends Institut Belge de Culture Française and meets Marie Closset (who published as the poet Jean Dominique).

1926	Graduates from Shady Hill School. Enters Cambridge High and Latin School.
1927	Sarton and father see Eva Le Gallienne in Sierra's *The Cradle Song*, and MS falls in love with Civic Repertory Theatre.
1929	Graduates from Cambridge High and Latin School. Publishes first poems, sonnets, in *Harp* and then in *Poetry*.
1929-33	Joins Eva Le Gallienne's Civic Repertory Theatre as apprentice, then member, and director of apprentices in New York, instead of going to Vassar on scholarship.
1931	Travels to Paris for first unchaperoned visit, studying theater and writing poems; marks the beginning of yearly trips abroad. Parents spend winter of 1931-32 at American University in Beirut, where George Sarton studies Arabic.
1932-33	Is Eva Le Gallienne's understudy for the White Queen in *Alice in Wonderland*, performing when Le Gallienne becomes ill. Later Sarton takes over briefly as Varya in *The Cherry Orchard*. Civic Repertory Theatre closes later that year.
1933-36	Founder and director, Apprentice Theatre, New York. New School for Social Research engages company to produce ten modern European plays never seen in U.S. Director of Associated Actors Theatre and produced five plays at the Wadsworth Atheneum, Hartford, Connecticut. Company fails in 1936, and MS resolves never to return to theater.
1934	Father receives Honorary Doctorate from University of Upsala, Sweden.

1936   In June, at 5 Clarence Terrace, London, the home
            of Elizabeth Bowen, meets Bowen, Isaiah Berlin,
            and David Cecil. Later meets Virginia Woolf, Vita
            Sackville-West, and James Stephens. April-August in
            Europe.

1937   *Encounter in April,* first volume of poetry pub-
            lished, poems written from 1930 to 1936. Becomes
            friends with Elizabeth Bowen. Frequently sees
            Julian and Juliette Huxley (who becomes a Muse
            for Sarton) as well as S. S. Koteliansky. April-
            September in Europe.

1937-40   Teaches creative writing and choral speech at the
            Stuart School in Boston.

1938   *The Single Hound* (novel). Spends April-July in
            Europe.

1939   *Inner Landscape* (poetry), poems written from
            1936 to 1938. Completes *Fire in a Mirror* (unpub-
            lished novel). Spends June-August in Europe.

1940   Directs *Trelawney,* Concord Academy. Begins
            annual lecture/poetry-reading tours.

1941   Sarton in Santa Fe for several months in the middle
            of first series of poetry readings.

1943   Organizes poetry readings at the New York Public
            Library. Works at Pearl Buck's East and West
            Society. Lectures for Asian scholars.

1944-45   Works in the U.S. Office of War Information,
            writing scripts for documentary films (propaganda
            films about American life which were translated into
            twenty-six languages).

1945	Edward Bland Memorial Prize (*Poetry,* Chicago). Awarded the Golden Rose of the New England Poetry Society. Meets H.D. and Bryher at 49 Lowndes Square, in London.
1946	*The Bridge of Years* (novel). Poet-in-Residence, Southern Illinois University, summer.
1947	*The Underground River* (a play). Spends April-July in Europe.
1948	Teaches short story, Bread Loaf Writers' Conference, Middlebury, Vermont. *The Lion and the Rose* (poetry). April-September in Europe.
1949	April-August in Europe.
1950	Teaches short story, Bread Loaf Writers' Conference. May-June in Europe. Mabel Sarton dies. *The Leaves of the Tree* (poetry). *Shadow of a Man* (novel). May-June in Europe.
1950-53	Briggs-Copeland Instructor in Composition, Harvard University.
1951	Teaches the novel, Bread Loaf Writers' Conference.
1952	*A Shower of Summer Days* (novel). June-September in Europe.
1953	Meets Louise Bogan. *The Land of Silence* (poetry). Named Lucy Martin Donnelly Fellow, Bryn Mawr College. Receives Reynolds Lyric Award, Poetry Society of America. Lecturer, Boulder Writers' Conference, Colorado.
1954	Receives Guggenheim Foundation Fellowship in Poetry. August-November in Europe.
1955	*Faithful Are the Wounds* (novel). Named Honorary Phi Beta Kappa at Radcliffe, and receives the Tidewater Prize.

1956	George Sarton dies.
1956-58	Teaches creative writing, Radcliffe College Seminars, "The Art of the Short Story."
1957	*The Birth of a Grandfather* (novel). *The Fur Person* (tale). May-July in Europe.
1958	Sells father's house in Cambridge and buys eighteenth-century home and barn on thirty-six acres in Nelson, New Hampshire. *In Time Like Air* (poetry). Nominated for National Book Award in poetry and in fiction. Fellow, American Academy of Arts and Sciences.
1959	*I Knew a Phoenix* (memoir). Honorary Doctor of Letters, Russell Sage College. June-August in Europe.
1959-60	Named a Phi Beta Kappa visiting scholar.
1960	Danforth visiting lecturer, College Arts Program.
1960-64	Teaches creative writing at Wellesley College.
1961	*The Small Room* (novel). *Cloud, Stone, Sun, Vine* (poetry). Johns Hopkins Poetry Festival Award. March-July in Europe.
1962	Marks fiftieth birthday with trip around the world.
1963	*Joanna and Ulysses* (tale).
1964	Visits Yaddo. August in Europe.
1965	*Mrs. Stevens Hears the Mermaids Singing* (novel). Poet-in-Residence, Lindenwood College.
1966	*A Private Mythology* (poetry), poems written between 1961 and 1966. *Miss Pickthorn and Mr. Hare* (fable). Emily Clark Balch prize for poems. April-June in Europe.

1967	*As Does New Hampshire* (poetry). Receives a National Foundation of the Arts and Humanities Grant. September-October in Europe.
1968	*Plant Dreaming Deep* (memoir). Writer-in-Residence, Lindenwood College.
1969	*The Poet and the Donkey* (tale).
1970	*Kinds of Love* (novel). Spends August in Bermuda and Europe.
1971	*A Grain of Mustard Seed* (poetry), written from 1967 to 1971. Honorary Doctor of Humane Letters, New England College.
1972	*A Durable Fire* (poetry). Writer-in-Residence, Agnes Scott College. Sarah Josepha Hale Award, Newport, New Hampshire.
1973	Moves to "Wild Knoll" in York, Maine. *Journal of a Solitude* (journal). *As We Are Now* (novel).
1974	*Punch's Secret* (juvenile book). *Collected Poems (1930–1973).* September-October in Europe.
1975	*Crucial Conversations* (novel). Alexandrine Award from College of St. Catherine. Honorary Doctor of Letters, Clark University and Thomas Starr King School of Ministry.
1976	*A Walk Through the Woods* (juvenile book). *A World of Light* (memoir). Honorary doctorates from the University of New Hampshire, Colby College, and Bates College.
1977	*The House by the Sea* (journal). July-August in Europe.
1978	*Selected Poems; A Reckoning* (novel).

1979	Spends May in England and December in Switzerland.
1980	*Halfway to Silence* (poetry). *Recovering* (journal). Honorary Doctor of Letters, Nasson College.
1981	*Writings on Writing* (essays). Honorary doctorate, University of Maine. Deborah Morton Award, Westbrook College. June in Europe.
1982	Judith Matlack dies, 22 December. *Anger* (novel). *A Winter Garland* (poetry). Writer-in-Residence, Colby College. Richard D. Perkins Memorial Award, Thoreau School, Eastern Connecticut State College. Unitarian-Universalist Women's Federation "Ministry to Women" Award.
1983	Ware Lecturer, Unitarian-Universalist Assembly. Avon/COCOA Pioneer Woman Award. Honorary doctorate, Bowdoin College.
1984	*At Seventy* (journal). *Letters from Maine* (poetry), includes thirteen poems that had appeared in a 1983 issue of *Paris Review*. Fund for Human Dignity Award. Honorary Doctor of Letters, Union College.
1985	*The Magnificent Spinster* (novel). Sabbatical from lecture tour. American Book Award for *At Seventy*. Human Rights Award. Honorary doctorate, Bucknell University.
1986	Cancels spring lecture tour because of stroke. *Letters to May* (letters from Mabel Sarton, selected, edited, and introduced by May Sarton). Receives Maryann Hartman Award from the University of Maine.
1987	*The Phoenix Again* (poetry). Resumes lecture tour.

1988   Retires from lecture tours/poetry readings. Spends March in England. *After the Stroke* (journal). *Honey in the Hive* (portrait of Judith Matlack). *The Silence Now* (poetry). "In Honor of May Sarton," meeting of the Modern Language Association, 29 December 1988.

1989   *The Education of Harriet Hatfield* (novel). Honorary Doctor of Letters, Rhode Island College.

1990   Honorary Doctor of Letters, Centenary College. New England Booksellers Author of the Year Award.

1991   *Sarton Selected: An Anthology of Journals, Novels, and Poems of May Sarton* (anthology). *Conversations with May Sarton* (interviews).

1992   Travels to London. Honorary Doctor of Letters, Westport College. "May Sarton at Eighty: A Celebration of Her Life and Work," a conference sponsored by Westbrook College, Portland, Maine. *Coming Into Eighty* (poetry). *Now I Become Myself* (poetry). *Endgame: A Journal of the Seventy-Ninth Year* (journal).

1993   *That Great Sanity: Critical Essays on May Sarton* (full-length critical study on Sarton); edited by Susan Schwartzlander and Marilyn R. Mumford. *Encore* (a journal). *May Sarton: Among the Usual Days: Illustrated Portrait of the Poet in Unpublished Letters, Journals and Poems,* edited by Susan Sherman. The Women's Press, London, publishes *Halfway to Silence* (includes in one edition three volumes of poetry: *Halfway to Silence, Letters from Maine,* and *The Silence Now.*) *Collected Poems: 1930–1993* (new edition to include last three books).

Bibliography

Works by May Sarton

"After All These Years." *Anthology of Magazine Verse and Yearbook of American Poetry*. Ed. Alan F. Pater. Palm Springs, Calif.: Monitor Book Co., 1981.

"After the Palaces." *Eye's Delights: Poems of Art and Architecture*. Comp. Helen Plotz. New York: Greenwillow Books, 1983.

"All Day I Was With Trees." *America in Literature: The North-East*. Ed. James Lape. New York: Charles Scribner's Sons, 1979.

Anger. New York: Norton, 1982.

As Does New Hampshire and Other Poems. Peterborough, N.H.: Smith, 1967.

As We Are Now. New York: Norton, 1973; London: Gollancz, 1974.

At Seventy. New York: Norton, 1984.

The Birth of a Grandfather. New York: Rinehart, 1957; London: Gollancz, 1958.

"Boulder Dam" and "Prayer Before Work." *Saturday's Children*. Comp. Helen Plotz. New York: Greenwillow Books, 1982.

The Bridge of Years. Garden City, N.J.: Doubleday, 1946.

"A Celebration of May Sarton," including the poems: "Because What I Want Most Is Permanence," "Now I Become Myself," "Old Lovers at the Ballet," and "The Consummation" from *Sarton Selected*. *Ms.* 1 (1991): 26–27.

Cloud, Stone, Sun, Vine: Poems, Selected and New. New York: Norton, 1961.

Collected Poems (1930–1973). New York: Norton, 1974.

Collected Poems (1930–1993). New York: Norton, 1993.

Coming Into Eighty. Concord, N.H.: William B. Ewert, 1992.

Conversations with May Sarton. Ed. Earl G. Ingersoll. Literary Conversation Series. Jackson: UP of Mississippi, 1991.

Crucial Conversations. New York: Norton, 1975; London: Gollancz, 1976.

Crucial Conversations. New York: Norton, 1980.

"Death and Transfiguration." *Vogue* 170 (1980): 96, 203.

"Der Abschied," "The Lady and the Unicorn," "Muse and Medusa," "My Sisters, O My Sisters," and "On a Winter Night." *Early Ripening: American Women's Poetry Now.* Ed. Marge Piercy. New York: Pandora Press, 1987.

A Durable Fire. New York: Norton, 1972.

"Dutch Interior." *Strong Measures: Contemporary American Poetry in Traditional Forms.* Ed. Philip Dacey and David Jauss. New York: Harper and Row, 1986.

The Education of Harriet Hatfield. New York: Norton, 1987.

Encore. New York: Norton, 1993.

Encounter in April. Boston: Houghton Mifflin, 1937.

Endgame: A Journal of the Seventy-Ninth Year. New York: Norton, 1992.

Faithful Are the Wounds. New York: Rinehart, 1955; London: Gollancz, 1958.

The Fur Person. New York: Rinehart, 1956; London: Muller, 1957.

A Grain of Mustard Seed. New York: Norton, 1971, 1984.

Halfway to Silence. New York: Norton, 1980.

Halfway to Silence. Includes *Halfway to Silence, Letters from Maine,* and *The Silence Now.* London: The Women's Press, 1993.

The House by the Sea. New York: Norton, 1977.

I Knew a Phoenix: Sketches for an Autobiography. New York: Rinehart, 1959; London: Owen, 1963.

In Memoriam. Brussels: Presses de W. Godenne, 1957.

Inner Landscape. Boston: Houghton Mifflin, 1939; London: Cresset P, 1939.

In Time Like Air. New York: Rinehart, 1957.

Joanna and Ulysses. New York: Norton, 1963; London: Murray, 1963.

Journal of a Solitude. New York: Norton, 1973.

Kinds of Love. New York: Norton, 1970.

The Land of Silence. New York: Rinehart, 1953.

The Leaves of the Tree. Mount Vernon, Iowa: Cornell College UP, 1950.

Letters from Maine. New York: Norton, 1984.

"Letters to H.D." *H.D.: Woman and Poet.* Ed. Michael King. Orono, Maine: National Poetry Foundation, 1986. 49–57.

The Lion and the Rose. New York: Rinehart, 1948.

The Magnificent Spinster. New York: Norton, 1985.

May Sarton: Among the Usual Days: Illustrated Portrait of the Poet in Unpublished Letters, Journals, and Poems. Ed. Susan Sherman. New York: Norton, 1993.

Miss Pickthorn and Mr. Hare. New York: Norton, 1966; London: Dent, 1968.

Mrs. Stevens Hears the Mermaids Singing. New York: Norton, 1965; London: Owen, 1966.

Now I Become Myself. Burlington, Vt.: Rumble Press, 1992.

The Phoenix Again. Concord, N.H.: William B. Ewert, 1987.

The Poet and the Donkey. New York: Norton, 1968, 1984.

Plant Dreaming Deep. New York: Norton, 1968,

A Private Mythology. New York: Norton, 1966.

Punch's Secret. New York: Harper & Row, 1974.

A Reckoning. New York: Norton, 1978; London: Gollancz, 1980.

Recovering. New York: Norton, 1980.

Sarton Selected: An Anthology of the Journals, Novels, and Poems of May Sarton. Ed. Bradford Daziel. New York: Norton, 1991.

Selected Poems of May Sarton. Ed. Sue Hilsinger and Lois Brynes. New York: Norton, 1978.

A Self-Portrait. New York: Norton, 1982.

Shadow of a Man. New York: Rinehart, 1950; London: Cresset, 1951.

A Shower of Summer Days. New York: Rinehart, 1952; London: Hutchinson, 1954.

The Silence Now: New and Uncollected Earlier Poems. New York: Norton, 1988.

The Single Hound. Boston: Houghton Mifflin, 1938.

The Small Room. New York: Norton, 1961; London: Gollancz, 1962.

"The Snow Light" and "Eine Kleine Snailmusik." *Norton Book of Light Verse.* Ed. Russell Baker. New York: Norton, 1986.

"There Was in Your Voice, Astonishment." *Under Another Sky: An Anthology of Commonwealth Poetry Prize Winners.* Ed. Alastair Niven. Toronto: Carcanet Press, 1987.

The Underground River: A Play in Three Acts. New York: Play Club, 1947.

A Walk Through the Woods. New York: Harper & Row, 1976.

A Winter Garland. Concord, N.H.: W. B. Ewert, 1982.

"Winter Thoughts." *New York Times* 24 Jan 1982: 21E.

A World of Light. New York: Norton, 1976.

Writing on Writing. Orono, Maine: Puckerbrush Press, 1981.

Selected Criticism, Interviews, and Reviews since 1978

Allen, Frank. Rev. of *Sarton Selected,* ed. Bradford Daziel. *Library Journal* 15 May 1991: 83–84.

Bakerman, Jane S. "Work Is My Rest: A Conversation with May Sarton." *Moving Out* 7.2 (1979): 8–12, 87.

Balin, George. "The Sacred Game." Rev. of *Writing on Writing,* by May Sarton. *The Puckerbrush Review* 4 (Summer 1981): 26–29.

Balin, George. "A Shining in the Dark: May Sarton's Accomplishment." *May Sarton: Woman and Poet.* Ed. Constance Hunting. 264–80.

Bauer, Grace. Rev. of *The Silence Now,* by May Sarton. *Library Journal* 1 Nov. 1988: 97.

Blouin, Lenora P. "A Revised Bibliography." *May Sarton: Woman and Poet.* Ed. Constance Hunting. 283–319.

Bulkin, Elly. " 'A Whole New Poetry Beginning Here': Teaching Lesbian Poetry." *College English* 40.8 (1979): 874–88.

Connelly, Maureen. "Metaphor in Five Garden Poems by May Sarton." *May Sarton: Woman and Poet.* Ed. Constance Hunting. 187–92.

Creange, Renee. "The Country of the Imagination." *May Sarton: Woman and Poet.* Ed. Constance Hunting. 85–99.

Dirham, Sharon. Rev. of *Sarton Selected,* ed. Bradford Daziel. *L.A. Book Review* 26 May 1991: 8.

Eddy, Darlene Mathis. "The Sculptor and the Rock: Some Uses of Myth in the Poetry of May Sarton." *May Sarton: Woman and Poet.* Ed. Constance Hunting. 179–86.

Eder, Doris L. "Woman Writer: May Sarton's *Mrs. Stevens Hears the Mermaids Singing.*" *International Journal of Women's Studies* (1978): 150–58.

Fowler, Sigrid H. "A Note on May Sarton's Use of Form." *May Sarton: Woman and Poet.* Ed. Constance Hunting. 173–78.

Frank, Charles E. "May Sarton: Approaches to Autobiography." *May Sarton: Woman and Poet.* Ed. Constance Hunting. 33–41.

Rev. of *Halfway to Silence,* by May Sarton. *Booklist* 1 Sept. 1980: 26.

Rev. of *Halfway to Silence,* by May Sarton. *Kliatt* 14 (Fall 1980): 22.

Rev. of *Halfway to Silence,* by May Sarton. *North American Review* 265 (December 1980): 70.

Hammond, Karla. "A Further Interview with May Sarton." *Puckerbrush Review* 2 (1979): 5–9.

Hammond, Karla. "To Be Reborn: An Interview with May Sarton." *Bennington Review* 3 (1978): 16, 18–20.

Heilbrun, Carolyn G. "May Sarton's Memoirs." *May Sarton: Woman and Poet.* Ed. Constance Hunting. 43–52.

Hershman, Marcie. "May Sarton at 70: A Viable Life Against the Odds." *MS* 11 (1982): 23–26.

Huber J. Parker. "A Magic Encounter with May Sarton." *Thoreau's Journal* 2:4 (1982). N. pag.

Hunting, Constance. "May Sarton: Reaching the Lighthouse." *The Puckerbrush Review* 2.1 (1979): 1, 3, 4–5.

Hunting, Constance, ed. *May Sarton: Woman and Poet.* Orono, Maine: National Poetry Foundation, University of Maine at Orono, 1982.

Hunting, Constance. "The Risk Is Very Great: The Poetry of May Sarton." *May Sarton: Woman and Poet.* Ed. Constance Hunting. 201–9.

Johnson, Manley. "Verse." Rev. of *Halfway to Silence,* by May Sarton. *World Literature Today* 55 (Spring 1981): 319.

Kallet, Marilyn. Rev. of *The Silence Now: New and Uncollected Earlier Poems; Letters from Maine;* and *Halfway to Silence,* by May Sarton. *Before Columbus Review: A Quarterly Review of Multicultural Literature* 1 (1990): 18–21.

Kaplan, Robin, and Shelley Neiderbach. "An Interview with May Sarton." *Motherroot Journal: A Women's Review of Small Presses* 1:4 (1979): 1, 10–11.

Rev. of *Letters from Maine,* by May Sarton. *Booklist* 15 Feb. 1985: 818.

Rev. of *Letters from Maine,* by May Sarton. *Book World* 17 Feb. 1985: 11.

Rev. of *Letters from Maine,* by May Sarton. *Kliatt* 19 (Fall 1985): 31.

Lydon, Mary. "A French View of May Sarton." *May Sarton: Woman and Poet.* Ed. Constance Hunting. 71–77.

McDermott, Debi. "An Interview with May Sarton." *Cocoon: A Journal for Emerging Women* 1.7 (1979): 9.

Nishimura, Kyoko. "May Sarton's World." *Kyushu American Literature* 20 (1979): 35–41.

Otis, Danielle. "Sarton's 'Because What I Want Most Is Permanence." *Explicator* 47 (1989): 55–57.

Ringold, Francine. Rev. of *Letters from Maine* and *At Seventy,* by May Sarton. *World Literature Today* 59 (Autumn 1985): 597–98.

Rev. of *Sarton Selected*. ed. Bradford Daziel. *Advocate* 2 July 1991: 101.

Rev. of *Sarton Selected*, ed. Daziel. *Bloomsbury Review* 11 (April 1991): 3.

Rev. of *Sarton Selected*, ed. Daziel. *Booklist* 1 May 1991: 1688.

Rev. of *Sarton Selected*, ed. Daziel. *Lambda Book Review* 2 July 1991: 22.

Rev. of *Sarton Selected*, ed. Daziel. *Publishers Weekly* 5 April 1991: 135.

Sarton, Eleanor Mabel. *Letters to May*. Ed. May Sarton. Orono, Maine: Puckerbrush Press, 1986.

Saum, Karen. "The Art of Poetry XXXII: May Sarton Interview." *Paris Review* 89 (1983): 80–110.

Shelley, Dolores. "A Conversation with May Sarton." *Women and Literature* 7 (1979): 33–41.

Rev. of *The Silence Now*, by May Sarton. *Booklist* 15 Oct. 1988: 359.

Rev. of *The Silence Now*, by May Sarton. *Publishers Weekly* 21 Oct. 1988: 46.

Rev. of *The Silence Now*, by May Sarton. *Stand Magazine* 31 (Fall 1990): 48.

Rev. of *The Silence Now*, by May Sarton. *Virginia Quarterly Review* 65. (Summer 1989): 99.

Schwartzlander, Susan, and Marilyn R. Mumford, eds. *That Great Sanity: Critical Essays on May Sarton*. Ann Arbor: UP of Michigan, 1993.

Springer, Marlene. "As We Shall Be: May Sarton and Aging." *Frontiers: A Journal of Women's Studies* 5 (1980): 46–49.

Straw, Deborah. Interview with May Sarton. *Belles Lettres* 6 (1991): 34–38.

Strong, Lennox and Teri Cook. "Poetry of Lesbiana: Lesbian Poets." *Lesbian Lives: Biographies of Women from the Ladder*. Ed. Barbara Grier and Coletta Reid. Maryland: Diana Press 1976. 228–56.

Taylor, Henry. "The Singing Wound: Intensifying Paradoxes in May Sarton's 'A Divorce of Lovers.'" *May Sarton: Woman and Poet*. Ed. Constance Hunting. 193–200.

Thyng, Deborah. "The Action of the Beautiful: The Concept of Balance in the Writings of May Sarton." *May Sarton: Woman and Poet*. Ed. Constance Hunting. 79–89.

Trzaskos, Alexandra. "Thanking the Light." Rev. of *Halfway to Silence*, by May Sarton. *The Puckerbrush Review* 3 (Fall/Winter 1980): 22.

Upton, Lee. "Fierce Integrities." Rev. of *The Silence Now*, by May Sarton. *Belles Lettres* 4 (Summer 1989): 10.

Wheelock, Martha. "May Sarton: A Metaphor for My Life, My Work, and My Art." *Between Women: Biographers, Novelists, Critics, Teachers, and Artists Write About Their Work on Women*. Ed. Carol Ascher, Louise DeSalvo, and Sara Ruddick. Boston: Beacon, 1984. 413–29.

Woodward, Kathleen. "May Sarton and Fictions of Old Age." *Women and Literature* (1980): 108–27.

Rev. of *Writings on Writing,* by May Sarton. *English Journal* 78 (Feb. 1989): 55.

Video Tapes

Robitaille, Stephen, and Bill Suchy, directors and producers. *Writing in the Upward Years.* The Florida Media Arts Center, 1990.

Saum, Karen, producer. Elaine Goldberg, director. *May Sarton: She Knew a Phoenix.* Maine: Women's Media Network, Inc., 1981.

Simpson, Marita, and Martha Wheelock. *World of Light: A Portrait of May Sarton.* New York: Ishtar, 1979.

Audio Tapes

"As We Are Now." May Sarton reads excerpts from *As We Are Now* and *Journal of a Solitude.* Interview with Kay Bonetti. Columbia, MO: American Audio Prose Library, 1982.

"Delights of the Poet." Smithsonian. 29 Sept. 1985.

"Jonah: A Cantata." Poetry by May Sarton. J. J. Hollingsworth.

"May Sarton Hears the Mermaids Singing." Los Angeles: Pacifica Tape Library, 1983.

"May Sarton: My Sisters, O My Sisters." Washington, D.C.: Watershed Foundation Retrospective. Poets Audio Center. C–1170. 1984.

"May Sarton Reading Her Poetry." Great American Poets. Caedmon. CPN–1810, 1987.

Contributors

BETH CASEY is coordinator for special programs in the College of Arts and Sciences at Bowling Green State University. Prior to coming to Bowling Green, she served as associate dean of Hobart & William Smith Colleges, where she gave her first poetry reading. She holds a Ph.D. in English and comparative literature from Columbia University and teaches American literature, particularly contemporary modern American and British poetry. She is finishing a book on Wallace Stevens and preparing a first book of poems to be entitled *The Promised Land*.

RICHARD CHESS has published poetry in a variety of journals, including *Poetry*, the *American Poetry Review*, the *American Voice, Tikkun*, the *Missouri Review*, the *New England Review*, and many others. He has also published several essays on contemporary poets, including essays on Philip Levine and Gerald Stern. He is an assistant professor of literature and language at the University of North Carolina at Asheville, where he also directs the Center for Jewish Studies.

CATHERINE B. EMANUEL is currently working on her Ph.D. at the University of Tennessee, with a concentration in eighteenth-century British literature and contemporary southern literature. Her poems have appeared in *The Anthology*, the *Cold Mountain Review*, and the *Phoenix*. In 1988 she won *Cold Mountain Review*'s first-place poetry award, and in the same year, she was a runner-up for The Writer's Workshop poetry contest.

SUSAN V. FACKNITZ holds an M.F.A. in poetry from the University of Virginia, where she studied with Gregory Orr, Donald Justice, and Carolyn Forché. She is an assistant professor of English at James Madison University in Harrisonburg, Virginia, where she teaches twentieth-century poetry and creative writing. Her manuscript of poems, *The Limits of Love,* is under revision, and she is beginning a book on the poetry of Lola Ridge. She is married to the fiction writer Mark Facknitz and lives with him and their two children on a sheep farm in McGaheysville, Virginia.

PAT ADAMS FURLONG lives in Knoxville, Tennessee, where she is pursuing a master of arts in English with writing emphasis at the University of Tennessee. Her poetry has been published in *Daughters of Sarah, Visions of the Soul,* and many other magazines. *Giving Voice,* her first volume of poetry, is now in its second printing.

CHARLOTTE MANDEL is a poet, editor, and independent scholar. Her books of poetry include two poem-novellas that re-vision biblical women: *The Life of Mary* (Foreword by Sandra M. Gilbert, Saturday Press, 1988) and *The Marriages of Jacob* (Micah Publications, 1991). Her poems, short fiction, and critical essays have been published in *Iowa Review, Seneca Review, Nimrod, Women's Studies, Indiana Review,* and numerous other journals nationwide. She coordinates the Eileen W. Barnes Award Series of first books by women poets over forty, and edited the contest award anthology, *Saturday's Women.* She has published a series of articles on the role of cinema in the life and work of the poet H.D.

JANE MILLER has written several books of poetry, including *American Odalesque,* from Copper Canyon Press, and most recently, *Working Time: Essays on Poetry, Culture, and Travel,* from the University of Michigan's Poets on Poetry Series. Her honors include a Guggenheim Fellowship and the Lila Wallace-Reader's Digest Award. She works in Tucson, Arizona.

KEITH S. NORRIS is a native Virginian who currently lives, writes, and studies in Knoxville, Tennessee. He reviews poetry for *American Book Review,* and has published poetry in *Salmon.*

KAREN OHNESORGE-FICK was born in Oak Ridge, Tennessee, amongst scientists. Though still haunted by biology and its manifestations, she has turned to art and words. She studied art and writing at the University of Tennessee in Knoxville and has her master's in English from New York University, where she studied with Sharon Olds. She now teaches basic skills, art, and composition, and directs the Achievement Center at Ottawa University in Kansas. Her poetry has appeared in *Ploughshares,* among other magazines. Her husband Marlon is a poet, and they have a son, Walt.

LINDA PASTAN was born in New York City, graduated from Radcliffe College in 1954, and received an M.A. from Brandeis University in 1957. She has published eight volumes of poetry. The most recent, *Heroes in Disguise,* was published by Norton in 1991. She has won the Di Castagnola award (Poetry Society of America), the Bess Hokin Prize (*Poetry* magazine), and the Maurice English Award, and has had grants from the National Endowment for the Arts and from the Maryland Arts Council. In 1991 she was appointed Poet Laureate of Maryland. She is on the staff of the Bread Loaf Writers' Conference.

KENNETH G. POBO'S most recent poetry collections are *Ferns on Fire* from Nightshade Press (1991), and *Yes: Irises* from Singular Speech (1992). Dr. Pobo serves as poetry editor for *Widener Review* from Widener University, where he is an associate professor of English. His work appears in magazines such as *Nimrod, Colorado Review, University of Windsor Review, Dalhousie Review,* and *Hawaii Review.*

BOBBY CAUDLE ROGERS, a native of McKenzie, Tennessee, was educated at Union University, the University of Tennessee at Knoxville, and the University of Virginia, where he held a Henry Hoyns Fellowship in Creative Writing. His poems have appeared in the *Southern Review,* the *Georgia Review, Shenandoah,* and other magazines. He currently is instructor of English at Union University on their Baptist Memorial Hospital Campus in Memphis.

WILLIAM STAFFORD has won not only the National Book Award but also the Award in Literature of the American Academy of Arts and Letters, and the Shelley Memorial Award. He has served as Consultant in Poetry for the Library of Congress and on the Literature Commission of the National Council of Teachers of English. Among his recent volumes of poetry from HarperCollins are *An Oregon Message,* published in 1989 and *Passwords,* published in 1991. Stafford's tenth book of poems, *My Name is William Tell,* won the 1992 Western States Book Award for Lifetime Achievement in Poetry. His new children's book is *The Animal That Drank Up Sound,* from Harcourt Brace. He and his wife Dorothy live in Lake Oswego, Oregon.

MARJORIE STELMACH lives in St. Louis and teaches at Ladue High School and Washington University. She received her M.F.A. from the Washington University Writer's Program and has been a Fellow at the Virginia Center for the Creative Arts. Her poetry has appeared in *Yankee, Southern Poetry Review, Union Street Review, River Styx, Ascent,* and *West Branch.* She has won a number of awards for her poetry, including the *Malahat Review* long-poem contest in 1990 and again in 1992, the First Annual Missouri Biennial Award in 1988, the First Chelsea Award in 1988, and the Billee Murray Denny Award in 1987.

About the Editor

MARILYN KALLET is director of creative writing at the University of Tennessee in Knoxville. Her first two books of poems were published by Ithaca House, and her poems have appeared in many national magazines, including *Denver Quarterly, Greensboro Review, New Letters, Seneca Review,* and *Tar River Poetry.* In 1988 she won the Tennessee Arts Commission Literary Fellowship in Poetry, and she is codirector of the Tennessee Writers Alliance. She received her Ph.D. in comparative literature from Rutgers University. Kallet translated Paul Eluard's *Last Love Poems* (LSU Press, 1980), and is the author of a critical study on William Carlos Williams, *Honest Simplicity in William Carlos Williams' "Asphodel, That Greeny Flower"* (LSU Press, 1985).

Index